42.95

# YEARBOOK IN EARLY CHILDHOOD EDUCATION

Bernard Spodek  •  Olivia N. Saracho
EDITORS

VOLUME 1
**Early Childhood Teacher Preparation**
*Bernard Spodek and Olivia N. Saracho, Editors*

## YEARBOOK IN EARLY CHILDHOOD EDUCATION
### EDITORIAL ADVISORY BOARD

Dr. Anne Haas Dyson
School of Education
University of California, Berkeley

Dr. David Elkind
Professor of Child Study, and
  Senior Resident Scholar
Lincoln Filene Center
Tufts University

Dr. Joe L. Frost
Parker Centennial Professor
  in Education
Department of Curriculum
  and Instruction
University of Texas at Austin

Dr. Eugene E. Garcia
Chair/Professor
Board on Education
Merril College
University of California, Santa Cruz

Dr. Celia Genishi
Associate Professor
Ohio State University

Dr. Alice Honig
Professor of Child Development
College of Human Development
Syracuse University

Dr. Sharon Lynn Kagan
Bush Center for Child Development
  and Social Policy
Yale University

Dr. Anthony D. Pellegrini
Professor
College of Education
University of Georgia

Dr. Donald L. Peters
Ann Rextrew Professor of
  Individual and Family Studies
College of Human Resources
University of Delaware

Dr. Douglas R. Powell
Department of Child Development
Purdue University

Dr. Joseph H. Stevens, Jr.
College of Education
Georgia State University

Dr. Edward F. Zigler
Psychology Department
Yale University

The *Yearbook in Early Childhood Education* is to be a series of annual publications. Each volume will address a timely topic of major significance in the field of early childhood education, and will contain chapters that present and interpret current knowledge on aspects of that topic, written by experts in the field. Key issues—including concerns about educational equity, multiculturalism, the needs of diverse populations of children and families, and the ethical dimensions of the field—will be woven into the organization of each of the volumes.

YEARBOOK
IN
EARLY CHILDHOOD EDUCATION
VOLUME 1

# EARLY CHILDHOOD
# TEACHER PREPARATION

Bernard Spodek • Olivia N. Saracho

EDITORS

Teachers College, Columbia University
New York • London

Published by Teachers College Press, 1234 Amsterdam Avenue
New York, NY 10027

Copyright © 1990 by Teachers College, Columbia University

All rights reserved. No part of this publication may be reproduced or transmitted in any form or by any means, electronic or mechanical, including photocopy, or any information storage and retrieval system, without permission from the publisher.

*Library of Congress Cataloging-in-Publication Data*

Early childhood teacher preparation / Bernard Spodek, Olivia N. Saracho, editors.
    p. cm. — (Yearbook in early childhood education ; v. 1)
    Includes bibliographical references and index.
    ISBN 0-8077-3042-4 (alk. paper) : $42.95. — ISBN 0-8077-3041-6 (alk. paper : pbk.) : $19.95
    1. Early childhood education.  2. Teachers—Training of.
I. Spodek, Bernard.  II. Saracho, Olivia N.  III. Series.
LB1139.23.E29   1990                                                              90-37961
370'.71'22—dc20                                                                          CIP

Printed on acid-free paper

Manufactured in the United States of America

97  96  95  94  93  92  91  90        8  7  6  5  4  3  2  1

# Contents

Introduction ... vii
    *Bernard Spodek* and *Olivia N. Saracho*

CHAPTER 1 **Historical Foundations of Early Childhood Teacher Training: The Evolution of Kindergarten Teacher Preparation** ... 1
    *Dorothy W. Hewes*

CHAPTER 2 **Preparing Early Childhood Teachers** ... 23
    *Bernard Spodek* and *Olivia N. Saracho*

CHAPTER 3 **Non-Baccalaureate Teacher Education in Early Childhood Education** ... 45
    *Douglas R. Powell* and *Loraine Dunn*

CHAPTER 4 **The Content of Early Childhood Teacher Education Programs: Child Development** ... 67
    *Donald L. Peters* and *Dene G. Klinzing*

CHAPTER 5 **The Content of Early Childhood Teacher Education Programs: Pedagogy** ... 82
    *Jan McCarthy*

CHAPTER 6 **Early Childhood Teacher Preparation in Cross-Cultural Perspective** ... 102
    *Olivia N. Saracho* and *Bernard Spodek*

CHAPTER 7 **Research Horizons and the Quest for a Knowledge Base in Early Childhood Teacher Education** ... 118
    *Daniel J. Ott, Kenneth M. Zeichner,* and *Gary Glen Price*

CHAPTER 8 **Setting and Maintaining Professional Standards** 138
*Susan Bredekamp*

CHAPTER 9 **Issues in Recruitment, Selection,
and Retention of Early Childhood Teachers** 153
*Barbara T. Bowman*

CHAPTER 10 **The Influence of Recent Educational Reforms
on Early Childhood Teacher Education Programs** 176
*James M. Cooper* and *Corinne E. Eisenhart*

CHAPTER 11 **Issues in the Preparation of Teachers
of Young Children** 192
*Lilian G. Katz* and *Stacie G. Goffin*

CHAPTER 12 **Preparing Early Childhood Teachers
for the Twenty-First Century:
A Look to the Future** 209
*Bernard Spodek* and *Olivia N. Saracho*

**About the Editors and the Contributors** 223

**Index** 231

# Introduction

Bernard Spodek
Olivia N. Saracho

Early childhood teacher preparation in the United States has gone through considerable change since the field was established in the latter half of the nineteenth century. At the beginning, kindergarten teachers were prepared in a form of apprenticeship, in teacher training programs attached to kindergarten programs for children. Along with the study of Froebel's philosophy and workshops in kindergarten methods, novice teachers essentially learned their craft by working alongside experienced teachers, who became their models.

By the turn of the century, most kindergarten teachers were being prepared in normal schools, the majority of which also prepared teachers for elementary school teaching. In the last half of the nineteenth century and the first half of the twentieth century, the normal schools evolved into normal colleges, which, unlike the normal schools, required completion of secondary education for admission. Since the end of World War II, the normal colleges have evolved into multipurpose universities. With this change, the preparation of teachers, including early childhood teachers, became one of many responsibilities of large state and private universities. In addition, private institutions specifically organized to prepare early childhood personnel have all but disappeared.

During this period, the preparation of teachers became less practice-based and more theory-based. The hours in the teacher preparation program devoted to working in classrooms and to the practical activities of the teacher were reduced. A large portion of the teacher preparation program was devoted to general education—that portion of the university program that offers students general cultural knowledge expected to be attained by all educated individuals and required of students in all university programs—and to educational foundations. Studies in child development also took on increased importance in early childhood teacher education programs. In addition, programs at the community college level were established to prepare early childhood practitioners, primarily for work in child care centers.

These changes in the preparation of early childhood teachers reflected changes in the field of early childhood education as well as changes in society at large. Kindergartens moved from being separate educational institutions to becoming part of the public elementary schools. Kindergarten teachers were expected to have the same qualifications as teachers in the elementary or secondary grades. They were required to be graduates of teacher preparation programs with at least a bachelors degree and to hold a state teachers certificate. Nursery schools were established for children below kindergarten age, and new programs of education for special populations, such as Head Start, were established outside the education establishment. There was also a major expansion in child care programs. Teachers in these non-public school programs were not expected to be certified or to have similar preparation as public school teachers. In addition, early childhood education was seen as a comprehensive period in the life of children. Programs for children from birth through about age 8 were seen as related to one another, even though these programs might be offered in different institutional settings. Thus, the field of early childhood education, more than any other field of education, came to be served by practitioners who range from having little or no preparation for their teaching responsibilities to those that have the same level of preparation as do teachers in public elementary and secondary schools.

During the last several years there has been increasing criticism of the preparation of all teachers. That criticism—regarding the inadequate level of education required of teachers as well as the inadequate preparation for particular teaching tasks—could be applied more strongly to the preparation of early childhood teachers. Early childhood education practitioners as a whole are less well educated and less well prepared for their teaching tasks, yet early childhood teachers may have an even greater influence on their pupils than do teachers at any other level. Increasingly the importance of the early years and the educational experiences provided to children in these years, both formally and informally, has been brought to the attention of both professionals and the lay public.

In the context of these concerns, this volume was designed to explore what we know about the preparation and certification or credentialing of early childhood practitioners. It is also designed to explore the issues that face the field regarding the nature of early childhood practice and the preparation of practitioners, and the need to address these issues as the field prepares for the future.

Chapter 1 constitutes an introductory section that provides readers with the context in which to interpret the chapters that follow. Present day early childhood teacher education programs evolved from those of the past. That chapter describes the preparation of kindergartners, as kindergarten teachers were called in the past century, thus presenting the antecedents of contemporary programs.

The next five chapters present a description of contemporary programs preparing early childhood personnel both at the bachelor's degree level and below that level. Descriptions of the educational knowledge and the knowledge of the field of child development that should be included are also offered. In addition, early childhood teacher education programs in other countries are described so that one can compare how American early childhood practitioners are prepared with how similar practitioners are prepared in other countries.

The final six chapters deal with the many issues related to the preparation of early childhood personnel. There is a need to identify a knowledge base of practice for early childhood education and for the preparation of early childhood practitioners. This knowledge base is sought both in the evolving research in the field of education as well as in our increased knowledge of practice itself. We need to improve the selection, recruitment, and retention of early childhood personnel, especially among minority populations and in the area of child care, where the turnover is so great.

Standards must be set in the field, both for the quality of programs offered for young children and for the personnel who staff these programs. Professional associations have a major role to play in establishing these standards. As we look to the reforms of teacher education that have been suggested for the field of education as a whole, we need to sensitively assess them, sorting out those that are appropriate for early childhood education and working to implement them. There are many other issues that need to be addressed in the preparation of early childhood teachers, and these are also explored.

Finally, any book of this kind needs to be focused as much on the future as on the past. Knowledge that is accumulated needs to be applied so the field of early childhood education can create, or at least influence, its own future.

It has often been said that the quality of an educational program is dependent to no small degree on the quality of the teachers who staff it. The quality of teachers results not only from their personal characteristics but from the preparation for teaching they have received. Our hope is that the knowledge provided in this book can be used to improve the quality of programs preparing early childhood teachers, so that teachers in the future will be better prepared and young children in the future will be better educated.

CHAPTER 1

# Historical Foundations of Early Childhood Teacher Training
THE EVOLUTION OF KINDERGARTEN TEACHER PREPARATION

## Dorothy W. Hewes

It is generally agreed that widespread training of teachers for early childhood education began with the Froebelian kindergarten in the 1870s. However, attitudes and policies affecting today's teacher education programs in the United States were established during the colonial and immediate post-Revolutionary period. The training of kindergarten teachers evolved as Froebel's system became more widespread. Teachers for the first kindergartens, small private classes enrolling children aged two or three to seven, were prepared through an apprenticeship system in which they assisted the more experienced "kindergartner" in her classroom. With the proliferation of larger private and philanthropic kindergartens in the 1880s, independent kindergarten training schools based on Froebel's German system became popular. By the 1920s, after two decades of a nationwide movement toward compulsory elementary education and the adoption of kindergartens into public schools, most students preparing to be kindergarten teachers attended the same normal schools and colleges as those preparing to be elementary teachers.

## SCHOOLING IN EARLY NORTH AMERICA

Regional variations in schooling have existed since earliest colonial times and have been well documented by educational historians. There is general agreement that the earliest settlers, seeking freedom to practice their own denominational religions, gave serious attention to the development of educational systems consistent with their beliefs

(Cremin, 1951; Dexter, 1904; Heatwole, 1916; Martin, 1894). Ellwood Cubberly (1920) developed the generally accepted categories of colonial education. One was a parochial school system established in the middle and Spanish colonies. A second was found in Virginia and other southern colonies, where a distinct class system led to private tutors and private schools for children of the gentry while education for poor children was limited to occupational training and occasional philanthropic schools.

The third major approach, compulsory education with public funds, became nationally accepted by the late nineteenth century. It was introduced by the Puritans, those Calvinist dissenters from the English national church who established Massachusetts Bay Colony in 1620. The Massachusetts Law of 1642, the first legislation in the English-speaking world to order that all children within a geographic area must be taught to read, established an important precedent by imposing on parents the legal responsibility for the education of their children. It was followed in 1647 by a law requiring each town of 50 families to raise money for a schoolteacher and each town of 100 householders to provide a Latin grammar school because "the old deluder Satan" kept people from knowledge of the Scriptures (Kotin & Aikman, 1980).

Parents in Massachusetts were responsible for teaching their children to read before grammar school entrance at about seven or eight years of age. Reading lessons often started at age 2 or 3, and there are many reports of precocious young children who not only read the Bible fluently but were well along in Latin and Greek. Early children's books emphasized Christian responsibilities and the sovereignty of God. Religious indoctrination dominated the curriculum of the grammar schools. Although some teachers reflected these high moral standards, it is generally agreed that "at the close of the eighteenth century, as at the beginning of the sixteenth, teachers were, by any standard of general education, for the most part ignorant men and women, often deficient in moral character and almost universally lacking in any special training for the office of school-teaching" (Reisner, 1930, p. 272).

Harvard, and the eight other colleges established before 1776, were designed to educate ministers, not teachers, although many of the men who attended them were schoolmasters at some time in their lives. They and their families became influential in disseminating "The American Way" when the frontiers expanded westward from the colonial enclaves. Their belief system, transmitted to the late 1800s, and applied to children and the training of their kindergarten teachers, helped create a dichotomy between European trained Froebelians and those who were White Early American Protestants.

During the colonial period, however, formal schooling was relatively unimportant for most of the American settlements and the general populace in European nations. Indeed, an encyclopedic world geography stated that "in New England, learning is more generally diffused among all ranks of people than in any other part of the globe; arising from the excellent establishment of schools in every township. A person of mature age who cannot both read and write is rarely to be found" (Guthrie, 1795, p. 824).

Even colonial New England was characterized by an absence of formal teacher training and a lack of awareness that early childhood was a period with special learning needs. It was assumed that any literate person could become a grammar school teacher, and only rare individuals were respected for their achievements as schoolmasters. As for the women who conducted dame schools for the teaching of basic reading skills, this was considered to be a rather menial extension of their maternal function.

When the colonies declared their independence from England, most of the men involved in setting up the United States of America had been educated by private tutors and in private schools. They recognized the diversity of religions in the new republic and determined that church and state should be kept separate. They repeatedly stressed the need for an educated electorate, but there was no mention of education in the Constitution and no national educational policy was established. Cubberly (1920) made a state-by-state analysis of public education during the post-Revolutionary period and found little interest expressed before about 1820 and the Jacksonian era of the common man.

## THE BEGINNING OF TEACHER EDUCATION

In the early 1800s, the development of teacher training classes for young women seems to have depended on market demand. One reason was financial, of course, since women were less expensive teachers than men. They were first hired during summers when older boys were at work, but when Locke's more tolerant disciplinary measures were adopted, schools no longer required strong males to carry out the whippings that had been common in colonial schools. By mid-century women were teaching regular terms. During this period there was also a growing recognition that teachers needed schooling beyond that of public grammar schools. That schooling was first available in the private academies. Marr (1959) estimates that there were about 50 in 1800 and at least 6,000 by mid-century, with the period of greatest growth between 1830 and 1865. Most were for males, with an age range of 12 to 30, but a few were for young women of today's high school age, and a very few were coeducational. Original emphasis in the female academies was on embroidery, music, and other domestic studies, but literature, science, and mathematics were soon added. By the 1830s, these private academies began to provide teacher preparation classes, although little methodology was taught in them. Not until Page's *Theory of Teaching* was published in 1847 was there a specific text on pedagogy.

One of the earliest advocates of professional training for teachers was the Swiss educator Johann Heinrich Pestalozzi (1746-1827). Although his teacher training institute was opened in 1801, it was not until the 1820s that Americans became aware of his writings. Educators visiting Europe brought back favorable reports of his work and of the Prussian educational system based on it. The first normal schools in the United States, in Massachusetts in 1838, "were directly traceable to the influence of German practice" based on Pestalozzi's work (Cubberly, 1920, p. 281). An 1851 report by Henry Barnard commented on these and six additional teacher training schools. He felt they were "doing much good" but didn't compare with similar training schools in Europe (p. 5).

The greatest impetus for Pestalozzi's ideas came after the 1861 opening by E. A. Sheldon of the Oswego (New York) Training School. Because Pestalozzi had been strongly influenced by Rousseau's ideas about education based on children's natural development, he advocated "thinking love" instead of corporal punishment, and viewed pupils as beings whose mental, moral, and physical development must be tenderly nurtured. He stressed object teaching, activity, and development of the senses and intended that children's first experiences with reading and other curricula should begin at the primary level. Pestalozzi urged his teachers-in-training to read nothing and discover everything through a whole child concept designed to train the head, the hand, and the heart.

Pestalozzi's more secular educational view fit into the newly legislated separation of church and state in American public schools. A modified Pestalozzian system spread from Oswego to other teacher training programs across the nation and by mid-century had become widely accepted. Instead of memorizing moral tracts to be recited individually, children were led to "developing their faculties" and expressing their ideas. For the first time, teachers had to acquire professional skills in asking questions and had to learn the subject matter they taught rather than simply make sure that the children gave the prescribed answers. They had to develop lesson plans and strategies for keeping children interested and under control. This was the beginning of professional teacher education in America.

## KINDERGARTEN APPRENTICESHIP TRAINING

Kindergartens, originally conceived by Friedrich Froebel (1782–1852) as only one segment of lifelong education beginning at birth, introduced humanistic ideas of early childhood education and teacher training into the United States. Since Froebel had studied with Pestalozzi, there were many similarities in their ideas. By the time kindergartens were introduced into public schools in the 1880s, many Oswego graduates were in positions of prominence and were more receptive to Froebelian innovations than traditionally trained administrators (Rogers, 1961).

From 1855 until 1870, the kindergarten (with a single exception) was limited to German-American schools. One historian of the public school movement, in explaining why the kindergarten became so well established in Europe before it was known in the United States, stated that "when one contemplates the opposition to [Horace] Mann's advocacy of new methods and more lenient discipline, support for a school in which play and enjoyment were the only observable results seems inconceivable" (Binder, 1974, p. 116).

The 10 kindergartens of 1870 increased to about 400 by 1880 and to about 4,000 in the peak year of 1894. The success of the Froebelian kindergarten was due in part to the favorable economic and social conditions of the times. This was a period of prosperity, with an emerging group of very wealthy families and an expanding middle class. The Civil War not only had led to organized charities but had given many women their first taste of leadership in community activities. By the early 1880s, thousands of women were organized into loosely linked associations whose sole purpose was the establishment and maintenance of kindergartens (Hewes, 1985).

Expositions of what is commonly called "The Kindergarten Crusade" have been detailed by various authors for the past century (Barnard, 1890; Bowen, 1897; Downs, 1978; Kilpatrick, 1916; Kreige, 1876; Ross, 1976; Shapiro, 1983; Snyder, 1972; Weber, 1969). American publications have been based primarily on writings of those who attempted to systematize and improve upon Froebel's philosophy and methods. Recent research at the Froebel Archives in East Berlin and elsewhere in Europe indicates that at his death Froebel was still in the process of developing the songs, games, and sequenced Gifts and Occupations that were standardized by both admirers and critics (Heiland, 1982; Konig, 1982; Liebschner, 1976). European teacher training programs, with less emphasis on Froebelian manufactured materials and more understanding of his basic philosophy about creative play, seem to have remained closer to the original philosophy than have those in the United States (Lawrence, 1953; Morgan, 1981; Ojala, 1988).

When American kindergartens began to attract attention in the 1870s, little had been published in English about the Froebel system. There was wide diversity, therefore, in its interpretation. Several kindergartens operated by European-trained Froebelians were the first to provide apprenticeship training for those seeking to enter the field. These were soon followed by others, some with little understanding of the method. Training sometimes meant working a year or so in what we would now call an aide or assistant teacher position. In 1900, Nora Smith criticized this system.

> Miss A trains a class including Miss B, who is not a thinker but repeats and imitates. She trains Miss C, who begins to teach long before she has digested her experience as a student. With lightning rapidity, Miss D arrives on the scene, sees the work as agreeable, and immediately seeks for others around whom she can wreathe her octopus arms and to whom she can impart the tricks of the trade. This continues with Misses F, G, H, I, J, and K. (pp. 113-14)

Despite their limitations, many of the kindergarten apprenticeships appear to have been excellent. One example, the 1876-77 Los Angeles kindergarten of German-trained Emma Marwedel, was described by Nora Smith's sister, Kate Douglas Wiggin. She and two other young women worked with the class of 20 children in the mornings, then studied Pestalozzi, Rousseau, Spencer, and Froebel. They made books of manual work, "the execution of which was to prove the student's ability to conduct the kindergarten occupations with the children," and had classes in games and story telling (Swift, 1931, p. 167).

Many "kindergartners," as these pioneer early childhood educators called themselves, developed lifelong support networks through the system. Anna Louise Jenkins recounted her conversation in 1912 with Ruth Burritt, who had taught the demonstration class at the 1876 Philadelphia Exposition and was by then an elderly lady. Burritt immediately asked, "Who trained you?" and when she heard that it had been Eliza Blaker exclaimed, "Why, you are my granddaughter then. Eliza is one of my girls" (Hewes' audiotaped interview with Jenkins, Oct. 27, 1972). Autobiographical writings and other papers confirm that this familial relationship was common among the early kindergartners.

Unification and promotion of the Froebel kindergartens in the United States between 1860 and the late 1870s is generally attributed to Elizabeth Peabody (1804-94). Descendent of an original Puritan family, she had lived in "genteel poverty" all her life. Her mother had opened a school in their home when Elizabeth was four, and when she was sixteen she was running it. She was always fascinated by radical new ideas, and she adopted the kindergarten with typical enthusiasm in her late fifties. Her interpretation of Froebel was influenced by her earlier experiences with infant schools, American adaptations of Pestalozzian schools that had briefly flourished in the 1820s. When Peabody and her widowed sister Mary Mann opened the first English-language kindergarten in 1860 and co-authored the *Moral Culture in Infancy and Kindergarten Guide* in 1864, Pestalozzian methods were presented under the guise of being Froebelian. Peabody later recognized that her early kindergarten work was an "ignorant" and "premature attempt" and asserted that she had learned true Froebelian methods when visiting European kindergartens in 1867-68 (Barnard, 1890, p. 10; Ronda, 1984, p. 363). However, the version she transmitted seems to have been based more on the materials and activities than on Froebel's underlying philosophy.

Peabody promoted training and attempted to develop and enforce standards for kindergarten teachers. She wrote innumerable letters such as one sent in 1870 to William Torrey Harris, Superintendent of Schools in St. Louis, trying to convert him to the system and emphasizing the necessity of a new Primary Education as "the underpinning for the Public school System — this will require a new special normal training" (Ronda, 1984, pp. 358-59). Peabody authored and translated books, published, at irregular intervals, a *Kindergarten Messenger*, arranged with Milton Bradley for Froebel's Gifts and Occupations to be manufactured and sold, and made inspiring speeches when she passed out diplomas to graduating classes. Although her understanding of Froebel was overly sentimental, her enthusiasm and energy were a critical contribution in the formative years of kindergarten teacher training in the United States.

## KINDERGARTEN TRAINING SCHOOLS

Froebel started courses for "child leaders" in Keilhau and Bad Blankenburg, in what is now the German Democratic Republic, when he opened the first classes for young children in 1837. By 1847, he had written the prospectus for his model training institute, despite the hilarious laughter at an all-male conference when he suggested that women should be educated as teachers. In 1849, Froebel and his associates acquired the use of a mansion belonging to the Duke of Saxe-Meiningen as a training school for both child-attendants (nursemaids) and child guides (kindergarten teachers). Applicants were to have good prior education and preferably would be between 17 and 20 years old. "More important than age and school education," wrote Froebel, "is the girlish love of childhood and ability to occupy herself with children, as well as a serene and joyful view taken of life in general. There ought also to be a love of play and playful occupations, a love and capacity for singing." The course had to be limited to six months because those who wanted to take it could not afford longer, although he asserted,

> Nothing but inexorable necessity could have enforced such a reduction of time, rendering next to impossible the acquisition of even such knowledge as is absolutely indispensable. Every part of the course must be shortened too much in order to render it possible to reach the end at all. (Heinemann, 1893, p. 73)

Under Froebel's plan, student teachers lived on the school premises. Their day began at 7:00 with a morning service that included a lesson in religious education. The hour from 9 to 10:00 was spent in teaching "the science of the phenomena and laws of the evolution of the child; of the essential nature of the child, and the requirements for his nursing and education." From 10 to 12:00, the previous theory was applied in the kindergarten, with appropriate language, singing accompanied by motions, and similar areas of emphasis. An afternoon session was devoted to practice in handling the gifts for play and occupation. From 5 to 6:00 the students assisted in "plays" and games with children who assembled for that purpose, and the next hour was spent practicing the "plays," games, and occupations that had been carried out during the day. After supper, the students again reviewed and practiced, with Froebel and his staff assisting them (see Heinemann, 1893, pp. 74–76).

Several other training programs soon opened, but this was a time of political unrest in Europe. An aborted revolution in 1848 caused some of Froebel's supporters to emigrate, and in 1851 the Prussian government officially outlawed kindergartens and their training schools. One of Froebel's subversive activities apparently was his insistence on the training of female teachers. After his death in 1852, his young widow and other followers continued teacher training programs in Geneva, Brussels, Dresden, and other locations.

In the United States, Froebel's model strongly influenced the kindergarten training schools. Although most retained much of the personal element that had characterized the earlier apprenticeship system, they were organized to educate teachers for both private kindergartens and those that were being started in public schools. For example, Nora Smith and Kate Douglas Wiggin opened the California Kindergarten Training School on Silver Street in San Francisco in 1880 with some policies remarkably like those of Froebel's model. The 10-month course of study included lectures on Froebelian methods and materials, observation and practice in the kindergarten, and the execution of full books of work in his "occupations," such as paper folding. A key part of the school's philosophy, which came through Froebel from Pestalozzi, was the belief that students could not learn simply from studying books. They must experience kindergarten with the children (Silver Street Kindergarten Society, 1891).

In New York, there were 1,200 graduates of the Krause Seminary for Kindergartners between 1873 and 1914, many of whom moved quickly into leadership positions. In addition, Froebel-trained John Krause and Maria Krause-Boelte were kindergarten activists in the National Educational Association (NEA) from 1872 onward. John Krause criticized the idea that only women should become teachers, since in Froebel's kindergarten men and women worked together. He also said that in Germany a "garden" was a place of recreation and he promoted the kindergarten as a play school to develop individuality. Rather than emphasizing books and theory, student teachers at the Krause Seminary were told to study the children to understand the laws of development. Although the sequenced Froebel materials were used, teachers suggested ideas only after the children had explored and experimented freely (Barnard, 1890; Krause-Boelte & Krause, 1877).

Instead of following Froebel's model, St. Louis Superintendent of Schools William Torrey Harris proposed a large room with one supervising teacher training about ten students, each of them responsible for ten to fifteen children at a long table. Susan Blow, his unsalaried kindergarten supervisor, was able to forestall this scheme. In 1873, after a year's study at the Krause Seminary, she was given a rent-free room at the Normal School, with only 20 children enrolled and 12 kindergartners trained. When those children finished three years of primary school in their first year after kindergarten, Dr. Harris gave approval for expansion. By 1880, there were 52 kindergartens in St. Louis, each with volunteer student assistants from the free training classes (Barnard, 1890). Although she was later criticized as a "traditionalist" who was obstructing scientific progress, Susan Blow's writings indicate her rejection of what she termed Froebelian fetish-worship and suggest the difficulties inherent in the St. Louis system (Blow, 1909). One of the teachers who had studied with her suggested that

> a number of her students showed by their work that they had grasped details only, instead of fundamental principles, and consequently did not have the flexibility and freedom necessary for creative work founded on the selection of educative environments, the experiences, and the culture background of each group of children; consequently, their work became formal and non-creative. (Harrison, 1930, p. 71)

Some training schools, like the one established in Peabody's Boston kindergarten, had other problems. Matilda Kriege and her daughter Alma, Froebelians Peabody had met in Germany, opened it in 1868 but were unsuccessful in part because they were unable to communicate clearly in English. Other training programs during this initial period included correspondence courses and private kindergartens that added teacher training to help pay their expenses. Kindergarten publications carried repeated warnings about spurious training schools, and even as late as 1894 the presidential address of the NEA Kindergarten Department was devoted to the "dangerous possibilities staring us in the face" with "so-called 'trainers'" who were establishing themselves in the "lucrative business" of turning out all graduates with enough money to pay for a course (Mackenzie, 1895, p. 685).

Two of the successful leaders in developing more structured kindergarten training schools were William Hailmann (1836–1920) and Eudora Hailmann (1838–1905). He was German-Swiss, educated in a Pestalozzian school and the Cantonal College in Zurich before emigrating to the United States in 1852, and began work in Pestalozzian German-American schools in 1857. A trip to Zurich in 1860 introduced him to what he called the marvels of Froebel's message. Four years later, as principal for a new school in Louisville, he designed a kindergarten room and hired a German kindergartner. Eudora Hailmann got her initial training as a participating mother in that classroom and then studied in Europe briefly in 1866 and for a full year in 1871. The Hailmanns, joined by their three children when they were older, worked together through the next 25 years to promote an educational system of self-realization and self-discipline. William Hailmann (1888?) wrote, "As if the true kindergarten methods were tied to the gifts and occupations of Froebel! Kindergarten methods may apply to any subject and to any material of instruction. . . . Indeed, I have frequently seen more true kindergarten methods in schools wholly destitute of kindergarten material than in some thoroughly stocked with Bradley's best." Translator of Froebel, author of a dozen books, co-editor with his wife of *The*

*New Education* from 1876 until 1893, prolific writer and speaker, organizer of the Froebel Institute as the first organization of kindergartners in 1882, and instigator of its 1885 merger with the National Educational Association, William Hailmann was a tireless worker for his version of the kindergarten crusade until his death in 1920 (Hewes, 1975).

As her husband moved from city to city, becoming administrator of increasingly larger school systems, Eudora Hailmann developed kindergarten associations, opened bilingual English-German training schools, was president of the Kindergarten Department of the National Educational Association, devised wooden beads and paper weaving mats, popularized the sand table and child-size furniture, co-authored with her daughter Elizabeth a popular school songbook, wrote pamphlets, lectured in colleges, designed exhibits in World's Fairs, and engaged in other activities to promote kindergartens and the training of their teachers. She felt that training schools for kindergartners should take into account the youth of the students, since many were only 14 or 15 years old. They needed a comfortable boarding house close to the kindergarten, with good food and comfortable furniture. She was concerned with the smallest details—the dining room walls should have fruit or harvest scenes, for example, instead of the popular pictures of dead fish and fowl. And, in her opinion, even a three-year course of study needed an additional year of full-time supervised work before a student was ready for employment (Hewes, 1975). One of Eudora Hailmann's former students wrote that

> Some students of Froebel's doctrine were attracted by his mysticism and believed that kindergarten essentials were grounded in symbolism. Those of us who were fortunate enough to come under the tutelage of Mrs. Hailmann (who soundly denounced all such worship of gifts and occupations) became saturated with her sane ideas. . . . The seed of spontaneous child initiative sown by Mrs. Hailmann began to take root, kindergarten ideals were more fitting for little children and although there were still some gross errors committed under the name of kindergarten principles, time has eliminated many of them. (Hosmer, 1942)

The distinction between Elizabeth Peabody's need to maintain God-given adult domination in the kindergarten and the Hailmanns' faith that each child would develop through careful nurturance remains difficult to explain. In current terminology, the European-influenced kindergartners had faith in children's intrinsic abilities, while many Americans depended on extrinsic motivation. The ideas of Peabody,

Harris, Blow, and many others in the kindergarten crusade reflected the New England Puritan work ethic. Their backgrounds predisposed them to believe that children should be taught to be aggressively competitive and to labor industriously so that they might obtain the possessions necessary for a good life. This was incompatible with Froebel's concept of self-determined joy, his blurring of distinctions between work and play, and his belief that one should do only what is creatively self-fulfilling.

The ability to identify with Froebel's philosophical position was only one of the problems met in transferring his method from Germany to the United States. In both the apprenticeships and the training schools, kindergarten teacher education showed wide variations according to the available sources of knowledge about the system, the ability of its American advocates to read idiomatic German or of the Europeans to communicate readily in English, and the basic personality characteristics or management skills of leaders. Elizabeth Peabody was enthusiastic and dedicated, but her financial affairs were always chaotic and haphazard. Matilda and Alma Kriege, with limited English and little public support, found it difficult to transmit the method. John Krause and Maria Krause-Bolte had extensive preparation, seem to have been skilled managers, were psychologically and socially able to accept children's autonomy, and not only had the ability to read and understand the German literature in the field but could pass it on to teachers in training. The Hailmanns, financially astute and able to utilize organizational networks, were oriented toward such liberal causes as the women's suffrage and anti-slavery movements, had no limiting religious orientation, and were able to assimilate from their observations and readings a developmental perspective that they applied to persons of all ages and backgrounds. By the mid-1890s, however, these originators of kindergarten training programs were no longer in leadership positions. The widely diverse versions of kindergarten and the training of kindergarten teachers left the system disorganized and open to criticism.

## KINDERGARTEN PREPARATION IN NORMAL SCHOOLS

It was not until after the Civil War of the early 1860s that public elementary schools with primary classes became widely established. Compulsory education, age-graded and systematized, was one of many innovations during the last half of the nineteenth century, a period in which it was assumed that all social problems were solvable and that schooling was the panacea for most of them. The nation's population of children was rapidly increasing through immigration, a rising birth rate, and a decline in infant mortality. For the first time, America faced serious problems of urban poverty and delinquency. Rather than serving spiritual salvation or vocational accomplishment, schooling was seen as a means of social reform and a way to assimilate immigrant families (Hewes, 1985).

School administrators who had gone to Germany for advanced studies brought back the methodology of Johann Frederick Herbart (1776–1841) as a solution to the problems of elementary schools. As adapted and promoted by American normal schools, the Herbartian method included five formal steps: Preparation, Presentation, Association, Generalization, and Application (Herbart, 1909). The Herbartian teacher's role was in direct contrast to that of the Froebelians, who were outspoken in their concerned criticism. A major debate at the NEA Department of Superintendence meeting in February 1895 was followed by a packed auditorium at the summer conference to hear Toronto's Froebelian superintendent of schools, James Hughes, compare Froebel and Herbart. He concluded by saying that

> Herbart studied the child to mold it; Froebel studied it to guide it in its growth. . . . Herbart saw the need of control much more clearly than the need of freedom; Froebel saw the harmony between freedom and control. Herbart made will result from action; Froebel made action result from will. (p. 544)

Many other attempts were made to distinguish between the two systems, as when Susan Blow (1909) described a kindergarten teacher "pouring herself out during the first hour of the day toward a passive circle of 60 children," who then moved to directed block constructions and to acting out the life of Lincoln with "more pouring out of the teacher's words" (p. 7). She attributed this to "a mixed marriage between Froebelian aims and methods" and "the Ziller-Rein school of Herbartian educators" (p. 11). Selleck (1968) summarized the distinction.

> Herbart's five formal steps became the marching song for a vast array of American teachers who had been reluctant to step out to the tune of Froebel's games and songs. Perhaps it is easier for a system to gain acceptance when the teacher—like a drillmaster—can call the cadence for her class. The Froebelians, playing with the children, lost that authority. (p. 264)

Because Herbartian child study was based on measurable aspects of performance, there was added impetus to require more formal theoretical study and less supervised experience in working directly with children. Not until they re-emerged as the progressive education of John Dewey did Froebelian concepts of children's self-determination and self-activity receive prominence in the teacher training institutions of the United States.

Dissemination of Herbartian methods was facilitated by the proliferation of normal schools for the training of elementary school teachers during the last half of the nineteenth century. The nine normal schools reported by Barnard in 1850 increased to 20 by 1860 and to 100 by 1870. Perkinson (1968) found 12 state-supported teacher training institutions prior to 1869, with many cities establishing their own soon after the Civil War. Most were in regular high schools, although San Francisco opened a postgraduate department for this purpose and St. Louis established a separate school. Some academies evolved into state normal schools. For example, St. Lawrence Academy in New York opened in 1816 with one room and one teacher. Ten years later, it added a substantial stone structure and started teacher education. Another building was required by 1836, and then all were demolished in 1867 to make room for the state-funded Potsdam Normal School (Potsdam Academy, 1895). Like many other normal schools, Potsdam is now a state university.

The transition of teacher training from academies and private training schools to colleges and normal schools was almost complete by the end of the century. An 1895 survey revealed 356 normal schools with about 12,000 students. An additional 6,000 students were enrolled in college teacher training departments, with virtually none in private academies or in the public high schools that had replaced them (Hollis, 1898).

The introduction of kindergarten teacher training into these normal schools was gradual, with initially poor results. One of the first was a short-lived training school in conjunction with New York Normal College that opened in 1870. Adolph Douai, previously a school administrator in Germany with minimal Froebelian background, was employed to conduct a kindergarten in its Model School. One reason for its failure was the age of the children enrolled — all were between seven and eleven. Douai and his daughter, who assisted him, had strong German accents, which made communication difficult. In addition, the principal was antagonistic, ridiculing the idea of learning through play (Barnard, 1890). Primarily, however, Douai seems to have lacked understanding about the system. His 1871 manual (Douai, 1871) described rote methods, strict discipline, and "toys and games" distributed as necessary to keep children from becoming unruly. The New York Normal College kindergarten was successfully reopened in 1874 with a Krause-Boelte graduate as the supervising teacher.

During the 1880s, observation kindergartens were opened in eight normal schools, primarily to familiarize primary teachers with kindergarten ideas. By 1913, 147 institutions offered kindergarten training, about half of them public and half private (U.S. Bureau of Education, 1914). Also in 1913, at a time when the Froebelians were going through a period of unusual controversy within their membership and were being criticized by the more scientific Herbartians, Nina Vandewalker opened her presidential address to the International Kindergarten Union by pointing out that questions about the quality of some programs were justified. Although she believed that some of the best training schools were of college rank, it was essential that standards be raised and that regular college credits be established. Although Vandewalker did not mention it, pay equity with elementary school teachers was perhaps a strong motivation for raising standards, since the inadequate and inferior training of kindergarten teachers in the public schools was frequently used to justify their lower salaries. Raising standards did not mean abandoning the basic Froebelian methodology, however. The purpose of the kindergarten was to develop creative self-activity on the part of the children, she pointed out, but instruction of student teachers often "violated Froebel's dictum that education must not be arbitrary, categorical, and interfering" (Vandewalker, 1914).

A detailed U.S. Bureau of Education report (1916) stated that of 126 teacher training programs registered in 1915, only 24 were identifiable as freestanding kindergarten training schools. All the others were in normal schools or colleges, but they had no uniformity of admissions requirements, curriculum, length of course of study, or certification. Although about half of these training programs provided a two-year curriculum for the teaching credential, employed teachers often spread the required courses over several summer vacations. The committee of kindergarten leaders who compiled this report recommended a two-year program following high school graduation as the minimum requirement for kindergarten teachers. Not more than one year should include supervised teaching, since this would take away from classes in theory. Applicants needed to be of good health, and should possess general culture, fine character, a sympathetic attitude toward young children, and musical ability.

By the 1920s, as kindergarten teacher training became more like that of the primary grades, Benson's (1922) survey of approximately 10,000 teachers, who were graduates from 22 training programs between 1915 and 1921, indicated that the only differences between kindergarten teachers and those at other levels was that a higher proportion of those in kindergarten had had specific preparation for their level. A slightly later study noted that the similarity of traits ascribed to the different types of teachers was remarkable; the study failed to distinguish teachers at the kindergarten level from those of higher grades (Charters, 1929).

The 1920-22 Biennial Survey of the U.S. Bureau of Education summarized changes reported by 305 schools "engaged in the business of preparing teachers." Feminization of teaching was apparent. In 1889-90, about one-third of the 11,684 students were men. Total enrollments for men remained fairly constant, with a high of 3,334 reported for 1921-22. However, enrollments of women students during this period almost tripled, with 23,413 reported in 1921-22. Requirements remained minimal for teacher training programs, with five of the normal schools requiring only eighth-grade graduation for entrance in 1921-22. Some others did not ask for high school completion. Of the 382 teacher training schools located by the Bureau of Education in 1920, 80 were classified as teachers colleges, 110 as state normal schools, 34 as city normal schools, and 95 as county normal schools. No kindergarten training schools were found, although it was noted that the National Kindergarten and Elementary College in Chicago had just made the transition from kindergarten training school to college (U.S. Bureau of Education, 1925, pp. 457, 498-501).

As would be expected, there continued to be many different versions of Froebelian philosophy and methodology as kindergarten training moved into the normal schools. In some, the spirit of the original German kindergartens was maintained. Because Eudora Hailmann was instrumental in establishing their kindergarten departments in 1880 and 1881, the Wisconsin State Normal School in Oshkosh and Minnesota State Normal School at Winona still expected student teachers to learn through creative self-activity and to follow Froebel's dictum, "Come, let us live with our children." In other cases, small kindergarten training schools like Wheelock College in Boston and the National College of Education in Chicago transformed themselves into colleges with much of their Froebelian philosophy intact. Some normal schools that added kindergarten training merely had an acquaintance with Froebel's writings, cursory practice with the Gifts and Occupations, limited experience with supervised observation and teaching, and an expectation that teachers would somehow incorporate these into the overall structure of Herbartian formal planning.

Some Froebelian methods were widely incorporated into training programs for elementary teachers, partly because of Pestalozzian influence and partly due to the demands of parents who had been exposed to the kindergartens through the national network of support associations, the Women's Christian Temperance Union, demonstration classes at World's Fairs, and popular periodicals. Elementary schools and teacher training programs were also affected by international and national expositions.

In a few pioneering school systems, notably that of La Porte, Indiana, where William Hailmann was superintendent from 1883 to 1894, the Froebel method was used from kindergarten through normal school; those schools were given widespread acclaim by popular writers such as Joseph Mayer Rice (1893). Vandewalker (1908) gave great credit to the summer Chautauqua camps, which added Teachers' Retreats in 1879 and demonstration kindergartens in 1881. She also noted that kindergarten songbooks helped primary level teachers become aware of children's bodies, and that studies revealed relationships between health and education. In addition, she wrote, an elementary teacher observing the kindergarten down the hall in her school would start to ask questions.

> Recognizing that there was possible an order of things quite different from that to which she was accustomed, she determined to profit from the lesson. If kindergarten procedure could be made so interesting, why not school procedure as well? Why, she asked, could there not be pictures upon the walls and plants in the windows? Why should the kindergarten children have bright-colored materials and the primary children none? (p. 218)

By the mid-1890s, Vandewalker notes,

> The fundamental principle of the kindergarten — that of education through activity — had been recognized as the principle upon which primary teaching should be based, since an acquaintance with the kindergarten had shown its validity. The external features of the kindergarten, its hand work, its songs and games, its nature work and its stories, had been adopted in many schools. The methods of art education had been radically reconstructed as a result of its influence, and a reconstruction of the methods of teaching music, nature study, and physical training was well under way. (pp. 230–31)

From the 1890s onward, as kindergartens in public school systems experienced rapid growth, some school districts followed the St. Louis plan of providing rooms, but with funding through associations and parent fees. In others, kindergarten was fully incorporated as the entering grade of compulsory elementary school. Just before World War I, which aroused strong feelings against anything with German origins and extinguished most financial support to the Froebelian associations, the federal Commissioner of Education prefaced a detailed analysis of the nation's kindergartens with a summary of their growth.

> Within the decade from 1902 to 1912 the number of kindergartens in the United States increased from 3,244 to 7,557, and the number of children enrolled . . . increased from 205,432 to 353,546, a gain of 133 percent in the number of kindergartens and of 72 percent in the number of enrolled children reported. The total number of kindergarten teachers in 1912 was 8,856. (U.S. Bureau of Education, 1914, p. 5)

This increase was almost all in public school kindergartens, and the demand for teachers with credentials was a critical factor in the transfer of their training from Froebelian training schools to normal schools. In addition, there was a need for a different type of training. Unlike the 1870s, when women entering the field tended to be well educated despite the lack of formal academics, the normal school students of the 1890s and later were more likely to be upwardly mobile daughters of working class families whose need for academic studies required a different method of preparation.

By the 1920s, tax-supported public education had extended downward to include kindergarten in most large American cities. No national policy for kindergarten education had been established, but, as Lazerson (1971), Shapiro (1983), and others have documented, kindergarten goals had changed from the play curriculum of the 1880s to the serious business of controlled preparation for first grade. Froebel's concept of kindergarten as a joyous play program for children between their second and seventh years had become an entry level class that would prepare four- and five-year-olds to enter a rigidly age-graded school. Their credentialed teacher incorporated some Froebelian materials and activities into the daily schedule, but primarily used Herbartian techniques and the methodology of twentieth-century child study theorists. The training of teachers of kindergarten children had entered an era in which both the children and their teachers were integrated into the elementary school systems of America.

## REFERENCES

Barnard, H. (1851). *Normal schools and other institutions, agencies, and means designed for the professional education of teachers.* Hartford, CT: Case, Tiffany & Co.

Barnard, H. (Ed.) (1890). *Papers on Froebel's kindergarten.* Hartford, CT: American Journal of Education.

Benson, C. E. (1922). *The output of professional schools for teachers.* Baltimore: Warwick & York.

Binder, F. M. (1974). *The age of the common school.* New York: John Wiley.

Blow, S. (1894). *Symbolic education: A commentary on Froebel's "Mother Play."* New York: D. Appleton.

Blow, S. (1909). *Educational issues in the kindergarten.* New York: D. Appleton.

Bowen, H. C. (1897). *Froebel and education through self-activity.* New York: Scribner.

Charters, W. W. (1929). *The Commonwealth teacher-training study.* Chicago: University of Chicago Press.

Cremin, L. A. (1951). *The American common school: An historic conception.* New York: Alfred A. Knopf.

Cubberly, E. P. (1920). *Public education in the United States.* Boston: Houghton Mifflin.

Dexter, E. G. (1904). *History of education in the United States.* New York: Macmillan.

Douai, A. (1871). *The kindergarten: A manual.* New York: E. Steiger.

Downs, R. B. (1978). *Friedrich Froebel.* Boston: Twayne.

Guthrie, W. (1795). *A new geographical, historical, and commercial grammar and present state of the several kingdoms of the world* (15th Ed.). London: Printed for Dilly & Robinson.

Hailmann, W. N. (1888?). Handwritten unpublished manuscript. Hailmann Collection, Research Library, University of California at Los Angeles. Box 3.

Primary references for this chapter included personal papers and publications in the William Hailmann Collection at the University of California at Los Angeles, the Los Angeles City Schools Kindergarten Memorial Library, the archives of the Association for Childhood Education International in Wheaton, Maryland, and the archives of the Froebel Institute College in London.

Portions of this chapter presented at the 10th session of the International Standing Conference for the History of Education, University of Joensuu, Finland, July 27, 1988 were published in Ojala (1988) and as "Kindergarten teacher training in the United States from 1870 to 1920" in the *Journal of the National Association of Early Childhood Teacher Educators,* 9(3) (Fall 1988).

Harrison, E. (1930). *Sketches along life's road.* Boston: Stratford.
Heatwole, C. J. (1916). *History of education in Virginia.* New York: Macmillan.
Heiland, H. (1982). *Friedrich Froebel.* Hamburg, FRG: Rowohlt.
Heinemann, A. H. (Ed.) (1893). *Froebel's letters to his wife and others.* Boston: Lee and Shepard.
Herbart, J. F. (1909). *Outlines of educational doctrine.* (A. F. Lange, Trans.) New York: Macmillan.
Hewes, D. W. (1975). W. N. Hailmann: Defender of Froebel. *Dissertation Abstracts International, 36,* 750-A. (University Microfilms No. 75-15, 939)
Hewes, D. W. (1985). The kindergarten as an assimilation program for immigrants to the United States, 1880-1900. In *Historia infantiae, International annual for the history of early childhood education II* (pp. 12-28). Budapest: Eötvös Loránd University.
Hollis, A. P. (1898). *The contribution of the Oswego Normal School to educational progress in the United States.* Boston: D. C. Heath.
Hosmer, E. (1942). Letter in unpublished collection. (M. Conlin, Compiler.) *Honoring the work—Eudora L. Hailmann, Pioneer educator, teacher of kindergartners, La Porte, Indiana 1883-1893.* Los Angeles City Schools Kindergarten Memorial Library.
Hughes, J. L. (1895). Comparison of the educational theories of Froebel and Herbart. *Journal of Proceedings and Addresses, National Educational Association* (pp. 541-45). St. Paul, MN: NEA.
Kilpatrick, W. H. (1916). *Froebel's kindergarten principles critically examined.* New York: Macmillan.
Konig, H. (1982). *Friedrich Froebel, 1782-1852.* Berlin, GDR: Volk und Wisser Volkseigener.
Kotin, L., & Aikman, W. F. (1980). *Legal foundations of education.* Port Washington, NY: National University Publications.
Krause-Boelte, M., & Krause, J. (1877). *The kindergarten guide.* New York: E. Steiger.
Kriege, M. H. (1876). *Friedrich Froebel.* New York: E. Steiger.
Lawrence, E. (Ed.). (1953). *Friedrich Froebel and English education.* New York: Philosophical Library.
Lazerson, M. (1971). *Origins of the urban school: Public education in Massachusetts, 1870-1915.* Cambridge: Harvard University Press.
Liebschner, H. J. (1976). Script of a lecture given to the Michaelis Guild. *The Link—Newsletter No. 66.* London: Michaelis Guild.
Mackenzie, C. (1895). President's address. *Journal of Proceedings, and addresses. Session of the year 1884.* (pp. 682-85). St. Paul, MN: NEA.
Marr, H. W. (1959). *The old New England academies founded before 1826.* New York: Comet.
Martin, G. H. (1894). *The evolution of the Massachusetts Public School System.* New York: D. Appleton.

Morgan, M. (Ed.). (1981). *Friedrich Froebel, 1782-1982*. London: Froebel Institute College.

Ojala, M. (Ed.). (1988). The history of preschool teachers' profession. *Conference Papers for the 10th Session of the International Standing Conference for the History of Education. Bulletins of the Faculty of Education, no. 28*. Joensuu, Finland: University of Joensuu.

Peabody, E. P., & Mann, M. (1864). *Moral culture in infancy and kindergarten guide*. Boston: T. O. H. P. Burnam.

Perkinson, H. J. (1968). *The imperfect panacea: American faith in education, 1865-1965*. New York: Random House.

Potsdam Academy. (1895). *First quarter-centennial history of the State Normal and Training School, Potsdam, N.Y., 1869-1894*. Potsdam, N.Y.: Elliot Fay.

Reisner, E. H. (1930). *The evolution of the common school*. New York: Macmillan.

Rice, J. M. (1893). *The public school system of the United States*. New York: Century.

Rogers, D. (1961). *Oswego: Fountainhead of teacher education*. New York: Appleton-Century-Crofts.

Ronda, B. A. (1984). *Letters of Elizabeth Palmer Peabody*. Middletown, CT: Wesleyan University Press.

Ross, E. D. (1976). *The kindergarten crusade: The establishment of preschool education in the United States*. Athens, OH: Ohio University Press.

Selleck, R. J. W. (1968). *The new education*. London: Sir Isaac Pitman.

Shapiro, M. S. (1983). *Child's garden — The kindergarten movement from Froebel to Dewey*. University Park, PA: Pennsylvania State University Press.

Silver Street Kindergarten Society. (1891). *Ninth annual statement for the year ending December 31, 1890*. San Francisco: Silver Street Kindergarten Society.

Smith, N. A. (1900). *The children of the future*. Cambridge, MA: Riverside Press.

Snyder, A. (1972). *Dauntless women in childhood education, 1856-1931*. Washington, DC: Association for Childhood Education International.

Swift, F. (1931). Emma Marwedel: Pioneer of the kindergarten in California. *University of California Publications in Education* 6(3), 139-216.

U.S. Bureau of Education. (1914). *Kindergartens in the United States*. Bulletin no. 6. Washington, DC: Government Printing Office.

U.S. Bureau of Education. (1916). *Kindergarten training schools*. Bulletin no. 5. Washington, DC: Government Printing Office.

U.S. Bureau of Education. (1925). *Biennial survey of education, 1920-1921*, Vol. 2. Washington, DC: Government Printing Office.

Vandewalker, N. C. (1908). *The kindergarten in American education*. New York: Macmillan.

Vandewalker, N. C. (1914). The standardizing of kindergarten training. In U.S. Bureau of Education, *Kindergartens in the United States*. Bulletin no. 6 (pp. 114–18). Washington, DC: U.S. Government Printing Office.

Weber, E. (1969). *The kindergarten: Its encounter with educational thought in America*. New York: Teachers College Press.

CHAPTER 2

# Preparing Early Childhood Teachers

## Bernard Spodek
## Olivia N. Saracho

Early childhood teachers function in kindergartens, prekindergartens, or primary grades of public elementary schools as well as in non-public school settings, such as child care centers, Head Start programs, and nursery schools. While some early childhood teachers work with normal young children, others work with exceptional children, such as gifted children, bilingual children, children of migrant workers, or children who have been identified as being at-risk of later school failure.

These distinctions in programs reflect their purposes, the populations served, and the programs' sponsorship. They are reflected in the teacher requirements, including preparation and expected levels of skills, understandings, and competencies. Distinctions are also reflected in the levels of compensation (1) between public school-sponsored programs and non-public school programs, whether sponsored by public or private agencies and (2) between teachers in child care programs and educational programs. Most often, early childhood teachers in public school education-oriented programs have the same level of preparation and meet similar standards for certification as do teachers in elementary or secondary school programs. Teachers in other early childhood programs may be graduates of one- or two-year programs at community or junior colleges, have completed a preparation program at a vocational center, or have had no preservice preparation at all. Teachers with the same qualifications working in child care programs earn less than their counterparts in educational programs, even when the child care programs are sponsored by public schools (Mitchell, Seligman, & Marx, 1989).

The distinction between *teacher* and *child caregiver* was identified more than 60 years ago when the authors of the 28th Yearbook of the

National Society for the Study of Education viewed day nurseries—as child care centers were then called—as serving a relief function for families rather than being primarily concerned with the needs of young children (Whipple, 1929). Whether those who work with young children in child care centers should have higher, lower, or equal preparation to those who educate young children was still being discussed a decade later (Beer, 1938) and continues to be discussed today—some five decades later (Kagan, 1989).

An acceptable level of preparation for practitioners in early childhood education is presently determined by employers or by state agencies—either those who supervise education or those who supervise child welfare programs. Typically, the requirements, which are established by child care licensing agencies for work in child care programs, are lower than those for work in public educational programs, whose requirements are set by the state education agencies. Teachers who meet higher academic requirements than child care workers and who receive a state teaching certificate are often considered professionals. The preservice preparation of these teachers, who are expected to complete teacher education programs in four-year colleges or universities and who receive at least a bachelors degree, is the focus of this chapter. Powell and Dunn (see Chapter 3) focus on those early childhood practitioners who are prepared in programs below the bachelors degree level. In the pages that follow, the content and structure of teacher education programs will be discussed, along with the possible consequences to the field of proposed reforms in teacher education programs.

## THE CONTENT OF EARLY CHILDHOOD TEACHER PREPARATION PROGRAMS

It would be logical to assume that the content of early childhood teacher education programs would be determined by early childhood educators themselves. However, in establishing educational criteria for employment in the field, state teacher certification standards heavily influence the nature of all teacher education programs, including those in early childhood education. These certification standards reflect a great number of different influences, those of early childhood educators, but also those of other interested groups. Changes in certification requirements have been the single most important influence on changes in early childhood teacher education programs, more so, in fact, than the professional knowledge of early childhood educators (Spodek, Davis, & Saracho, 1983).

Along with state teacher certification guidelines, program accreditation guidelines, such as those of the National Council for Accreditation of Teacher Education (NCATE), and position statements, such as those of the National Association for the Education of Young Children (NAEYC), also influence the content and structure of early childhood teacher education. These varied guidelines generally determine the structure of teacher education programs more than their content. Such guidelines are based on judgments about what content and training experiences would develop the knowledge, attitudes, skills, and ethics required of a teacher of young children. Judgments also need to be made about the sequencing of learning experiences for those preparing to teach, as well as about the standards of accomplishment to be applied to beginners in the field and about what learnings might best be postponed to later in an individual's career rather than before beginning one's career. Thus, there is a developmental as well as a substantive issue to be addressed in dealing with the preparation of teachers of young children.

There is also a belief that a teacher is more than a technician. Teachers are expected to be well-educated persons. They also should have a strong enough knowledge base to make professional decisions regarding the education of the children within their charge. The first of these requirements has led to the belief that good teachers must have strong programs of general education along with professional preparation. Thus, general education is increasingly being viewed as an important part of teacher preparation. There is also the belief that the professional part of the program should consist of something more than passing on the practical lore of experienced teachers. Identifying the knowledge base of early childhood education and of early childhood teacher education, including educational and developmental theory, is increasingly being seen as a high priority task for the field.

There are four components of four-year teacher education programs: general education, foundations, instructional knowledge, and practice (Saracho & Spodek, 1983). Each of these is discussed below.

## General Education

The general education portion of early childhood teacher education programs is common to all higher education programs, whether liberal arts or professionally oriented. This portion typically constitutes from two-thirds to three-fourths of the teacher education program. Its content is determined by what knowledge is expected of any well-educated person, not by what one is required to know as a teacher. In some programs the general education component is broadly conceived, with required courses widely distributed across scholarly disciplines. In other programs, a specialization or minor field of study is required, which focuses a large proportion of the students' general education work in one discipline or core of subjects. Typically, general education courses are heavily concentrated in the first two years of the teacher education program, with professional courses making up a greater proportion of the work in the last two years of the program.

The general education component should not be considered an add-on to the preparation of early childhood teachers. Because teachers at this level are teachers of general education, it represents the core of the subject matter that teachers of younger children must master. The early childhood teacher is not a teacher of child development, but one who uses child development knowledge in making decisions both about what to include in an early childhood program and how to present that content to a particular group of children. Sometimes the content of the general education component is modified to reflect the portions that are relevant to young children. Children's literature and music for children, for example, may be required along with adult literature and music.

In recent years, there has been increased criticism and controversy over the nature of general education in higher education. Some educators have argued that there is no single core of knowledge that all individuals in our society should master. This view has led to a proliferation of general education requirements in colleges and universities. Electives, sometimes within required areas of scholarship, have been offered to students as a way of meeting general education requirements.

Among the spokespersons for an alternative view have been E. D. Hirsch, Jr. (Hirsch, 1987). In his book, *Cultural Literacy*, Hirsch argues that individuals need to share a common core of schema with others in a community to participate in the discourse and activities of a culture. Whether there is a clearly identifiable core that should be required of all educated persons or whether this core is related to subcultural groups or is even a matter of personal taste continues to be argued. Indeed, there have been serious controversies on many campuses about the nature of that core, which traditionally has reflected Western culture as well as the products of male scholars from the majority cultural group.

However, there is common agreement that those who will teach young children should be knowledgeable in a variety of areas: the humanities—including history, language, and literature—the sciences, the social sciences, and the arts. The level of knowledge they should acquire in each field and whether what they learn should reflect Western majority society or include non-Western cultures and give adequate representation to the contributions of women and members of cultural minorities is being argued on many university campuses.

These issues are at least as, if not more, important for those who are preparing to become teachers as for those who are being educated for other careers. Teachers are given the responsibility for socializing children and for transmitting our culture to the next generation. The depth and range of the teachers' knowledge will be reflected in what they teach. Thus, if teachers are familiar only with Western culture and the contributions of white male Americans, then the programs they prepare will probably exclude the contributions of non-Westerners, members of minority groups, and females. The content of the general education program can be used as a vehicle to provide social justice within our children's schools.

## Educational Foundations

The foundational component of the teacher education program is concerned with knowledge about education rather than with professional techniques. This component draws heavily on the disciplines of history, philosophy, psychology, sociology, economics, political science, and anthropology. It tends to be theory- and policy-oriented.

In early childhood education, child development makes up a large portion of the foundational knowledge that teachers are expected to learn. Sometimes the justification for this is the view that early childhood education is the practical application of child development research and theory (Caldwell, 1984). Thus, the greater the knowledge of child growth and development teachers acquire, the better teachers of young children they will be.

Many leaders in the field have felt that child development knowledge is more necessary for early childhood teachers than for teachers of older children. Others take the view that while early childhood education as a field represents a broader core of knowledge, the field of child development has made and continues to make a significant contribution to the field of early childhood education, possibly a greater one than the other foundation areas. Children at this younger age level change quickly, and, more than at any other age, their capability to learn is heavily dependent on their level of development. Child development knowledge is viewed as necessary for teachers to plan learning activities that are developmentally appropriate for children in their classes.

The conventional wisdom reflecting the close relationship of child development research and theory to early childhood curriculum and to teaching methodology in the classroom, as well as the application of child development knowledge to teacher training, has been challenged by a number of educators and psychologists. Sylva (1986) argues that we cannot trace the emphasis on exploration and play to the influence of Piaget. She traces the preschool practices of Susan Isaacs, for example, to those of John Dewey and to her own experiences as a classroom teacher. She also suggests that the High/Scope curriculum, which has been identified by its developers as Piaget-based, uses the work of Bruner and Smilansky at least as much as the theories of Piaget, with all these theories being more germinal than central to the curriculum.

Similarly, Desforges (1986) sees limited use of developmental psychology in teacher training. He identifies reservations in the degree to which psychologists and others accept each developmental theory and suggests that given these reservations the theories are not sound enough for educators to use. In addition, the fact that contemporary developmental research and theory have given little attention to their applicability to education makes their application limited with regard to teacher education. Such criticism suggests the need to rethink the relationship of developmental theory to early childhood education that has been articulated in such documents as NAEYC's *Developmentally Appropriate Practice in Early Childhood Programs Serving Children from Birth Through Age 8* (Bredekamp, 1987).

Providing foundational studies only in child development limits the areas of knowledge that teachers will have for functioning in their many capacities, both within the classroom and outside it. Additional areas of foundational knowledge include the other social sciences as well as philosophy of education. Teachers work with children in groups. They should know about the nature of groups, how groups function, and the roles and relationships among members. This kind of knowledge comes from the areas of sociology and social psychology. Early childhood teachers are becoming increasingly involved in policy issues related to children and families. Knowledge of how governments work and how legislatures and government agencies function, and of how legislation and regulation can be influenced, is reflected in political science. Since education is a moral activity reflecting the values of the community, philosophic foundations would help teachers put their professional knowledge into a broader perspective in making classroom decisions. All these areas and more should be reflected in the educational foundations of a teacher education program.

## Instructional Knowledge

Within the instructional knowledge component, prospective teachers are helped to gain specific knowledge and skills to be used in planning and implementing educational programs. The courses students take within this component include early childhood curriculum and instruction. These courses are needed to plan programs and to teach music, art, language, and other subjects. Courses in classroom management, working with parents, and dealing with handicapped children in regular classrooms are also generally part of such programs. Typically, these courses are offered in regular college classes. Sometimes, a practicum may be associated with each methods course.

Most of the research on teacher education has been done on the instructional knowledge and practice components of teacher education programs. Unfortunately, little of this research has been conducted on programs preparing early childhood teachers or their components. Thus, our knowledge of early childhood teacher education programs is generally extrapolated from studies of programs preparing elementary teachers (Spodek & Saracho, 1982).

The content of courses in the instructional knowledge component is rooted in curriculum theory and instructional theory as well as developmental theory and learning theory. These courses cannot be completely theory-based, however, since no theory or set of theories can adequately justify classroom practice. Thus such courses are also rooted in the practical knowledge that teachers develop from working directly with children in classes. According to Elbaz (1983), practical knowledge is related to teaching and learning. It is integrated by each individual teacher from his or her accumulated teaching experience, the educational theories learned, and the individual's values and beliefs. The importance of practical knowledge is attested to by the fact that most teacher education programs require that faculty who teach courses related to instructional knowledge have prior experience in teaching children.

One approach to determining the nature of instructional knowledge was taken early in the evolution of the child development associate (CDA) credential. This approach attempted to identify teaching competencies through a task analysis and observations of teachers in action, and was rooted in the performance-based or competency-based teacher education movement of the 1970s. Essentially, the belief was that competent teachers can be identified by what they do. By observing competent teachers as well as less competent ones, one could identify those behaviors that are associated with high levels of competence and could train novices in these behaviors or competencies so that they would become competent themselves. This approach of using a behavioral profile of highly qualified teachers as a basis for a teacher education program, while superficially very attractive, poses a number of problems.

The consortium's broad description of a competent professional did not result from actual observations of competent teachers in action. In addition, the competencies identified do not describe what an effective teacher needs to know. Diversity and individual differences must be valued and respected. Performance skills must be integrated with a body of knowledge and theory in which teachers need to be immersed. When teachers plan and evaluate instruction, they implement such knowledge in the classroom. Also, what teachers know helps them to select and sequence instructional strategies and develop educational goals for young children. The integration and understanding of knowledge provide a broad perspective and make teaching relevant. In addition, there are significant differences between how competent veteran teachers and competent novice teachers function in the classroom (Saracho & Spodek, 1983; Spodek & Saracho, 1988). To train novice teachers to perform teaching tasks like veterans may create problems for them since they function at a different level.

Rather than doing a task analysis of teachers in action to identify necessary teacher competencies, Saracho (1984) suggested a conceptual analysis of teaching using the roles early childhood teachers assumed to obtain knowledge of classroom practice. Through a role analysis, Saracho (1984) found the following roles of a teacher:

1. *Diagnostician*. Teachers need to assess children's strengths and needs in order to plan the proper match of successful learning experiences for children.

2. *Curriculum designer*. Teachers develop curricula for young children within their capabilities based on theories and practices of early childhood education as well as the learnings that the community considers important.

3. *Organizer of instruction*. Teachers use their outcomes from long-range and short-range planning to organize classroom activities to achieve educational goals. Teachers inquire about appropriate available resources and make the best use of these resources.

4. *Manager of learning.* Teachers facilitate learning by creating a learning environment and offering learning experiences that are relevant and of interest to the children.

5. *Counselor/Advisor.* Teachers continuously interact with children and provide them with caretaking, emotional support, and guidance, as well as instruction. Teachers also help children to learn socialization skills.

6. *Decision maker.* Teachers constantly make a range of decisions about children, materials, activities, and goals. Some are instantaneous decisions, while others reflect decisions as teachers plan, select, and implement from among alternatives.

These roles, which are summarized in Table 2.1, are directly related to both the teacher's preactive and interactive professional performance. If the role of the teacher is conceptualized beyond classroom responsibilities, other roles (for example, child advocate, adult educator, or supervisor) may be added.

The identification of roles indicates that successful performance of each role requires that teachers of young children acquire a range of knowledge, skills, and attitudes. As teachers acquire knowledge and understanding, they can apply the principles and practices of early childhood education to practical situations.

In a series of studies, Saracho (1987, 1988a, 1988b, 1988c, 1988d) tested through observations and interviews the different roles of the early childhood teacher. She found an equal balance in the teacher's roles as curriculum designer, organizer of instruction, and counselor/advisor. Rather than identify a separate decision-making role, however, the role of decision maker was integrated within those roles. Thus, each of the first five roles has within it both a decision-making function and a performance function related to carrying out the decisions that teachers make.

The results of these studies provide insight into the roles teachers assume in the classroom and help to integrate theory and practice. Role theory was modified in several ways.

1. Organizer of instruction and manager of learning were integrated. The tasks seem to differ, but in actual practice both roles must be integrated.
2. Unsophisticated tasks like cleaning are also the teacher's responsibility, even if the teacher delegates this responsibility to students. Teachers need to model appropriate behavior, and some cleaning tasks can be performed only by the teacher.

*(continued on p. 37)*

**Table 2.1.** Summary of the Different Roles of the Teacher

| Roles | Knowledge | Skills | Attitudes |
|---|---|---|---|
| Decision maker | Curriculum of early childhood education<br>Content and methods of different subject areas | Organizing the classroom<br>Planning the curriculum<br>Matching materials and methods to children | Community's values |
|  | Child development | Meeting individual needs<br>Obtaining techniques to work with children<br>Obtaining information about children | Behavioral style<br>Teaching style |
|  | Theories of play | Knowing how to use play as a tool of learning | Play as educational |
|  | Recent research, development, and practice in early childhood education | Acquiring research skills | Objectives |
|  | Role of the teacher | Teaching duties, responsibilities, obligations, functions | Ethics, attitudes, ideological position, self-image, membership and reference group, commitment to the profession |
| Organizer of Instruction | Child development—Process of development and learning | Knowing how certain procedures affect children and teachers<br>Integrating information within some structure to give meaning | Behavioral style<br>Teaching style |

|  |  |  |
|---|---|---|
|  |  | Developing materials |
|  |  | Operating equipment |
|  |  | Locating resources for a variety of materials |
|  |  | Working with other adults in the classroom |
|  | Evaluation methods | Evaluating materials, resources, and equipment |
|  |  | Knowing self-evaluation |
|  |  | Knowing evaluation of teaching and programs |
| Curriculum Designer | Curriculum theory | Selecting scope, sequence, and balance |
|  |  | Adapting content to individual differences |
|  |  | Knowing different methods of teaching |
|  |  | Selecting materials and equipment without demeaning individuals |
|  |  | Planning long-range and short-range goals |
|  |  | Establishing goals, content, and teaching techniques |
|  |  | Matching goals, methods, and experiences |
|  |  | Locating resources |
|  |  | Community's values |
|  |  | Cultural values |
|  |  | Teacher's ideology of early childhood education |
|  |  | Ethnic groups |
|  |  | Teacher's values |
|  |  | Teaching style |

*(continued)*

**Table 2.1.** (Continued)

| Roles | Knowledge | Skills | Attitudes |
|---|---|---|---|
| | Child development theory | Knowing developmental norms to group children for appropriate experiences | |
| | Knowledge of curriculum areas (language, reading, mathematics, social studies, etc.) | Selecting concepts from a mixture of different forms of knowledge | |
| | | Integrating knowledge with understanding | |
| | | Integrating curriculum areas and teaching practice | |
| | Philosophy | Integrating activities with the different disciplines | |
| Diagnostician | Child development | Judging children's maturation stages, achievement of prior learnings, behavior, and so on | Concern for individual differences |
| | | Collecting, analyzing, and interpreting data | |
| | | Becoming aware of individual skills, abilities, interests, and behavior | |

|  | Assessment techniques | Using: |
|  |  | Sociometric scales |
|  |  | Observation techniques |
|  |  | Interviews |
|  |  | Selecting appropriate experiences, materials, and equipment |
|  | Curriculum and methods | Selecting activities |
|  | Psychology of learning | Creating an attractive educational environment |
|  |  | Awareness of individual differences such as cognitive styles, interests, and needs |
| Manager of Learning | Curriculum theory | Planning and implementing learning activities |
|  | Child development | Guiding children's behavior in performing educational tasks |
|  |  | Establishing work routines |
|  |  | Presenting subject matter |
|  |  | Providing educational tools and classroom displays |
|  |  | Offering a wide range of learning alternatives |
|  |  | Scheduling and implementing transitions |

*(continued)*

**Table 2.1.** (Continued)

| Roles | Knowledge | Skills | Attitudes |
|---|---|---|---|
| Counselor/Advisor | Child psychology | Knowing different methods of interacting | Teacher's values and priorities |
| | Child development | Creating an environment that motivates the child's exploration and discovery | Accept individual differences |
| | Sociology | Helping children make decisions | Provide warmth and emotional support |
| | Anthropology | Promoting children's creative growth and self-actualization | Present a sense of trust and security |
| | Philosophy | Manifesting their personality in an authentic way | Society's values |
| | Psychology of learning | Searching their educational and teaching values | |

*Source:* Saracho, O. N. (1984). Perception of the Teaching Process in Early Childhood Education Through Role Analysis. *Journal of the Association for the Study of Perception, International, 19*(1), pp. 35–38.

Although the results of these studies supported the roles identified by Saracho (1984), such a role analysis does not by itself lead to a particular set of instructional knowledge components that should be required of each person in a teacher preparation program. Teaching is a creative process, not a mechanical art. It demands more than just assimilating the behavior of a role model. There are several methods of teaching, and one is not better than the others. The rational basis of teaching is definitely not learned through modeling. In addition, there is insufficient research evidence to support some teacher behaviors or specific models of good teaching.

Saracho's (1984) descriptions of the different roles provide some insight into the theory, knowledge, and practice teachers need for the different roles. The descriptions also provide teacher education programs a way to evaluate their goals, content, and field experiences. The goals should be restated to reflect the impact of issues on the preparation of effective teachers. Similarly, the teacher education program should be evaluated in light of the changing society and the integrative nature of teaching behaviors rather than segmented courses that are generally taught in isolation. Several evaluation strategies in a variety of situations determine the teacher's progress throughout the different stages of the preparation program.

In the near future, teachers and those educators concerned about young children will make public their priorities as the issues of quality and control become increasingly important to them. They will take stands and demonstrate what they believe to be right, true, and good for young children. Such demonstrations will affect the future of teacher education in the United States and its educational framework.

Teacher education programs must modify their conceptual framework, including their content, practice, and methodology. The accumulated faculty enterprise must change its instructional processes. A new teacher education program that is responsive to the need to prepare teachers for their multifaceted roles within our society can produce effective teachers.

## Practice

The practice component of a teacher education program that includes prestudent teaching field experiences as well as student teaching is generally the part in which instructors in teacher education institutions collaborate with practitioners in children's programs. Field experiences in early childhood schools or centers allow teachers-in-training to relate what they are learning in their college or university classes to actual classroom practice. Both observation and participation are important. This component typically culminates in the novice assuming total responsibility for teaching a group of children.

Observation helps the student become aware of all of the elements of classroom teaching: the role of the teacher, the behaviors and interactions of students, the uses of materials and equipment, and the importance of scheduling and room arrangement. Participation, including assuming full responsibility for classroom practice and the decisions related to that practice, enables students to integrate the professional knowledge that they have gained from their studies, along with their own values, understandings, and sensitivities, and create their own core of personal practical knowledge that will guide their teaching.

Four-year teacher education programs might require as many as 600 clock hours of student teaching, in at least two early childhood educational settings. They often also require 100 or more clock hours of prestudent teaching field experiences. Over the years, the reduction in the number of laboratory schools on college and university campuses has shifted the placement of student teachers away from campus-controlled settings. Most student teaching experiences now take place in off-campus sites, including public schools and non-public preschools.

The practice component of teacher education programs has long been considered an important part of teacher education programs. Among its positive outcomes, student teaching

1. improves teacher behavior and performance;
2. increases teachers' professional orientation, positive attitudes, and commitments to teaching;
3. increases preservice teachers' abilities to determine readiness levels, clarify program objectives, and motivate and evaluate students;
4. facilitates teachers' understandings and acceptance of at-risk children;
5. increases teachers' use of indirect teaching methods;
6. increases teachers' orientation to democratic teaching styles (Becher & Ade, 1982).

There may also be negative consequences of student teaching. Student teachers may project what they have observed in their practice situations as the only or proper way of dealing with classroom situations, even if inappropriate, and may avoid seeking new knowledge and skills (Feiman-Nemser, 1983; Katz, 1984). Although there are questions about the negative impact of less-than-ideal student teaching placements, it is clear that the practice component is primarily a positive experience. It allows prospective teachers to apply the theoretical knowledge they receive from classes and textbooks to real classroom situations. It also allows them to construct and modify their own knowledge, skills, and personal-professional theories and understandings about teaching and learning.

Successful completion of all of the components of a teacher education program that has been approved by the state education agency leads to the individual's becoming a certified teacher. Students typically have demonstrated their knowledge through meeting particular course requirements, which often include tests and course papers. They have also demonstrated their ability to function as novice teachers in the practice component of their programs. They have been observed and evaluated by both classroom practitioners who serve as cooperating teachers and college or university supervisors. In many states today, graduates of these programs seeking teacher certification must also pass state tests — sometimes tests of basic academic skills, sometimes tests of pedagogical knowledge, and sometimes a combination of both.

While bachelors degree programs have been described here, vocational programs, at the community college and high school level, also prepare early childhood practitioners. There are few descriptions of these programs in the literature. Typically, however, they consist of instruction in child growth and development, and laboratory experience with young children. Instructors in such programs are often certified vocational home economics teachers or persons with experience in the child care field (see Powell & Dunn, this volume).

## REFORMS IN THE PREPARATION OF EARLY CHILDHOOD TEACHERS

There have been a number of groups, concerned with the preparation of teachers at all levels, that have been dissatisfied with current practices in the preparation of teachers and have suggested ways of reforming these programs. Foremost among these has been the Carnegie Forum on Education and the Economy (1986) and the Holmes Group (1986). Cooper and Eisenhart, in Chapter 10, have identified some of the suggested reforms that might affect early childhood teacher education programs. They include

1. abolishing undergraduate teacher education degrees;
2. creating programs of teacher education that extend beyond the bachelors degree;
3. placing a cap on the number of credit hours in education that would be allowed toward a university degree;
4. extending the field experiences in teacher education programs;
5. creating an induction period or internship for novice teachers;
6. creating alternative approaches to teacher certification;
7. establishing more specific forms of teacher certification.

Abolishing undergraduate teacher education degrees and creating programs of teacher education that extend beyond the bachelors degree would make access to the early childhood teaching profession less available to many individuals. It would seriously hamper the creation of career ladders that might allow persons from minority and low income groups to move through the stages of early childhood professionalism, especially since many of these individuals have greater difficulty with the general education component of teacher preparation programs than with the professional components.

Placing a cap on the number of credit hours in education that would be allowed toward a university degree might make for a better educated teacher, but not necessarily a more professionally competent teacher. Teaching young children requires a great amount of professional knowledge. Limiting the number of courses that may be included in a program may also limit the amount of knowledge that can be gained by the students. A proposal for a cap, which might make sense for teachers at the secondary level, could actually weaken the early childhood teaching profession.

Extending the field experiences in teacher education programs might have a positive influence on those programs. It would probably result in a greater proportion of the teacher education program taking place in children's schools or centers. It would probably also allow practitioners to have a greater and more important role in the preparation of early childhood teachers. This should lead to programs that provide greater support for teachers' development of professional practical knowledge. Whether it will weaken the theoretical component of early childhood teacher education programs might depend on how such a proposal is implemented.

Creating an induction period or internship for novice teachers could have a positive impact on the field. In the normal course of events, once teachers complete an approved program and are certified, they are hired by schools or school systems and immediately assume the same responsibilities as experienced teachers. Seldom is a support system available for a reasonable period of time to allow for a more gradual transition to professional responsibilities. Some school systems have instituted formal mentor programs to allow experienced teachers to offer help and guidance to novices. At other times, informal mentoring may occur among colleagues in a school. A more systematic approach to induction might lessen the trauma of beginning teaching and could lead to greater retention of teachers in the field.

Providing alternative approaches to teacher certification could help many practitioners in the field move from lower to higher levels of professionalism. It might also allow the CDA credential to become a stepping stone to certification. Haberman (1988) sees a possible conflict arising from alternative approaches to certification. He predicts a situation where, on the one hand, teachers will be required to complete more rigorous and extensive programs of teacher education to be certified in the conventional manner. On the other hand, school systems would be able to hire as teachers individuals who have no pedagogical background. An effort is needed to avoid such a conflict before a proposal for alternative routes to certification is implemented.

Establishing more specific forms of teacher certification could improve the field of early childhood education. With broad certification now available, such as kindergarten through grade 6, or even grade 9, many persons teaching in early childhood programs were not actually prepared to teach in these programs, although their certificates allow them and suggest they are competent to do so. A narrower teaching certificate might better ensure that teachers teach the areas for which they have been prepared.

The suggestions noted above are designed to improve the quality of teachers in our schools. Yet, with the exception of the call for extended field experiences, they do not deal with improving the nature of the professional component of teacher education programs. Few would say that we have achieved the ideal content in our programs of early childhood teacher preparation. It would seem that this is an area where early childhood professionals need to identify problems or needs and come up with possible solutions.

We need to identify the specific knowledge that is critical for a professional early childhood teacher. What developmental theories should teachers know and how extensive should this knowledge be? What other foundational areas must early childhood teachers know? We also need to identify other areas of requisite knowledge, as well as the competencies expected. In addition, we need to test the effectiveness of our current programs to see how successful we are in preparing teachers to have the understandings and competencies we should expect. Perhaps we should be looking for alternative ways of preparing professionals as well as alternative ways of certifying them.

## CONCLUSION

This chapter has presented and discussed the framework of current early childhood teacher preparation programs as well as proposals for the reform of early childhood teacher education. The reforms presented here were designed to improve university-based, certification-oriented teacher education programs. Other efforts to improve practices and standards in early childhood teacher education have come from professional associations directly concerned with early childhood education (for example, NAEYC, 1982). Many early childhood practitioners, especially those who practice in child care programs, are not professionally trained. One of the dilemmas facing the field is that improving the professional preparation of early childhood teachers may not greatly affect the field as it is currently organized. For one thing, we are not currently preparing enough early childhood teachers at the professional level to staff all the early childhood classrooms that presently exist and that will exist in the future. Given this situation, practitioners would have to be hired who do not meet any standards that might be set for entering the field. In addition, professionally prepared early childhood teachers will not always accept positions in the places where they are available. Child care centers and other preschool programs do not pay enough to compete with public school systems in hiring teachers. Thus, certified teachers tend to accept employment within the higher paying public school systems. It also seems that many centers prefer not to hire professionally trained personnel. Instead, they prefer hiring individuals on an hourly basis, often at near minimum wage and sometimes on a less than full-time basis. In this way they can avoid the cost of employee benefits, such as sick leave, health insurance, and pensions.

No improvement in the preparation of early childhood teacher education programs will solve the personnel problem facing the field. Rather, we need to look at ways of increasing the expected level of professionalism in the field. This is a complex task (Spodek, Saracho, & Peters, 1988). Standards of practice and criteria for entry into the field would have to be established and monitored. Salaries, working conditions, and benefits of early childhood practitioners would have to be improved to make the field more attractive for qualified practitioners to enter and to wish to remain. The task ahead will require major modifications in the way that programs are sponsored and regulated. It will certainly raise opposition from a number of concerned groups. To what extent the field of early childhood education becomes more professionalized and requires standards of preparation will be determined by the actions of individuals and groups both within and outside the field.

## REFERENCES

Becher, R. M., & Ade, W. (1982). The relationship of field placement characteristics and students' potential field performance abilities to clinical experience performance ratings. *Journal of Teacher Education, 33*(2), 24-30.

Beer, E. S. (1938). *The day nursery.* New York: Dutton.

Bredekamp, S. (Ed.). (1987). *Developmentally appropriate practice in early childhood programs serving children from birth through age 8* (exp. ed.). Washington, DC: National Association for the Education of Young Children.

Caldwell, B. (1984). Growth and development. *Young Children, 39*(6), 53-56.

Carnegie Forum on Education and the Economy. (1986). *A nation prepared: Teachers for the 21st century.* New York: Carnegie Corporation.

Child Development Associate Consortium (1977). *Competency standards.* Washington, DC: Child Development Associate Consortium.

Desforges, C. (1986). Developmental psychology applied to teacher training. In J. Harris (Ed.), *Child psychology in action: Linking research and practice* (pp. 208-19). London: Croom Helm.

Elbaz, F. (1983). *Teachers' thinking: A study of practical knowledge.* New York: Nicholas.

Feiman-Nemser, S. (1983). Learning to teach. In L. S. Shulman & G. Sykes (Eds.), *Handbook of teaching and policy* (pp. 150-70). New York: Longman.

Haberman, M. (1988). Gatekeepers to the profession. In B. Spodek, O. N. Saracho, & D. L. Peters (Eds.), *Professionalism and the early childhood practitioner* (pp. 84-92). New York: Teachers College Press.

Hirsch, E. D., Jr. (1987). *Cultural literacy: What every American needs to know.* Boston: Houghton Mifflin.

Holmes Group. (1986). *Tomorrow's teachers: A report of the Holmes Group.* East Lansing, MI: Michigan State University.

Kagan, S. L. (1988). Current reforms in early childhood education: Are we addressing the issues? *Young Children, 43*(2), 27-32.

Katz, L. G. (1984). The education of preprimary teachers. In L. G. Katz (Ed.), *Current topics in early childhood education* (Vol. 5, pp. 209-28). Norwood, NJ: Ablex.

Mitchell, A., Seligman, M., & Marx, F. (1989). *Early childhood programs and the public schools.* Dover, MA: Auburn House.

National Association for the Education of Young Children. (1982). *Early child-*

hood teacher education guidelines for four- and five-year programs. Washington, DC: NAEYC.

Saracho, O. N. (1984). Perception of the teaching process in early childhood education through role analysis. *Journal of the Association for the Study of Perception, International, 19*(1), 26-29.

Saracho, O. N. (1987). An instructional evaluation study in early childhood education. *Studies in Educational Evaluation, 13*, 163-74.

Saracho, O. N. (1988a). An evaluation of an early childhood teacher education curriculum for preservice teachers. *Early Child Development and Care, 38*, 81-101.

Saracho, O. N. (1988b). A study of the roles of early childhood teachers. *Early Child Development and Care, 38*, 43-56.

Saracho, O. N. (1988c). Using observation to study the roles of the teacher. *College Student Journal, 22*(4), 396-400.

Saracho, O. N. (1988d). Assessing instructional materials in an early childhood teacher education curriculum: The search for impact. *Reading Improvement, 25*(1), 10-27.

Saracho, O. N., & Spodek, B. (1983). Preparing teachers for multicultural settings. In O. N. Saracho & B. Spodek (Eds.), *Understanding the multicultural experience in early childhood education* (pp. 125-46). Washington, DC: NAEYC.

Spodek, B., Davis, M. D., & Saracho, O. N. (1983). Early childhood teacher education and certification. *Journal of Teacher Education, 34*(5), 50-52.

Spodek, B., & Saracho, O. N. (1982). The preparation and certification of early childhood personnel. In B. Spodek (Ed.), *Handbook of research in early childhood education* (pp. 399-425). New York: Free Press.

Spodek, B., & Saracho, O. N. (1988). Professionalism in early childhood education. In B. Spodek, O. N. Saracho, & D. L. Peters (Eds.), *Professionalism and the early childhood practitioner* (pp. 59-74). New York: Teachers College Press.

Spodek, B., Saracho, O. N., & Peters, D. L. (Eds.). (1988). *Professionalism and the early childhood practitioner*. New York: Teachers College Press.

Sylva, K. (1986). Developmental psychology and the preschool curriculum. In J. Harris (Ed.), *Child psychology in action: Linking research and practice* (pp. 127-42). London: Croom Helm.

Whipple, G. M. (Ed.). (1929). *Preschool and parental education, 28th yearbook of the National Society for the Study of Education*. Bloomington, IL: Public Schools Publication.

CHAPTER 3

# Non-Baccalaureate Teacher Education in Early Childhood Education

Douglas R. Powell
Loraine Dunn

The conventional and minimum standard of professional preparation for practice in most educational and human services is a baccalaureate degree in the respective field. Yet the majority of individuals who work in programs of early childhood education and care do not have a bachelors degree in early childhood education or a related area. The federal government's largest direct investment in early childhood education — the Head Start program — does not require a bachelors degree for classroom teachers, and most state licensing regulations for entry level child care personnel do not require any professional education, let alone a baccalaureate degree. Not surprisingly, of the 1,309 classroom personnel interviewed at 227 child care centers in the 1989 National Child Care Staffing Study, only 12% had a bachelors or graduate degree in a field related to early childhood education (ECE); 38% had no ECE-related training, 24% had at least one high school course in ECE, 7% had ECE-related vocational training, and 19% had some college education related to ECE (Whitebook, personal communication, June 12, 1989).

This state of affairs reflects long-standing disagreements within and outside the early childhood education field about the types of personnel that should staff programs of early childhood education and care, what qualifications they should have, and how they should be prepared (Spodek & Saracho, 1982). At present, there is no convincing empirical evidence that a bachelors degree is a requisite for effectively teaching and caring for young children, and the nation's rapidly growing need for early childhood personnel continues to surpass the ability of baccalaureate early childhood education programs to produce the needed staff. Research findings are clear, though, that increased levels of professional education in early childhood education or child development are associated with improved outcomes in young children (Ruopp, Travers, Glantz, & Coelen, 1979; see also, Phillips, 1987). Thus, the field is confronted with a critical challenge: How to upgrade the competence of the nation's early childhood personnel, many of whom have had no or extremely limited experiences in higher education? The task is further complicated by the autonomy and diversity of settings in which the education and care of young children take place.

The absence of a minimum professional preparation standard as a requirement for work with young children elevates the significance of the non-baccalaureate training received by staff in early childhood education programs. This training is a principal vehicle for improving the quality of early childhood education programs in this country. For many practitioners, participation in an in-service educational experience is not a supplement to preservice education but an initial encounter with professional education.

This chapter reviews initiatives of the past two decades directed at preparing early childhood personnel primarily through the provision of non-baccalaureate education. Three areas are considered: the Child Development Associate credential; associate degree and vocational education programs; and professional development activities, including in-service training, professional journals, and conferences and workshops. Needed directions in non-baccalaureate education for early childhood educators also are suggested.

## CHILD DEVELOPMENT ASSOCIATE CREDENTIAL

The creation of the child development associate (CDA) credential is the field's most extensive effort to improve the quality of early childhood settings by improving staff competence. It is an innovative initiative that originally bypassed institutions of higher education—the conventional pathway and gatekeeper of entrance into a profession. The CDA program serves the educationally disenfranchised (Peters, 1988), and thus has the potential to exert influence on the hundreds of thousands of individuals who wish to work with children but have limited levels of formal education.

## Origins and Current Status

The CDA program was initiated in 1971 by the U.S. Office of Child Development (OCD), now the Administration for Children, Youth and Families. In response to the rapidly growing number of early childhood programs, particularly Head Start, and the concomitant need for competent personnel to deliver these programs, OCD convened a task force to examine the possibility of establishing a national credential for early childhood staff. The task force recommended a system that would "identify basic competencies (or skills) needed by staff to provide competent care; provide training for caregivers in these competencies; and evaluate the work of caregivers on the basis of these national standards and recognize them with a national 'credential' or award" (CDA National Credentialing Program, 1988, p. 41).

In 1972, the Child Development Associate Consortium was formed by 39 professional organizations. Following the recommendations of the task force, the Consortium developed the original competency structure and procedures used to evaluate early childhood personnel for the credential. The first credentials were awarded by the Consortium in 1975. The Consortium operated the CDA program until 1979. Between 1979 and 1985 the program was administered through the Bank Street College of Education. Since 1985, the CDA program has been under the guidance of the National Association for the Education of Young Children, which established the Council for Early Childhood Professional Recognition (the Council) as a separate entity to administer the program. (For a discussion of the early history of the CDA, see Trickett, 1979.)

The 13 functional areas in which individuals are assessed for the CDA credential fall into 6 competency goals. The competency goals are

1. to establish and maintain a safe, healthy learning environment;
2. to advance physical and intellectual competence;
3. to support social and emotional development and provide positive guidance;
4. to establish positive and productive relationships with families;
5. to ensure a well-run, purposeful program responsive to participant needs;
6. to maintain a commitment to professionalism.

The competency areas were developed through extensive field testing and with the input of task forces and more than 1,000 early childhood practitioners. Indirect empirical support for their validity is found in a substudy of the National Day Care Study (Ruopp et al., 1979), in which a checklist based on 11 CDA functional areas was used to observe more than 100 classrooms. A factor analysis of the observational data yielded factors similar to the CDA competency areas; more important, the factors were found to be positively correlated with the children's total scores on the Peabody Picture Vocabulary Test and the Pre-school Inventory (Goodrich, 1979).

By the end of 1989, some 30,000 individuals had received the CDA credential. Currently, 40 states plus the District of Columbia include the CDA credential in their licensing codes as a means of meeting staff qualification requirements. Moreover, the CDA competency areas have served as a guideline for the content of education programs in two-year colleges and other educational institutions. A 1988 survey found 140 institutions of higher education offering CDA training and another 201 with early childhood course work structured around the CDA competency areas (Phillips, personal communication, May 31, 1989).

The CDA program was designed to accommodate individuals who might not qualify for or succeed in traditional baccalaureate teacher education programs. It does so by focusing on performance rather than on the completion of course work or the accumulation of academic credit hours; by permitting considerable local control in the interpretation of competency standards; and by not prescribing the type of training one needs to receive a credential. Hence, the CDA program is less exclusive than traditional teacher preparation programs ( that is, traditional academic standards are not applied) and, as a result, has the potential to create diversity among early childhood practitioners by making a teaching credential accessible to the educationally disenfranchised (Berk & Berson, 1981; Peters, 1988; Ward, 1976). Existing data suggest that the CDA program has been successful in reaching primarily poor women with considerable work experience in early childhood settings but limited formal education. A 1983 national survey of CDA recipients found that only 13 percent had a four-year college or graduate degree but slightly more than 50 percent had more than six years of work experience in early childhood settings at the time the credential was awarded. For the entire sample, the average level of early childhood experience was 7.7 years. When credentialed, the average age was 38.6 years, and most were female. A significant percentage (45%) represented ethnic minority populations (Granger, Lombardi, & Gleason, 1984).

Originally the CDA was available only to personnel working in center-based programs with three- to five-year-old children, including the option of a bilingual (Spanish) specialization. In the mid-1980s an expansion was initiated, and the credential is now available to center-based caregivers working with infants and toddlers, and to home visitors, and family day care providers working with three- to five-year-olds. As of April 1989, the overwhelming majority of individuals receiving the CDA credential have been assessed in preschool settings (Phillips, personal communication, May 31, 1989).

At present, the CDA assessment system works as follows: The caregiver (known as the "candidate" in CDA terminology) wishing to earn the credential applies to the CDA National Credentialing Program and verifies that three training experiences have been completed. These documented training experiences may be formal education such as high school, vocational or college courses, and/or informal experiences such as workshops or in-service sessions. The candidate also must verify that she or he has completed 640 hours of direct experience with young children over the course of the previous three years. The candidate identifies an advisor (an early childhood professional) and a parent/community representative to work with her throughout the assessment process as members of the Local Assessment Team. The candidate, advisor, and parent/community representative each gather information on the candidate's performance with young children. After all information has been collected, the candidate notifies the CDA National Credentialing Program that she is ready to be assessed. The national program then assigns a CDA representative to the Local Assessment Team.

The CDA representative visits the candidate's work site to gather additional information on her performance with young children. The four members of the Local Assessment Team (the candidate, advisor, parent/community representative, and CDA representative) then meet to discuss the candidate's performance and make a recommendation to the National Credentialing Program about the candidate's competence. All four members of the Local Assessment Team must agree that the candidate is competent in order for the credential to be awarded by the National Credentialing Program. The CDA credential is valid for three years after it is awarded, and may be renewed for periods of five years (CDA National Credentialing Program, 1988).

While nearly all candidates are recommended for the credential at the Local Assessment Team meeting, data gathered prior to 1985 indicate that 67 percent of the individuals who formally apply for the CDA credential complete the final meeting (Gleason cited in Granger & Lombardi, in press). Recent attrition data are not available because the CDA program no longer requires individuals to register when they begin the assessment process. Anecdotal reports in the literature indicate that some candidates have difficulty keeping the Local Assessment Team intact due to the mobility of advisors and parent/community representatives. Also, the financial cost of the assessment ($325 in 1989 dollars) is a deterrent to some prospective CDA recipients (Granger & Lombardi, in press). A study of a university-based CDA training program found that individuals were more likely to complete the training if they taught in private preschools or Head Start than in public schools, were married, were over 30 years of age, and had been teaching more than three years (R. Saltz, personal communication, June 27, 1989).

## Evaluation of Program Effects

Because the CDA credential offers a nontraditional alternative to the well-established and generally respected system of higher education, there has been significant pressure on the program to prove its value through research data. Unfortunately, there have been few empirical studies of the effects of the CDA effort. Some studies lack a control or comparison group, and others have employed a nonequivalent control group. There is heavy reliance on self-report measures, and most of the studies do not disentangle the effects of CDA training and assessment components.

Those studies that have been conducted have found that CDA participants experienced a positive change in self-confidence during the course of CDA training (Peters & Sutton, 1984) and one to three years after receipt of the credential (Granger et al., 1984; Pettygrove, 1981). Self-report data also indicate that an overwhelming percentage of CDA recipients believed the experience positively affected their work with young children and parents, relations with co-workers, and relations with their own children (Granger et al., 1984). Evaluations of university-based CDA training programs have found that participants experienced positive changes in self-assessed job performance, an increase in cognitively oriented, child-centered beliefs (Peters & Sutton, 1984), an increase in child development knowledge and improved classroom behaviors (Peters & Sutton, 1984; Saltz & Boesen, 1985), and increases in feelings of self-worth and in control over life events (Saltz & Boesen, 1985; Saltz, personal communication, June 27, 1989).

A national follow-up study of CDA recipients found that many of those holding the CDA credential became consumers of higher education. A significant majority indicated that the CDA program influenced them to continue their education through formal course work or enrollment in a college degree program. Also, 92 percent indicated that becoming a CDA made them feel more a part of the professional community (Granger et al., 1984). Other studies have found similar patterns (Peters & Sutton, 1984; Saltz & Boesen, 1985).

Research findings are inconsistent regarding the relation of the CDA credential to advances in salary and promotion. One national survey found that about two-fifths of the CDA recipients studied gained a salary increase when they earned the credential, with much of this probably due to a change in job title or responsibility (Granger et al., 1984). However, studies of CDA recipients in Illinois (Anderson, 1983) and in 10 midwestern states (Pettygrove, 1981) found few changes in position or salary after receiving the credential. An evaluation of a university-based CDA training program also found few extrinsic rewards in the form of pay increases and promotions (Peters & Sutton, 1984).

## Challenges

While the CDA achievements are noteworthy in view of serious financial and administrative difficulties encountered since its inception, the CDA initiative faces critical challenges in the years ahead with regard to issues of candidate quality, the status of the credential within the field of early childhood education, and the visibility and use of the credential in non-Head Start settings.

*Quality Control.* The structural flexibility of the CDA program and the circumventing of institutions of higher education as the locus of teacher preparation have prompted some to question the quality of the CDA plan. Specifically, Berk and Berson (1981) have suggested that the CDA program's primary emphasis on performance rather than knowledge "permits teacher preparation to be narrowly vocational, limited to training in collections of skills" (p. 37), and that the absence of standards for training allows for "substandard training sites, as well as training experiences which are haphazard, parochial, and limited to the trainee's employment setting" (p. 38). Berk and Berson also criticize the use of a lay person (parent/community representative) to assess individuals for a professional credential, and the presence of the candidate as an equal voting member in the Local Assessment Team. (See Granger & Gleason, 1981, for a response to the Berk & Berson criticisms.) The necessity of making a decision about the candidate's competence in the presence of the candidate is problematic for the other three members of the Local Assessment Team, something the Council has recognized through the provision of special guidance to CDA representatives on how to handle denial votes (Council for Early Childhood Professional Recognition, 1987).

Stronger mechanisms for quality control in the CDA program are present in a revision of the CDA assessment system proposed by the Council. The proposal calls for two routes to credentialing. The direct assessment route is designed for individuals currently working in the field who do not feel they need additional training or experience to be judged competent. Using this route, candidates would complete a written test on a Council Model curriculum based on appropriate methods of teaching and caring for young children, and would undergo a formal on-site observation. The Local Assessment Team meeting would be eliminated, and the Council would assume responsibility for determining whether a candidate should be awarded the CDA credential. The second route to credentialing would be a training program available to persons who may or may not be currently working in the field. It would involve structured field work, self-study under the supervision of a local early childhood professional approved by the Council, participation in course work at an approved training institution, a written test on the Council Model curriculum, and a formal on-site observation (Council for Early Childhood Professional Recognition, n.d.).

*Confusion about Status.* The CDA program was launched to create a middle level group of early childhood professionals who are knowledgeable about children and able to provide valuable experiences for preschool children. By design, the CDA was neither to replace the college-trained teacher, the master teacher, or supervisor, nor to serve as an aide (Zigler, 1971). Initiators of the CDA program were clear that the CDA credential was not to be equivalent to an associate or a bachelors degree, but rather a credential signifying adequate competence to assume full responsibility for the care and education of young children.

In reality, there is confusion as to whether the CDA is to be treated as a terminal teaching credential or a stepping stone to more traditional educational programs, including a college degree. For example, the National Association for the Education of Young Children (NAEYC, 1984) position statement on nomenclature of the early childhood profession indicates that an individual may enter the field as an early childhood associate teacher (Level 2) with a CDA credential *or* an associate degree in early childhood education or child development (ECE/CD). There is no mention of the CDA as a requirement for work as an early childhood teacher (Level 3), which requires a baccalaureate degree in ECE/CD, or as an early childhood specialist (Level 4), which requires a graduate degree in ECE/CD or a baccalaureate degree and three years of experience. Yet the roles and functions of Level 2 and Level 3 — responsibility for the care and education of a group of children — are similar.

Questions as to whether the CDA credential dilutes the value of a four-year college degree in early childhood education have been raised since the inception of the CDA program (Woolsey, 1977). Indirectly, such questions are fueled by self-report data suggesting no differences between individuals enrolled in a high-quality, university-based CDA training program and undergraduate students engaged in student teaching assignments in a four-year college degree program. The self-report data include measures of job performance, self-confidence, educational aspirations, and cognitively oriented, child-centered beliefs (Peters & Sutton, 1984).

Peters (1988) has argued that the CDA credentialing and training program is limited in its ability to establish a profession because it fails to make a commitment to an explicit knowledge base for practice, and because it replaces principal indicators of success — academic credits and degrees — with a credential of uncertain backing and value. He suggests that the concept of alternative entries into the profession is threatening to a field that is struggling to establish proper acknowledgment for its unique skills, especially when one of the entries does not follow the usual pattern set by other professions.

Treatment of the CDA as a way station for traditional academic preparation is prevalent. For instance, VanderVen (1988) indicates that individuals pursuing a CDA credential or an associate degree are in the "initial" stage of professional development and "obviously . . . do not hold complete professional credentials for practice" (p. 146). Also, the focus on academic preparation, coupled with the absence of reference to the CDA credential at Levels 3 and 4 of the NAEYC (1984) nomenclature statement, implies the credential occupies an entry level status in the organizational view of NAEYC. As noted earlier, research on the effects of the CDA program has found that one of its outcomes is participation in advanced academic course work and professional development activities (Granger et al., 1984; Peters & Sutton, 1984; Saltz & Boesen, 1985).

In part, limited clarity about the role of the CDA credential in the overall scheme of early childhood education personnel preparation reflects the lack of a well-functioning career ladder. We return to this matter in the final section of the chapter.

*Limited Scope.* A continuing challenge for the CDA program is to broaden its base of influence and support beyond Head Start and government programs. For example, the CDA initiative has yet to realize the vision of being a recognized credential that would make proprietary child care centers more attractive to consumer-parents (Zigler & Kagan, 1981). The vast majority of CDA holders are or have been employees of Head Start. This is partially due to inclusion of the CDA credential in the minimum standards for classroom personnel and the Head Start provision of financial support for CDA assessment and training costs. A 1983 national survey of CDA recipients found that 80% were Head Start employees (Granger et al., 1984), a pattern that continues to the present. Between 1985 and 1989, 80% of all individuals receiving the credential were employed by Head Start, 9% were employed in center-based child care programs, 7% were in half-day preschool programs, and 4% were family day care providers (Phillips, personal communication, May 31, 1989). Thus, the CDA program runs the risk of being perceived as a support for Head Start, thereby limiting its usefulness to other early childhood settings and reducing the likelihood of securing the support and involvement of private sector sources that view Head Start as a federal program responsibility (Granger et al., 1984).

In recent years efforts have been made to extend the CDA program to non-Head Start personnel. New initiatives include the CDA endorsement for work in infant-toddler family day care settings (Council, 1989), CDA training provided by the U.S. Army for its child care staff (Phillips, 1988b), CDA training programs available through the federal Job Training Partnership Act (JTPA Colloquium, 1988), 15 demonstration grants to community colleges awarded by the U.S. Administration for Children, Youth and Families in 1987–89 to help expand the availability of CDA training (New Community, 1987), and a CDA Scholarship Act approved by Congress in 1986 to make the credential accessible to a wider variety of early childhood staff by providing financial assistance (Phillips, 1988a). These efforts should help expand awareness of the credential beyond the Head Start population.

The future of the CDA credential as a viable influence on early childhood education, then, seems to rest largely on how well it meets the major challenges regarding quality control, clarification of status, and increased visibility and use in non-Head Start settings. As noted in the foregoing discussion, resolution of these problems is not confined to the CDA program alone but must be viewed and addressed as a manifestation of larger issues in the field of early childhood education and of society's stance toward the education and care of young children.

## ASSOCIATE DEGREE AND VOCATIONAL PROGRAMS

Associate degree and vocational training programs have mushroomed in the past two decades in response to the growing societal interest in early childhood education. Information does not exist on the numbers of early childhood personnel who have participated in two-year and vocational programs, but the growth in programs at this level of education suggests they represent a major delivery system for professional preparation.

### Associate Degree Programs

In 1985, NAEYC issued guidelines for early childhood personnel preparation programs in associate degree-granting institutions (NAEYC, 1985). The intent of the guidelines was to establish a standard for the associate degree in early childhood education as preparation for immediate entry into professional work with young children. The NAEYC (1984) position statement was formulated on the basis of papers prepared by eight leaders in associate degree programs, open meetings at two NAEYC annual conferences, and reviews of draft documents by more than 200 early childhood professionals.

The guidelines call for professional studies constituting a minimum of 50 percent of the student's degree work, plus a general education curriculum including courses in English composition, mathematics, science, the humanities, and social science. The professional studies curriculum should include courses and field experiences that provide both theoretical knowledge and practical skills in areas such as the following:

Child growth and development
Introduction to the early childhood profession
Curriculum planning
Methods of child guidance and group management
Work with special needs children
Relations with families and community
Child health and safety

The professional studies curriculum also should provide opportunities for students to apply their knowledge and skills, including child observation work and supervised practicum experiences totaling a minimum of 300 clock hours of contact time with children. Students should be placed in settings that reflect the best possible practices in early childhood education as well as the curricular diversity of the field.

The guidelines specify components to support the successful implementation of a two-year associate degree in early childhood education. For example, the position statement indicates that faculty members should have, or be working toward, an advanced degree in a field directly related to early childhood education or child development, and should have substantial direct experience with young children. Other components pertain to professional relationships within the program, cultural diversity, student services, administrative structure, and evaluation of students and the program.

Data do not exist on the uses or impact of the NAEYC associate degree guidelines. It is not known, for instance, what percentage of associate degree programs in early childhood education comply with the standards. There are anecdotal reports that the position statement has helped two-year college faculty make decisions about the content of an associate degree program in early childhood education (Dimmlich, personal communication, May 26, 1989). There also are reports that the guidelines are useful to faculty in appealing to college administrators for additional resources and courses in the early childhood area (Peterson, personal communication, May 26, 1989).

While the NAEYC guidelines can be used to design an associate degree curriculum, faculty still face the challenge of structuring courses to accommodate students with diverse needs. It appears that some courses contain both students who do not want a degree and prefer to learn all they can about early childhood in several courses, and students who wish to transfer their associate degree courses to a baccalaureate degree program.

### Vocational Training

Training for entry level early childhood personnel is also provided through vocational home economics programs. Typically referred to as occupational child care training, these programs are offered at the high school, vocational school, and community college level. Vocational child care training is intended to prepare students to assume the roles of child care assistants or aides in early childhood settings under the supervision of more experienced or educated staff members. While some students enter the work force in this capacity immediately after their training experience, others go on for additional postsecondary education and/or never enter the field of early childhood education.

All 50 states and 3 territories have vocational child care training programs, but the available funds are seriously limited. Each state receives funding through the Carl D. Perkins Vocational Education Act (P. L. 98–524), which may be used to supplement state and local funds supporting occupational training programs. In 1989, approximately $900 million was allocated for the Perkins Act (Kuntz, 1989), but only about 5 percent of this money was spent on occupational training programs, and training in child care is only one of many areas sharing this limited pool of funds (King, personal communication, June 6, 1989). These federal funds often are used for start-up costs to initiate nursery school or day care laboratory programs in high school settings.

The typical training program offers instruction in child growth and development, and a laboratory experience with young children. Training program instructors are certified vocational home economics teachers or persons with extensive experience in the child care field (Smith, personal communication, June 2, 1989). The laboratory programs take a variety of forms, including half-day nursery school and full-day child care. A few programs offer students experiences with infants and toddlers, but the majority of laboratory experiences are with preschool-age children.

Since the high school diploma is the highest level of education held by many individuals working in the early childhood field, vocational child care training programs hold the potential of providing individuals with formal exposure to child development principles that might not be secured otherwise.

## Challenges

One of the key challenges regarding courses offered in two-year college and vocational training programs is the consistency of course content and quality across postsecondary educational institutions. The issue surfaces most readily surrounding the transfer of academic credit from one institution to another. Some two-year institutions specifically state their course credits are vocational and nontransferable, while other institutions certify courses in early childhood education and child development as transferable. Four-year colleges and universities often are hesitant to accept credits earned in two-year colleges and vocational schools as comparable to courses available in four-year institutions of higher education.

The relative brevity of this chapter's coverage of personnel preparation programs at the two-year college and vocational training level underscores the dearth of available information on the depth and breadth of professional education that occurs in this arena. We address this need in the final section of the chapter.

## IN-SERVICE PROFESSIONAL DEVELOPMENT

Most occupational groups recommend or require professional development activities for individuals engaged in professional practice, including attendance at workshops and conferences, membership in professional organizations, and participation in in-service education programs. Early childhood education is no exception, with organizations such as NAEYC actively promoting various forms of continuing education. However, there is considerable variation in state policies as to whether and what type of professional development activities are required of persons who work with young children.

### Group-based Programs

Of the various avenues of professional development available to early childhood personnel, on-site, in-service education programs have the advantage of reaching all individuals and tailoring their content to the needs and interests of participants. Reliable data on the availability of in-service education programs are not available. An early study of Pennsylvania early childhood programs found that 77% of private child care centers and 85% of federally funded centers had some in-service programs, the majority offered at least one session per month (Cohen, Sonnenschein, & Peters, 1973). A recent study of personnel in licensed group child care programs in Indiana found that in-service education sessions were held infrequently at most centers; for 53% of the sample, in-service education was held 1 to 4 times yearly, and 27% of the sample indicated that in-service education was never conducted at the center. These data come from a nonprobability sample of 533 directors, teachers, and assistant teachers (Powell & Stremmel, 1989).

The Indiana study found limited involvement of child care center personnel in other conventional practices of professional development. Lay publications were a major source of information for nearly all workers. For example, 25% or more of the respondents had read one or more articles related to children in one or more of the following publications: *Redbook, Woman's Day, Working Mother, Better Homes and Gardens, Parents Magazine, Family Circle,* and *McCalls.* Overall, only

34% of the sample reported reading the leading practitioner journal in the field, *Young Children*, in the past six months. Job-related reading occurred more frequently as part of personal time than as part of activities at the center. While lay publications frequently include articles and columns on child development issues, questions must be raised as to whether these articles, usually written for parents, are of sufficient depth for individuals who work with children in a group setting (Powell & Stremmel, 1989).

Seventy-six percent of the Indiana sample reportedly attended a professional meeting or workshop in the past year. However, only 26% of the sample reported membership in a professional organization; 19% were members of NAEYC. Co-workers were rated as the most helpful information source for a majority of the child care workers in this study, although the center director was consulted as frequently as co-workers.

Involvement in conventional professional development practices was highest among personnel with higher levels of early childhood training and experience. In addition to reading professional publications and maintaining membership in a professional association, individuals with higher levels of training and experience also were more likely to use professional standards to determine their job effectiveness than to rely on the judgment of friends, relatives, and other lay persons. The findings suggested that training might play a distinctive role in facilitating professional development of early childhood personnel. Higher levels of early childhood training, but not experience, were associated with decreased use of center information sources, professional reading during nonwork hours, and reports of the helpfulness of conferences.

Data from the Indiana study provide partial support for the existence of a "trickle down" flow of child development and child care information from senior workers, especially the director, to those with no or limited training. Workers with no or limited training tapped a narrow range of information sources, generally using the center-based resources of the director, co-workers, and in-service training sessions. This finding is consistent with the suggestion of Spodek and Saracho (1982) regarding a two-tiered system of training in the early childhood field. Individuals who enter the field with the lowest levels of training are less likely to seek additional training than those entering the field with higher levels of training. Thus, the gap between minimally trained staff and more highly trained staff widens over time. The mean level of experience reported by assistants in a small study by Kontos and Stremmel (1988) supports this notion. Assistants reported an average of nine years experience in child care, yet they were still assistants; they had not moved up the career ladder.

The Powell and Stremmel findings suggest that work experience in the early childhood field is not a substitute for formal child-related training in maintaining a professional orientation to work with young children, particularly in the use of professional versus lay sources for information and determining work effectiveness. Hence, the study strengthens the argument for requiring postsecondary training of child care personnel: A greater number of professional indices were associated with increased training than with increased experience. In settings where workers possess less than college level training, the data suggest a need to improve center-based information sources for staff development purposes. Practices that enable staff members to attend conferences warrant support. Yet for individuals with no or limited training, conference attendance cannot be viewed as a substitute for high-quality, in-service training and direct consultation provided at the center. Because the study found that increased levels of training were related to the perceived helpfulness of conferences, it would appear that for individuals with no or limited training, center-based sources have greater potential to address particular interests and needs than the more diffuse resources of a conference.

## Family Day Care

Family day care providers — individuals who care for a small group of nonfamilial children in the provider's own home — are responsible for the out-of-home care of the bulk of the nation's children under five years of age. Yet this category of early childhood personnel is the most difficult to reach because family day care providers generally are isolated and often not known to institutions with early childhood education resources. Also, their work situation does not provide readily available substitutes so they can attend conferences, workshops, and meetings. Further, some family day care providers may not see their occupation ("babysitting") as an activity that is connected to or able to benefit from a professional knowledge base.

Fortunately, exemplary efforts to provide professional education to family day care providers have been carried out and provide a data base on which to design future efforts. For example, videotapes for providers working with infants and toddlers have been developed by J. Ronald Lally and Peter Mangione at the Far West Educational Laboratory in San Francisco in collaboration with the State of California's Child Development Division (Program for Infant-Toddler Caregivers, 1988). The Community Family Day Care Project launched by Pacific Oaks College in the 1970s is a training model that combined group meetings (in the evenings and Saturdays) with periodic one-on-one consultation with a project professional (Sale & Torres, 1971). As another example, the Neighborcare Project at Purdue University employs in-home training to assist providers in the integration of disabled preschool children into their family day care homes (Kontos, 1988).

## NEEDED DIRECTIONS

The early childhood education field is highly dependent on non-baccalaureate teacher education to improve and maintain the quality of early childhood programs. While the past two decades have been marked by innovative efforts to provide professional education to early childhood teachers in diverse settings, the field has a long way to go to integrate personnel preparation into the mainstream of professional practice. Energies need to be expended in four areas.

*Strengthen the Data Base.* The research base of non-baccalaureate professional education is woefully inadequate. As demonstrated by this chapter's review of initiatives, the field needs to know what conventional professional development activities exist, and how many individuals are engaged in these various activities (especially associate degree programs). Of no less importance is the need for studies of the effects of professional education, with particular attention to elements of the training initiative and to ways in which participant characteristics modify the effects of a training program.

*Assess Differentiated Staffing Levels.* Career ladders are at an infancy stage of development in the field of early childhood education and care. A comparison of reality with visions of desired differentiated staffing schemes (for example, the aforementioned NAEYC nomenclature position statement) raises questions about the utility of and barriers to implementing a career ladder in programs of early childhood education and care. Studies of child care working conditions indicate that a variety of titles such as director, teacher, and assistant teacher exist, but the responsibilities of individuals holding these positions are strikingly similar, as suggested in the NAEYC (1984) nomenclature statement. While teachers are expected to do more planning and interaction with parents, in actuality both teachers and assistant teachers spend similar amounts of time supervising children's play, guiding children's behavior, planning and implementing the curriculum, interacting with parents, preparing meals, and performing clerical and administrative tasks (Kontos & Stremmel, 1988; Whitebook, Howes, Darrah, & Friedman, 1982). Teachers frequently have higher levels of formal education than assistants, but not always. Teachers also tend to receive higher levels of compensation than assistants. Thus, there are some small differences in education and salary levels of personnel holding assistant teacher and teacher positions, but the duties each performs are essentially the same (Whitebook et al., 1982).

The task, then, is to clarify the need for and feasibility of differentiated staffing and training levels in diverse programs of early childhood education and care operating under different auspices. The NAEYC nomenclature position statement discussed earlier in this chapter provides a useful beginning point.

*Experiment with Training Methods.* The field needs to increase its level of experimental program development activity regarding the design and delivery of non-baccalaureate professional education. Further work is needed with nontraditional strategies for training hard-to-reach early childhood personnel, such as family day care providers and individuals with no or limited formal education who work as aides or teaching assistants. A challenge is to improve the quality of early childhood personnel without imposing conventional higher education requirements that essentially foreclose advanced training opportunities for mature individuals of poor and minority backgrounds. It is not uncommon for students enrolled in early childhood education teacher preparation programs to encounter difficulty with the general education courses, especially English and mathematics, but to excel in courses associated with the professional education curriculum. As Haberman (1988) has suggested, general studies requirements serve as an informal gatekeeper for older women, especially those of minority status, who wish to obtain college level preparation in early childhood education.

Methods of introducing child development and early education information to early childhood personnel also require work. Early childhood education practitioners are not blank slates eager to soak up technical information without question. Their rich and varied experiences with young children provide a cognitive construct system that serves as a filter for new information. Teachers' implicit theories of early childhood educational practice are a rich domain in need of careful investigation (Spodek, 1988). Much still needs to be done to act on Almy's (1975) suggestion that principles of adult education be incorporated into the professional education of early childhood educators.

*Strengthen the Commitment to Professional Development.* The field needs a strong commitment to professional development. There needs to be time provided during the workday for practitioners to reflect on their experiences, consult with others, examine reading materials, and plan new ways of working with young children. The developmental needs of early childhood personnel should also be addressed through the provision of time and resources for conference attendance and course work. These are not new recommendations, but they continue to be neglected.

Perhaps the most difficult challenge is to change the widespread misconception that work with young children can be carried out effectively without the benefit of specialized knowledge. To the extent that a love of children is viewed as sufficient background for entry into the early childhood field, efforts to provide professional education and upgrade personnel standards will continue to face a tumultuous battle.

## REFERENCES

Almy, M. (1975). *The early childhood educator at work.* New York: McGraw-Hill.

Anderson, E. T. (1983). The perceived effect of the Child Development Associate credential on recipients in Illinois. Edwardsville, IL: Southern Illinois University at Edwardsville. (ERIC Document Reproduction Service No. 266 868).

Berk, L. E., & Berson, M. P. (1981). A review of the Child Development Associate credential. *Child Care Quarterly, 10,* 9–42.

Child Development Associate National Credentialing Program. (1988). *Child Development Associate Assessment System and Competency Standards: Preschool caregivers in center-based programs.* Washington, DC: Author.

Cohen, A., Sonnenschein, S., & Peters, D. L. (1973). *Pennsylvania day care centers: A preliminary profile* (Report No. 20). University Park, PA: The Pennsylvania State University Center for Human Services Development.

Council for Early Childhood Professional Recognition. (no date). *The Council Model for CDA assessment and training.* Washington, DC: Author.

Council for Early Childhood Professional Recognition. (1987, November). *Child Development Associate Representative Training.* Presented at the annual meeting of the National Association for the Education of Young Children, Chicago.

Council for Early Childhood Professional Recognition. (1989). *National Directory of Early Childhood Training Programs.* Washington, DC: Author.

Dimmlich, P. (May 26, 1989). Personal communication. Instructor, Highland Community College, Freeport, IL.

Goodrich, N. (1979). An analysis of the CDA checklist data. In *National Day Care Study. Vol. IV-B: Measurements and methods*. Cambridge, MA: Abt Associates.

Granger, R. C., & Gleason, D. J. (1981). A review of the Child Development Associate credential: Corrections and comments. *Child Care Quarterly, 10*, 63–73.

Granger, R. C., & Lombardi, J. (in press). A review of the Child Development Associate competencies and assessment system. In S. L. Kilmer (Ed.), *Advances in early education and day care* (Vol. 5). Greenwich, CT: JAI Press.

Granger, R. C., Lombardi, J., & Gleason, D. J. (1984, April). The impact of the Child Development Associate program on CDAs: Results of a national survey. Paper presented at the annual meeting of the American Educational Research Association, New Orleans.

Haberman, M. (1988). Gatekeepers to the profession. In B. Spodek, O. N. Saracho, & D. L. Peters (Eds.), *Professionalism and the early childhood practitioner* (pp. 84–92). New York: Teachers College Press.

JTPA Colloquium (1988, November). *Competence: News for the CDA community, 5*(2), 4.

King, B. (June 6, 1989). Personal communication. Senior Education Program Specialist, Vocational Home Economics Education/Sex Equity. Office of Vocational and Adult Education, U.S. Department of Education, Washington, DC.

Kontos, S. (1988). Family day care as an integrated early intervention setting. *Topics in Early Childhood Special Education, 8*, 1–14.

Kontos, S., & Stremmel, A. J. (1988). Caregivers' perceptions of working conditions in a child care environment. *Early Childhood Research Quarterly, 3*, 77–90.

Kuntz, P. (1989). Congress to take hard look at vocational-training law. *Congressional Quarterly Weekly Report, 47*, 453–57.

National Association for the Education of Young Children. (1984). *NAEYC position statement on nomenclature, salaries, benefits, and status of the early childhood profession*. Washington, DC: Author.

National Association for the Education of Young Children. (1985). *Guidelines for early childhood education programs in associate degree granting institutions*. Washington, DC: Author.

New community college grantees (1987, October). *Competence: News of the CDA Community, 4*(1), 3.

Peters, D. L. (1988). The Child Development Associate credential and the educationally disenfranchised. In B. Spodek, O. N. Saracho, & D. L. Peters (Eds.), *Professionalism and the early childhood practitioner* (pp. 93–104). New York: Teachers College Press.

Peters, D. L., & Sutton, R. E. (1984). The effects of CDA training on the beliefs, attitudes, and behaviors of Head Start personnel. *Child Care Quarterly, 13*, 251–61.

Peterson, J. (May 26, 1989). Personal communication. Instructor, Reading Area Community College, Reading, PA.

Pettygrove, W. B. (1981). The Child Development Associate credential as a child care staff standard: Accuracy, career development, and policy implications. *Child Care Quarterly, 10,* 43–58.

Phillips, C. B. (1988a). *CDA Scholarship Act: Executive Summary.* Washington, DC: Council for Early Childhood Professional Recognition.

Phillips, C. B. (1988b). From the executive director. *Competence: News for the CDA Community, 5*(2), 2.

Phillips, C. B. (May 31, 1989). Personal communication. Executive Director, Council for Early Childhood Professional Recognition, Washington, DC.

Phillips, D. (Ed.). (1987). *Quality in child care: What does research tell us?* Washington, DC: National Association for the Education of Young Children.

Powell, D. R., & Stremmel, A. J. (1989). The relation of early childhood training and experience to the professional development of child care workers. *Early Childhood Research Quarterly, 4,* 339–55.

Program for Infant-Toddler Caregivers. (1988). Videotapes available from Child Development Division, California State Department of Education, 560 J Street, Suite 220, Sacramento, CA 95814.

Ruopp, R., Travers, J., Glantz, F., & Coelen, C. (1979). *Children at the center.* (Vol. 1, Final report of the National Day Care Study). Cambridge, MA: Abt Associates.

Sale, J. S., & Torres, L. L. (1971). *"I'm not just a babysitter." A descriptive report of the Community Family Day Care Project.* Pasadena, CA: Pacific Oaks College.

Saltz, R. (June 27, 1989). Personal communication. Professor, University of Michigan at Dearborn.

Saltz, R., & Boesen, C. (1985). Effects of a university CDA teacher education program. Findings of a three-year study. Dearborn, MI: University of Michigan at Dearborn. (ERIC Document Reproduction Service No. 264 018).

Smith, J. (June 2, 1989). Personal communication. Vocational Education State Supervisor, Home Economics Education. Division of Vocational Education, Indiana State Department of Education, Indianapolis.

Spodek, B. (1988). Implicit theories of early childhood teachers: Foundations for professional behavior. In B. Spodek, O. N. Saracho, & D. L. Peters (Eds.), *Professionalism and the early childhood practitioner* (pp. 161–72). New York: Teachers College Press.

Spodek, B., & Saracho, O. N. (1982). The preparation and certification of early childhood personnel. In B. Spodek (Ed.), *Handbook of research in early childhood education* (pp. 399–425). New York: Free Press.

Trickett, P. (1979). Career development in Head Start. In E. Zigler & J. Valentine (Eds.), *Project Head Start: A legacy of the War on Poverty* (pp. 315–36). New York: Free Press.

VanderVen, K. (1988). Pathways to professional effectiveness for early childhood educators. In B. Spodek, O. N. Saracho, & D. L. Peters (Eds.), *Professionalism and the early childhood practitioner* (pp. 137-60). New York: Teachers College Press.

Ward, E. (1976). The Child Development Associate Consortium's assessment system. *Young Children, 31*, 244-54.

Whitebook, M. (June 12, 1989). Personal communication. Executive Director, Child Care Employee Project, Oakland, CA.

Whitebook, M., Howes, C., Darrah, R., & Friedman, J. (1982). Caring for the caregivers: Staff burnout in child care. In L. G. Katz (Ed.), *Current topics in early childhood education*, Vol. 4 (pp. 211-35). Norwood, NJ: Ablex.

Woolsey, S. (1977). Pied piper politics and the child-care debate. *Daedalus, 106*, 127-45.

Zigler, E. (1971). A new child care profession: The Child Development Associate. *Young Children, 27*, 71-74.

Zigler, E., & Kagan, S. L. (1981). The Child Development Associate: A challenge for the 1980s. *Young Children, 36*, 10-15.

CHAPTER 4

# The Content of Early Childhood Teacher Education Programs

## CHILD DEVELOPMENT

Donald L. Peters
Dene G. Klinzing

This chapter is written from a particular perspective, one that is based on a developmental approach to early childhood teacher preparation (Elkind, 1989). Within this approach, child development is considered the core content and the basis of sound early childhood education practice (Cartwright & Peters, 1983; DeVries, 1974; Elkind, 1989; Vander-Ven, 1986). Knowing how children grow, develop, and learn is viewed as more critical than any particular content area. Indeed, knowledge, the what or content of early childhood curricula, is often viewed as the least important learning goal of early childhood programming (Katz, 1987). In essence, the early childhood teacher is expected to be an expert in and an applied practitioner of child development.

The central theme of the essential nature of child development knowledge runs through the many reports and publications designed to guide early childhood personnel preparation programs (Craig, 1978; Howard, 1968; NAEYC, 1982, 1985; Peters & Kelly, 1982; Peters, in press). Such knowledge has been considered essential in the movement toward professionalism of the early childhood field (Almy, 1975, 1988) and for those providing high-quality programming for young children. For example, the Accreditation Criteria and Procedures of the National Academy of Early Childhood Programs require that "the program is staffed by adults who understand child development and who recognize and provide for children's needs" (Bredekamp, 1984, p. 18).

## CHILD DEVELOPMENT: A DIVERSITY OF CONTENT

Such agreement concerning the importance of child development knowledge to the early childhood teaching field does not, however, mean that there is fundamental agreement on what constitutes the essentials of such knowledge as it is to be incorporated into the course sequences of teacher preparation programs. A recent telephone survey (Bailey, Simenson, Huntington, Cochrane, Crais, & Humphrey, 1988) confirms that there is major variability in the amount of child development course work required across the several disciplines associated with programming for young children and across preparation levels, for example, the associate, bachelors, and masters levels. Virtually no information is available concerning the content of courses that are required or what students learn (Peters, Cohen, & McNichol, 1974).

The plethora of child development texts published reflects the diversity of content and organizational structure available to those charged with imparting such knowledge to fledgling early childhood personnel and others. Textbooks differ in

1. structure—usually whether a topical (e.g., cognitive development, physical development, or social development) or a chronological or stage orientation (infancy, toddlerhood, and so on) is taken;
2. breadth or comprehensiveness (including both the age span included and the disciplinary knowledge represented or emphasized);
3. depth or detail of coverage (with some providing only generalized principles and others providing considerable detail of classical and contemporary research); and
4. adherence to a single theoretical perspective or advocacy for an eclectic approach.

The diversity of the conceptions of the content of child development is not surprising, but it is worthy of some comment. Such diversity is attributable to several factors. To some degree it simply reflects the audience or purpose of the course for which the text was designed. More important, however, it also reflects the nature of the field of child development.

### The Multidisciplinary Origins of the Field

From their beginnings, child study and early childhood education have been closely related. Both began by bringing together individuals of diverse backgrounds representing the fields of education, nursing, nutrition, psychology, and social work. These people, who were often from universities or university-related research institutions, had interests in the preschool child that sprouted from their professional contacts with children and families. They were brought together by their shared conviction concerning the importance of the early childhood years for later development and their desire to know more about the processes involved in the course of that development. Being from an academic tradition and sharing a common focus of interest, many of these pioneers gathered in 1925 at Teachers College of Columbia University. Subsequently, they formed the National Committee on Nursery Schools (1926), which became the National Association for Nursery Education in 1929, and the National Association for the Education of Young Children (NAEYC) in 1965, on the one hand, and the Society for Research in Child Development (1933), on the other (NAEYC, 1976; Peters, Neisworth, & Yawkey). Each of these organizations has maintained a multidisciplinary tradition to the present, and many of the current leaders in the field of early childhood education are active participants in both organizations.

Although the field of child development is multidisciplinary, many of its practitioners and researchers, including those who write or select textbooks, view the field from their own disciplinary viewpoint and from their own perspectives on their professional role. Not all are interested in early childhood education, and even among those who are, a wide range of disciplinary perspectives may be found.

## The Historical Divisions of the Field

The research base of modern child development reflects its multidisciplinary origins, but in its applications particular disciplines tend to dominate. Practitioners in health-related fields (pediatrics, pediatric nursing, nutrition), education-related fields (early childhood education, child care), psychology-related fields (child psychology, pediatric psychology), and sociology-related fields (social work, family sociology, family therapy) often have little overlap in the knowledge base they acquire during their preparation (Bailey et al., 1988). Even within the narrower domain of early childhood education, there has been a recurring distinction between knowledge of the subjects of early childhood education (that is, children and how they learn) and the processes of early childhood education (pedagogy). Within many institutions of higher education, the former is the purview of child development or child psychology, the latter the purview of education. That distinction is maintained in the organization of this book as well as in such things as the titles of professional organizations (the special interest group of the American Educational Research Association is called Early Education and Child Development) and professional journals (for example, *Early Education and Development*).

Throughout the years there have been numerous appeals for closer integration of the various disciplines and a berating of the effects of the dominance of narrow, single disciplinary views (Almy, 1975; Silin, 1988). Silin (1988) states, "Early education must become permeable to influences from many disciplines in addition to psychology. For example, greater attention to knowledge of sociology and history can serve to balance the often abstracted and decontextualized way that mainstream psychology looks at children. Without such a perspective, an unrealistic emphasis on individual development may dominate the field to the neglect of the social realities of everyday life" (p. 124). This broader historical, contextual view is taking hold in some areas, but unfortunately many of the disciplinary distinctions are strongly embedded in the structure of the institutions of higher education in this country, including those at the masters and doctoral levels—the source of those who will teach teachers (Cartwright & Peters, 1983; Peters, 1979, 1981, in press). Consequently, change in the near future is unlikely.

## Dramatic Increase in the Quantity of Child Development Research

The quantity of research in child development has grown by leaps and bounds during the last 25 years. This growth has been spurred on in part by historical, demographic, and philosophical changes affecting the way society looks at children, and in part by the rapid growth of early childhood education programs. The former have provided more public and private funding for both basic child development research and research and demonstration projects in early childhood education. The latter has produced a demand for more and better qualified early childhood teachers.

The press for more and better qualified teachers has created, in turn, an increase in the number of early childhood preparation programs, with a concomitant increase in the number of faculty and graduate students. For example, there are 272 early childhood education graduate degree programs and 84 child development graduate degree programs listed in Peterson's *Annual Guides to Graduate Study* (1988). Programs also may be found within university departments of curriculum and instruction, elementary education, home economics, and psychology. Many, if not most, of the faculty in these programs engage in some form of scholarship or research activity. The expectation generally is that the results of such scholarly effort should be disseminated.

As a result, there has been a rapid growth in the number of scholarly journals, books, newsletters, and periodicals. Not all the research and scholarship published is of equal quality, nor is it all relevant for inclusion in early childhood teacher preparation programs. However, the faculty and staff of the 1,488 two-year and four-year programs listed in the *National Directory of Early Childhood Training Programs* (Council for Early Childhood Professional Recognition, 1989) are certainly faced with an increasingly difficult task of sorting and selecting what should be in the curriculum for early childhood teachers.

## The Changing Ecology of Early Childhood Education

That the world of early childhood education has changed markedly and with great rapidity is so well understood that it need not be reiterated here. However, the sociodemographic changes of recent history have altered what early childhood educators need to know. A few of the key changes are worth noting.

1. Early childhood programs are involving younger children. Infant and toddler development is a field in and of itself, with its own rapidly growing research and theory base. It is no longer reasonable to assume that early childhood personnel need only to understand the development of three- to eight-year-olds.

2. Early childhood programs are serving an increasingly diverse clientele. Federal law (e.g., P.L. 94-142 and P.L. 99-457) and state initiatives are bringing more handicapped, developmentally delayed, and at-risk children into the mainstream of early childhood education. Understanding diverse patterns of development is as essential as understanding normative patterns of development.

3. Changing demographic and immigration patterns have continued to introduce a wider array of languages and cultures into our communities. An understanding of child development, either normative or nonnormative, requires an understanding of the context in which that development occurs—the family and the community—from a multicultural, multilinguistic perspective (Bowman, 1989).

4. Early childhood programs are providing, directly or indirectly, a wider range of services to children and families. These range from health and nutrition programs to the provision of speech and physical

therapy. Interagency coordination and collaboration will be the "buzz words" of the 1990s. Personnel working with children will need enough shared knowledge and terminology to communicate and negotiate with each other and with a wide range of related professionals in both the public and private sector.

Each of these changes in the ecology of the early childhood field during the past two decades has major implications for changes in early childhood personnel preparation program policies and curricula, including the content of child development courses.

## CHILD DEVELOPMENT:
## A DEFENSIBLE CONTENT OUTLINE

Given that there are important reasons for the diversity of the content of child development and that the potential content far exceeds what can reasonably be included in any teacher preparation program, some difficult decisions need to be made. Without belaboring the point, we reiterate our initial premise: Child development, broadly conceived, should be the core content of early childhood teacher programs. As such, we believe child development course work and related practica should represent the greatest investment of time and energy in the curriculum. How such content is organized into courses, learning modules, or sequences is too dependent on local conditions to be discussed here. However, we will discuss our rationale for including this content material, no matter how it is organized.

### Conceptual Framework

The developmental framework on which this chapter is based has some further implications for the parameters of the child development content that should be included in the education and training of teachers. In essence, the framework provides guidance for selecting particular content.

1. Although emphasis is placed on a particular age range of children with whom a teacher may work, it is essential that the child development content also include coverage of earlier and later periods. Only through such coverage can a perspective on the continuities and discontinuities of development be attained. The generalized or norma-

tive patterns of continuities and discontinuities across ages represent an important base of understanding about the general characteristics of children at different ages. An understanding of those patterns contributes to a teacher's expectations concerning what children at different ages can or will do, all other things being equal.

2. Understanding variability in development, including its causes, is important. Expectations derived from normative data will serve us only so far. When we interact with children, it is each child's individuality that impresses us and that we respond to. To be effective, a teacher needs to understand the origins (biological and environmental) and the meaning of this uniqueness.

3. The processes of development are an essential focus. The early childhood years are years of change. Developmentally appropriate teaching during these years involves structuring, guiding, and facilitating developmental change. To do so a teacher needs to know the how and why of development — the processes involved.

4. The environment in which development occurs is a continuous codeterminant of child development. The physical, social, and cultural environment provides the context for development; through that environment the commonalities and individual differences in development evolve.

5. No aspect of development proceeds entirely independently of all the others. Physical development is important for intellectual and emotional development. At the same time, intellectual ability and emotional states will influence how and when a child reacts with the environment. Teachers should not forget that they are trying to understand, relate to, and foster the development of the whole child.

Within the above framework, and with full recognition of the diversity of the field of child development and the reasonableness of the disagreements as to what might be most important, or even essential, for teachers, we provide the following commentary on content.

## Fundamentals of Child Development

Although there are arguments against starting off a student of any new field with the most abstract concepts in that field, we begin our outline with the fundamentals of child development. When and how often in the course of a program these fundamentals will be presented, discussed, and reinforced will depend on the length and intensity of the training program and the nature and background of the students enrolled. However, there are three broad concepts involved: principles, scientific basis, and conceptual integration.

The first concept might be called *principles* for understanding development. Within the framework presented above, this material sets the foundation for an understanding that normative development occurs through an orderly sequence of steps from conception to maturity, and that developmental changes are often permanent and not reversible. In addition, the material helps to foster an appreciation of children as valuable and unique members of society. The life-span perspective stresses the importance of the developmental histories as well as predicted futures of children. The systems perspective places the child in the context of the social and physical environment and stresses the dynamic relationship between the child and this environment. The historical perspective illustrates that children have not changed in their need for love, protection, and acceptance, but society's attitudes and treatments toward children have changed.

The second concept might be called the *scientific basis* for understanding child development. It includes information on a variety of research methodologies. The information stresses the importance and usefulness of carefully designed research in child development as a means for validly and reliably ascertaining developmental commonalities and differences, the processes of development, and the influences of the contextual and historical environment. The intent is to foster respect for systematic study in place of personal opinion and personal experience for deriving "truths" about children.

The third concept might be called *conceptual integration*. Here the emphasis is on the relationship between "fact," the bits and pieces of knowledge about a child or children more generally, and a broader understanding that permits the prediction of the outcome of a particular circumstance or action. Theories are portrayed as useful human constructions — conceptual integrations — that aid and extend our capabilities beyond immediate experience. The value of theory lies in its utility — whether it explains aspects or processes of development and directs our behavior. Examples of different theories or partial theories, indicating how they work for us and what we gain from them, are essential. For example, what does Piagetian theory tell us about the selection and organization of classroom materials or the structuring of time?

It is our belief that the fundamentals of child development are not a course or part of a course, but rather a set of recurring themes that are presented, re-presented, and reinforced throughout the early childhood teacher preparation program. The purpose is not to have students learn a set of names or definitions, but rather to develop a pattern of thinking that recognizes critical developmental issues, includes standards for admissible evidence, and values conceptual integration as a means and basis for action.

## Specific Child Development Content

It would be relatively easy to provide a laundry list of specific content. Our own program, again reflecting our developmental bias, requires students majoring in early childhood education to take one course in life-span development, three courses in child development (infancy, early childhood, and middle childhood), and one course in the exceptional child — a total of 15 semester hours of developmental course work. These courses are paralleled by methods courses ranging from child assessment to parent education and their associated practica. The developmental courses, the methods courses, and the practica are designed to build upon and integrate with one another.

Within this program, the major topical areas of genetic and prenatal development, physical and motor development, social development, personality and intrapersonal development, cognitive and intellectual development, and language development are thoroughly covered, with the emphasis shifting with the period under discussion.

Given the relative luxury of developmental course hours, as compared with some other teacher training programs, topics can be covered in considerable depth. Further, because of the close relationship between developmental courses, methods courses, and practica, there is frequently the potential for interplay between classroom discussion and actual experiences with different children. This is particularly useful for emphasizing and integrating the fundamentals of child development.

## TEACHING CHILD DEVELOPMENT

How best to teach child development to future teachers of young children is too broad and complex a topic to be handled well here. Readers interested in the topic are directed to sources such as Colvin and Zaffiro (1974), or Stallings and Stipek (1986), or to the many instructors' guides provided by textbook publishers. There are, however, two "methods" for teaching child development content that are considered essential: observation and direct experience (practica) with children (Heck & Williams, 1984).

## Observation

The use of direct observation in teaching child development is seen as doubly valuable. Assuming that opportunities are available for observing different age groups of children, observation can assist the student in gaining an understanding of the normative sequences of development while not losing sight of the individual differences that occur within any group of children. Guided observations can focus the learner on these commonalities and differences for each domain of development (language, play, and so on), thereby reinforcing classroom and text content.

Observation is considered a central skill of early childhood teaching. High-quality, developmentally appropriate teaching requires that the teacher be able to assess each child's abilities and plan to meet each child's needs (Beaty, 1986). Hence, systematic introduction into the "art and science of observation" serves to both (1) assist the student to make a connection between what is learned about normative developmental sequences and patterns and his or her understanding of the uniqueness of every child, and (2) reinforce the notion of systematic study as a way to understand children.

To be most useful, observation needs to be guided, focused, and fully integrated with the learning process. This means the purpose of the observation must be clearly understood, and there needs to be a set of operational definitions for the behaviors or actions to be observed, and a method of objective recording (Stallings & Mohlman, 1988). Further, the relation of the observation exercise to the lecture/course content should be explicit and properly sequenced.

## Practica

One of the most ancient and honorable methods of learning a skilled craft or profession has been actual experience with or apprenticeship to a master teacher. This method of teaching and learning through guided practice underlies a major portion of the education of early childhood personnel (Honig & Fears, 1974). It was the principle upon which university-based laboratory preschools were established (Benham, 1985), and is considered by most teachers to be the most important part of their training (Peters & Kostelnick, 1981). Such experience under supervision goes under many names. It is sometimes called practice teaching, student teaching, directed teaching, internship, apprenticeship, or field practicum, with the variations in terminology usually reflecting differences in duration and intensity of supervision. Regardless of what it is called, its purposes are to

1. provide an opportunity for novices to learn and employ knowledge of child development with children;
2. make meaningful and comprehensible the research and theory presented in other ways;
3. motivate students by permitting them to test their learning and try out their ideas under sheltered conditions;
4. assess the commitment and personal appropriateness of the individual for the teaching profession and for working with a particular age group (Honig & Fears, 1974).

Research on field experience, generally in education, has been relatively extensive and long-standing (Lanier & Little, 1986). As Lortie (1975) and others have documented, experienced teachers also stress the importance of field experience. Within early childhood education, field practica have been shown to influence future teachers' beliefs, attitudes, preferences, and behaviors (Cohen, Peters, & Willis, 1976), and it is clear that "desired" behaviors can be taught through field practica in ways that have generalizability across settings, time, and children (Thompson, Holberg, & Baer, 1978).

Much less is known, however, about the most appropriate or effective timing, duration, or settings for field experience. Researchers and practitioners alike are beginning to stress continuities of such experience and their integration throughout the education and training of teachers. Within the Child Development Associate training standards, for example, it is clear that academic and field experiences must be integrated and that 50 percent or more of the trainee's total training must be spent in supervised field work (Jones & Hamby, 1981). Given the manner in which the CDA competencies and training principles were established, this represents an overwhelming endorsement by the early childhood field.

There is also a growing awareness that there may be negative outcomes for the individual future teacher and for the profession associated with field learning. Lanier and Little (1986) outline the following:

1. By catering to the insecurities of prospective teachers the emphasis of field learning tends to be on discipline and group manage-

ment rather than on the developmental progress and learning of children.

2. A heavy emphasis on practica over classroom learning in teacher preparation programs suggests to future teachers that the way to learn more about teaching is through trial and error, not through knowledge of child development, careful thought, and scholarship. The focus is more on how things are done in the classroom than on why.

3. Too much emphasis on learning from experience and apprenticeship reinforces a "reflexive conservation" in education that inhibits innovation in the field and limits the ability of individual teachers to see the range of possible decisions and actions available to them in the teaching situation.

These problems or potential negative outcomes have become exacerbated in the early childhood field because the rapid growth of the field and rapid turnover have generated a pyramid that includes few experienced master teachers and many inexperienced teachers in need of mentoring. It also is clear that the time an individual has spent teaching does not mean that he or she has the knowledge, skills, or personality to supervise students (Caruso & Fawcett, 1986). Supervisors who are themselves inexperienced are more likely to stress classroom management, learning by trial and error, and "the way we were taught."

## A DEVELOPMENTAL PERSPECTIVE

Perhaps the most important change that has occurred in recent years in the teaching of child development is the recognition that the learners of child development, the prospective or neophyte teachers, go through a developmental process themselves. Indeed, it has been suggested that those engaged in teaching adults need to be cognizant of where the learners are in both their personal development *and* their professional development (Caruso & Fawcett, 1986; VanderVen, 1979, 1988). Recognition of the developmental needs of learners is as important in the teaching of child development as it is in the teaching of young children, and it has major implications for the focus, timing, and sequencing of observation and practica experiences (Peters & Kostelnick, 1981; Sutton & Peters, 1983; VanderVen, 1979, 1988). The developmental perspective in the teaching of prospective teachers provides a line of research that shows much promise for the future.

## REFERENCES

Almy, M. (1975). *The early childhood educator at work.* New York: McGraw-Hill.
Almy, M. (1988). The early educator revisited. In B. Spodek, O. Saracho, & D. Peters, (Eds.), *Professionalism and the early childhood practitioner* (pp. 44-58). New York: Teachers College Press.
Bailey, D., Simenson, R., Huntington, G., Cochrane, C., Crais, E., & Humphrey, R. (1988). Preparing professionals from multiple disciplines to work with handicapped infants, toddlers, and the families. University of North Carolina, Chapel Hill: Carolina Institute for Research on Infant Personnel Preparation.
Beaty, J. (1986). *Observing development of the young child.* Columbus, OH: Charles E. Merrill.
Benham, N. (1985). *An historical analysis of child study settings for policy research potential.* Unpublished doctoral dissertation, Pennsylvania State University.
Bowman, B. (1989). Educating language—minority children. *Phi Delta Kappan, 71*(2), 118-20.
Bredekamp, S. (1984). *Accreditation criteria and procedures of the National Academy of Early Childhood Programs.* Washington, DC: National Association for the Education of Young Children.
Cartwright, C., & Peters, D. (1983). Early childhood development. In H. Mitzel (Ed.), *Encyclopedia of educational research* (Vol. 1, pp. 477-89). Chicago: University of Chicago Press.
Caruso, J., & Fawcett, M. T. (1986). *Supervision in early childhood education.* New York: Teachers College Press.
Cohen, A., Peters, D., & Willis, S. (1976). The effects of early childhood education student teaching on program preferences, beliefs, and behaviors. *The Journal of Educational Research, 70,* 15-20.
Colvin, R., & Zaffiro, E. (1974). *Preschool education: A handbook for the training of early childhood educators.* New York: Springer.
Council for Early Childhood Professional Recognition. (1989). *National Directory of Early Childhood Training Programs.* Washington, DC: Author.
Craig, S. (1978). Pennsylvania competency based teacher education and specialized competencies for early childhood educations. Harrisburg: Pennsylvania Department of Education.
DeVries, R. (1974). Theory in educational practice. In R. Colvin & E. Zaffiro (Eds.), *Preschool education: A handbook for the training of early childhood educators.* New York: Springer.
Elkind, D. (1989). Developmentally appropriate practice: Philosophical and practical implications. *Phi Delta Kappan, 71*(2), 113-17.
Heck, S., & Williams, C. R. (1984). *The complex roles of the teacher: An ecological perspective.* New York: Teachers College Press.

Honig, A., & Fears, L. (1974). Practicum. In R. Colvin & E. Zaffiro (Eds.), *Preschool education: A handbook for the training of early childhood educators* (pp. 171-98). New York: Springer.

Howard, A. E. (1968). *Characteristics of early childhood teacher education.* Washington, DC: Association for Childhood Education International.

Jones, L., & Hamby, T. (1981). Comments on "A Review of the Child Development Credential." *Child Care Quarterly, 10*(1), 74-83.

Katz, L. G. (1987). Early education: What should young children be doing? In S. Kagan & E. Zigler (Eds.), *Early schooling: The national debate* (pp. 151-67). New Haven: Yale University Press.

Lanier, J., & Little, J. (1986). Research on teacher education. In M. Wittrock (Ed.), *Handbook of research on teaching* (3rd ed., pp. 527-69). New York: Macmillan.

Lortie, D. (1975). *School teacher.* Chicago: University of Chicago Press.

NAEYC. (1976). *NAEYC's first half century: 1926-1976.* Washington, DC: National Association for the Education of Young Children.

NAEYC. (1982). *Early childhood teacher education guidelines for four- and five-year programs.* Washington, DC: National Association for the Education of Young Children.

NAEYC. (1985). *Guidelines for early childhood education programs in associate degree granting institutions.* Washington, DC: National Association for the Education of Young Children.

Peters, D. (1979). Educational programs for early childhood personnel. *Children in Contemporary Society, 12*(2), 11-14.

Peters, D. (1981). Up the down escalator: Comments on professionalism and academic credentials in child care. *Child Care Quarterly, 10*(3), 261-69.

Peters, D. (in press). Graduate degree programs in early childhood education. In L. Williams & D. Fromberg (Eds.), *Encyclopedia of early childhood education.* New York: Garland.

Peters, D., Cohen, A., & McNichol, M. (1974). The training and certification of early childhood personnel. *Child Care Quarterly, 3,* 39-53.

Peters, D., & Kelly, C. (1982). Principles and guidelines for child care personnel preparation programs. *Child Care Quarterly, 11*(3), 22-35.

Peters, D., & Kostelnick, M. (1981). Current research on day care personnel preparation. In S. Kilmer (Ed.), *Advances in day care and early education* (Vol. 2). Greenwich, CT: JAI Press.

Peters, D., Neisworth, J., & Yawkey, T. (1985). *Early childhood education: From theory to practice.* Monterey, CA: Brooks/Cole.

*Peterson's Annual guides to graduate study: Graduate programs in the humanities and social sciences.* (1988). Princeton, NJ: Peterson's Guides, Inc.

Silin, J. (1988). On becoming knowledgeable professionals. In B. Spodek, O. Saracho, & D. Peters (Eds.), *Professionalism and the early childhood practitioner,* (pp. 117-36). New York: Teachers College Press.

Stallings, J., & Mohlman, G. (1988). Classroom observation techniques. In J.

Keeves (Ed.), *Educational research, methodology, and measurement: An international handbook*, (pp. 469-473). Oxford: Pergamon Press.

Stallings, J., & Stipek, D. (1986). Research on early childhood and elementary school teaching programs. In M. Wittrock (Ed.), *Handbook of research on teaching* (3rd ed., pp. 727-53). New York: Macmillan.

Sutton, R., & Peters, D. (1983). Implications for research of a life-span approach to teacher development. ERIC Document Reproduction Service #ED 253-309.

Thompson, C., Holmberg, M., & Baer, D. (1978). An experimental analysis of some procedures to teach priming and reinforcement skills to preschool teachers. *Monographs of the Society for Research in Child Development, 43*(4), Serial #176.

VanderVen, K. (1979). Encouraging personal and professional development of child care practitioners. *Children in Contemporary Society, 12*(2), 5-8.

VanderVen, K. (1986). The current status and emerging issues in training and education for child care practice. In K. VanderVen & E. Tittnick (Eds.), *Competent caregivers — competent children: Training and education for child care practice*, (pp. 13-32). New York: Haworth Press.

VanderVen, K. (1988). Pathways to professional effectiveness for early childhood educators. In B. Spodek, O. Saracho, & D. Peters (Eds.), *Professionalism and the early childhood practitioner* (pp. 137-60). New York: Teachers College Press.

CHAPTER 5

# The Content of Early Childhood Teacher Education Programs
PEDAGOGY

## Jan McCarthy

The knowledge base of pedagogy, derived from research on effective teaching and from clinical experiences, consists of those concepts and principles that influence and enlighten practice and that provide the context within which policies and judgments are formulated. During the last two decades extensive gains have been made in organizing the findings in a way that can inform how elementary and secondary teachers should be prepared and how they should carry out their responsibilities; however, little attention has been focused on early childhood education.

The lack of attention to the preparation of teachers of young children is rooted in the uniqueness of the field and in the philosophical, historical, and political views of society. The early childhood years are defined as including the span from birth to age 8. The kinds of experiences that enhance children's development during this growth period are extremely different from those that apply at other ages and require different teacher competencies. Hymes (1988) questions whether it is possible to prepare personnel to have the competencies to enter the profession and to meet the diverse role expectations associated with infant and toddler programs, preprimary education, and primary education.

The differing types of programs (child care, nursery schools, Head Start, kindergartens), the wide range of program sponsors (public, private, churches, business/industry), the diverse agencies (education, health, welfare) that monitor programs within states, and the array of institutions offering preparation of personnel have impeded unity of the field. For some practitioners and early childhood educators, the word *teaching* conjures a very didactic image, even though a more heuristic orientation dominates the literature and practice. These disparities are further complicated by low salaries, nonprofessionals carrying out program responsibilities, and a failure of society to recognize the early years as important. Therefore, early childhood educators have responded equivocally to preservice teacher preparation.

Teaching young children is a complex human activity. It is never a straightforward occupation or routine job without texture and emotion. It requires the depth of knowledge that develops artistry within those who choose this career—an artistry that must be sanctioned by the profession.

The intent of this chapter is to suggest the domains of knowledge and the concomitant implications for preparing beginning teachers not only to know, but to think and act in ways that are characterized as wise, sensible, and well advised. Both content knowledge and clinical (field) experiences are valuable. Neither, by itself, prepares individuals to respond intelligently in the myriad of situations they will face in their future professional roles as teachers.

## COMPLEMENTARY COMPONENTS OF PEDAGOGICAL KNOWLEDGE

The challenge for early childhood teacher educators is to develop a program of initial preparation for beginning teachers that will develop their propensity and capacity to engage in intellectual dialogue and principled action. For this to occur, two foundational elements must be accommodated in the program, namely, general and subject-matter studies and child development.

Teachers of young children have a responsibility for providing a range of experiences for children that encompasses all disciplines. This implies that teachers must have an appreciation for the disciplines, acquired through general studies, in addition to breadth and reasonable depth of study in the social sciences, biological and physical sciences, mathematics, fine arts, and literature in order to know what concepts, ideas, and principles make up the primary content in the disciplines. Shulman (1986) calls for teacher education to attempt to restore subject-matter knowledge as an integral and supporting component in the teacher education program. Teachers of young children are no exception. Only when teachers understand the interrelatedness among the disciplines will they be able to help young children make connections between and among bodies of knowledge.

Child development, which was discussed in detail in Chapter 4, is inextricably associated with the art and science of teaching young children. Understanding how young children develop, think, interact, and respond is the major source of information that guides assessment, planning, and evaluation, which in turn lead to developmentally appropriate practices. The ensuing discussion is built on the assumption that the aforementioned components will be incorporated with the pedagogical knowledge base in a manner that conveys the concept of teaching as an art to be viewed holistically.

## DOMAINS AND CONTENT OF PEDAGOGICAL KNOWLEDGE

Early childhood teacher education programs must be comprehensively designed to develop knowledgeable and reflective teachers empowered to give leadership to program development and withstand the pressures to include educational experiences that are developmentally inappropriate for young children. In order to construct a program of professional preparation for beginning teachers, Smith (1980) proposes identifying categories of performance for which the skills of pedagogy are to be developed. These categories, herein called domains, provide early childhood teacher educators with a meaningful framework for bringing together the general and subject-matter studies, professional studies, and clinical experiences, including student teaching, so that they will interrelate and inform teacher judgments.

Research should be included with instruction in each of the domains and in the clinical and student teaching components. Its application should be demonstrated and discussed in terms of the implications for practice. The sequential experience of having documented evidence to explicate practice increases the probability that students will be more effective in planning and evaluating as well as in developing a greater appreciation for research (Egbert, 1984).

### Conception of the Teaching and Learning Process

Each beginning teacher must develop a set of defensible professional beliefs about the teaching and learning process that will lead to consistency in practice. Eisner (1982) observes in his studies that what children learn has a great deal to do with what teachers believe about learning and the way in which those beliefs are reflected in the learning activities offered. Likewise, Spodek (1988) reports that teachers' decisions are primarily driven by value-oriented theories: Students preparing to teach have completed approximately 13 years of "teacher watching" and have developed personal beliefs about teaching from that apprenticeship. These are beliefs that will not be easy to alter.

A classification of the views of teaching is not clearly defined, but four broad categories are recognized, namely,

1. teaching as skill training;
2. teaching as transmitting knowledge;
3. teaching as fostering natural development;
4. teaching as producing conceptual change (Scardamalia & Bereiter, 1989).

Without a clear understanding of the underlying principles associated with each of the categories, beginning teachers tend to lose focus and engage in practices that confuse children and make the only classroom action that of problem minimizing.

When skill training is the beginner's conception of teaching, decontextualized activities, such as workbooks, are apt to become the tools for teaching. The novice tends to lack the breadth of experience to translate skill development experiences into activities built around children's natural interests and actions. Clark and Peterson (1986) point out that beginners are apt to feel driven to cover subject matter when transmitting knowledge is their perspective; published curriculum materials become the learning experience, with little consideration of what children are understanding.

Even though the remaining two categories—teaching as fostering natural development and teaching as producing conceptual change—are in consort with the dominant thinking in early childhood education, these views are not without problems for the beginner. Both views require the teacher to have an in-depth understanding of how children perceive information, see relationships, and draw conclusions. This understanding, derived from the study of child development, learning theory, and findings from research related to culture and social class, must be assimilated by the teacher and translated into meaningful practice. Extensive clinical experiences are essential in developing the competence with these two categories, which will sustain the beginner in the world of practice.

The challenge for teacher education is to create ways through which the preservice teacher can develop the expertise to function under the guidance of information and experiences drawn from many sources. Henderson (1988) points out that a teacher education curriculum focusing on professional development should engage students in reflective interplay between their personal predispositions and the diverse languages of professional growth associated with the profession's heritage. Drawing from the work of Henderson (1988) and Schön (1983), a strong recommendation is made for having students in teacher education engage in autobiographical inquiry. In this phase students would be encouraged to explore their past experiences, their prejudgments concerning teaching, and the reasons for their career choice. Awareness of one's values and beliefs and their relationship to teaching increases the possibility that teachers may develop a more principled way of performing.

## Foundations of Early Childhood Education: Philosophical, Psychological, and Historical

During the past century and a half, behavioral sciences, sociological research, philosophical views, economic and political conditions, and religious beliefs have all had an impact on program development for young children. Comprehension of the divergent practices existing today flows from an understanding of both the theoretical perspectives from which they have evolved and the historical context in which they occurred. Only through examining the basic ideas that have infused programs can teachers gain a firmer sense of the reasons for accepting or rejecting proposed classroom practices (Weber, 1984).

The knowledge base in the foundations of early childhood education should highlight the critical developments that have had an impact on the field. Understanding the ideas of Comenius, Rousseau, Pestalozzi, and Froebel calls attention to how their beliefs set the stage for late-nineteenth and early-twentieth-century initiatives in both Europe and America. These initiatives—stemming primarily from the works of G. Stanley Hall, Maria Montessori, Margaret McMillan, John Dewey, Arnold Gessel, Sigmund Freud, B. F. Skinner, and Lawrence Frank—influenced the evolution of early childhood education.

By the middle of the twentieth century a child development point of view was evolving, and principles of child development were being applied to curriculum planning. During this period, the work of Arthur Jersild, Jean Piaget, James Hymes, Erik Erikson, and Lawrence Kohlberg focused attention to cognitive, physical, emotional, moral, and social development, which has led to the formulation of numerous theories about the nature of children and how they learn. Applications of these theories in program development have produced educational models that range from uncompromisingly dissimilar to barely distinguishable.

Through methodically reviewing the past, students preparing to teach will not only note the diversity of ideas but develop a keener sensitivity for the persistence of some ideas and a clearer understanding of the supporting evidence. Furthermore, familiarity with the historical context in which changes occur leads to a better understanding of how policies and practices are influenced. By confronting the fallacies, limitations, and inconsistencies that permeate many of the practices, teachers will become more confident and effective in their roles as teachers and advocates for young children.

## Home, School, and Community Relations

Parent involvement has always been a hallmark in early childhood education, even though the nature of the involvement has changed extensively. Early parent programs focused on parent education and emphasized ways of improving relationships among children and family members, practical child rearing techniques, and how to aid the child's development. Conferences, directed observations, participation, and group meetings were the major ways of providing information to parents that would enable them to manage their roles.

The early intervention programs of the 1960s stimulated a different focus: one that viewed parents as important allies in the educational process. Even though all the interventionists acknowledged the influence of the family on the child's growth and development, each had somewhat different strategies for interacting with parents. Numerous models, which included a mix of modalities of involvement, were developed. Even though the previous strategies for working with parents were retained, the interactions between parents and teachers became more personal, individualized, and reciprocal. These strategies were supplemented by other types of involvement, such as home and school visits, parent networks, parents as teachers, parent advisory groups, child-help projects, and work projects.

In the late 1970s two new populations, young children with special needs and infants and toddlers, caused a re-examining of the parents' relationship with programs. As programs for children with special needs developed, it became clear that parents' views, abilities, capabilities, and difficulties had to be considered as an integral component in managing the children's needs. These were also important considerations when attempting to develop consistency in care giving for the very young and vulnerable infants and toddlers. The emerging trend seems to reflect a sense of partnership between families and professionals (Cataldo, 1987).

A review of research findings by Honig (1982) validates the effectiveness of parent involvement and indicates that the most successful programs are planned collaboratively with parents and tailored to the unique needs of the constituents of a particular program and community. Teachers will associate with many families whose life-styles, cultural values, beliefs, and mores are different from theirs. They must have understanding and deference in order to resolve discrepancies between their beliefs and values and those held by parents and to develop a collaborative teacher-parent program (Becher, 1985; Lyons, Robbins, & Smith, 1983; Powell, 1986). Responsive programs will be designed and maintained when teachers are knowledgeable about the relationships and practices inside families and are aware of ways to form a child-parent-teacher triad.

## Learning Experiences and Curricular Vision

Educational reforms proposed in the mid-to-late 1980s support the view that all learners—from infancy through high school—are active, interactive, constructive problem solvers. Early childhood educators have long championed this perspective, even though there are differing ways in which it is implemented in practice. Knowledge of child development provides the insight that guides planning of learning experiences and development of a curricular vision that links learning to the individual learner's needs and abilities. Young children should be stimulated by their sense of self-fulfillment and maintain the curiosity, inquisitiveness, and zest for learning that lead to the development of thinking, reasoning, and problem solving.

Furthermore, recognizing the value and importance of each individual means respecting and accepting each child's culture. The United States has the broadest range of cultural and ethnic groups in the world. A classroom may be composed of children from a wide range of cultural, ethnic, and religious backgrounds or it may be monocultural. Regardless of the group composition, a multicultural perspective should be evident in all learning experiences. Ramsey (1987) points out that multicultural education is not a set curriculum or a collection of activities. It is a world view, a way of interpreting behavior and events in which diversity among individuals is valued and all human differences are encompassed. Children should not be expected to abandon their own cultural values in order to participate in school experiences, or be subjected to cultural conflicts that result in alienation or school failure (Philips, 1983).

The following abbreviated discussion of subject areas serves to call attention to the breadth of experiences that constitute a well-rounded curriculum for young children and is not meant to imply that a program for young children should occur in narrowly defined, isolated subjects. Teachers must be in command of knowledge pertaining to each of the areas in order to select appropriate materials and equipment, to plan learning activities that are concrete and relevant to the developmental interests and abilities of children, and to structure a learning environment that is responsive to the integrative mode in which young children function.

*Play.* Play is central to and touches all aspects of young children's development. A theoretical understanding of play and the practical implications of that understanding facilitates the teacher's ability to implement developmentally appropriate learning experiences that are defensible and in consort with the young child's natural way of exploring, discovering, and learning (Bergen, 1987; Fein & Rivkin, 1986; Frost & Sunderlin, 1985; Johnson, Christie, & Yawkey, 1987; Monighan-Nourot, Scales, Van Hoorn, & Almy, 1987; Rogers & Sawyers, 1988; Saracho, 1986).

*Emergent Literacy.* During the 1980s, investigations of the competence of children as literacy learners have called for redefinition of thinking regarding language experiences for young children. The knowledge children bring to literacy experiences before they can read or write; the interdependence of reading, writing, and speaking; the social nature of language learning; the emergence of oral language in context; contextual cues and interpretation of print; and the role of children's books in the reading process are a few of the understandings that beginning teachers need in order to be effective in nurturing literacy (Ferreiro & Teberosky, 1982; Genishi, 1987; Goodman, 1986; Hall, 1987; Harste, Woodward, & Burke, 1984; Newman, 1985; Schickedanz, 1986).

*Science and Math.* Science and math curriculum in early childhood education is strongly influenced by the work of Piaget. The nature of these disciplines, in which meaningful learning occurs only when children are able to organize information in a way that is understandable to them, fits well with Piaget's theory of how children construct knowledge. A knowledge of the procedural misunderstandings that lead children to make faulty judgments and of the processes children use in arriving at correct decisions is valuable information for teachers. The knowledge base in science and math includes both understanding the process as well as appropriate learning experiences to nurture awareness and understanding of science- and math-related concepts (Berman, 1982; Carlin & Sund, 1980; Forman & Kaden, 1987; Ginsburg, 1983; Holt, 1977; Kamii, 1982, 1985, 1986; McCracken, 1987; McIntyre, 1984; Spodek, Saracho, & Davis, 1987).

*Social Studies.* It is difficult to find planned social studies experiences for young children in early childhood classrooms. To plan learning experiences that will develop new orientations for young children, teachers must have command of the knowledge and the ability to intentionally and selectively draw from the various disciplines: history, geography, sociology, anthropology, global studies, ecology, economics, and moral education. An understanding of the immediate physical environment, where materials come from, and what people do builds security, independence, and self-understanding as young children learn to function in an expanded world (Becker, 1979; Kendall, 1983; Ryan, 1980; Saracho & Spodek, 1983; Seefeldt, 1984; Spodek, Saracho, & Davis, 1987).

*The Arts.* The arts in early childhood education include music, movement, art, and dramatization, with emphasis on process skills that children are acquiring. The arts contribute to the development of multiple ways of expressing thoughts and ideas, while providing a way for children to put meaning to events, actions, and experiences during personal explorations (Brittain, 1979; McDonald, 1979). Teachers must understand how each of these areas contributes to the young child's development, be capable of expressing this information to other professionals and parents, and be able to defend the young child's need for creative expression as well as plan and implement a balanced program (Carpenter, 1986; Lasky & Mukerji, 1980).

## Organization and Management of the Learning Environment

One of the major concerns of beginning teachers is classroom organization and management (Veenman, 1984). Teacher education programs must engage students in analyzing attributes of effective classrooms, such as appropriate equipment and materials, arrangement of a total learning environment, daily schedules and time frames, transitions, grouping (when age appropriate), motivation, planning, peer relations, teacher-child interactions, and guiding behavior. Hill, Yinger, and Robbins (1981) found that preschool teachers spend many hours each week rearranging the physical environment when things go wrong. In this case simple cues become a substitute for thoughtful analysis of the content and structure of the learning experiences and their relationship to children's needs.

The pedagogy of classroom management is barely observable in teacher education programs, partially because of the context-specific nature of the programs and partially because the knowledge base is derived from several sources. Nevertheless, a range of experiences must be afforded students that will develop their ability to reflect, analyze conditions, consider consequences, and respond effectively to the many interactions that occur daily. Moving from being a team member to being in charge of orchestrating the social and academic system in a classroom can be an overwhelming responsibility (Decker & Decker, 1988; Gottfried, 1983; Leeper, Witherspoon, & Day, 1984; Loughlin & Suina, 1982; Marzollo, 1987; Spodek, Saracho, & Davis, 1987; Yonemura, 1986).

## Mainstreaming in Early Childhood Education

In 1975 Public Law 94-142, the Education for All Handicapped Children Act, was passed. The purpose of this legislation was to ensure that handicapped persons between the ages of three and twenty-one would receive free and appropriate education in the least restrictive environment. This means that children with special needs should receive an education that is individualized, closely approximates the experiences provided for normal children, and is in a regular classroom if that is the educational setting in which the child can function best. Often children between the ages of three and five did not receive public school services since states had discretion as to whether to provide services for this age group. Consequently, Public Law 99-457 was enacted in 1986 authorizing two new programs, the Federal Preschool Program and Early Intervention Program. The Federal Preschool Program mandated that services provided under P.L. 94-142 be extended to children between the ages of three and five by the 1990-91 school year or states will no longer receive funding under P.L. 94-142. The Early Intervention Program authorizes states to establish a grant program for handicapped infants and toddlers from birth to two years.

Implementation of this legislation has many implications for the classroom teacher, and therefore the knowledge base in teacher education must be responsive. Even though teachers must have an understanding of the legislative mandates, such as the role of parent and child in diagnosis, placement, and development of the individualized educational plan (IEP) and the rights of parents, their knowledge must transcend the legal aspects. They will be expected to

1. demonstrate an understanding of the various types of handicapping conditions and their relationship to the child's educational plan;
2. show awareness of resources available for assistance in meeting the child's needs;
3. exhibit proficiency in working with professionals such as physical therapists, psychologists, social workers, pediatricians, and special educators (see Allen, 1980; Fallen & McGovern, 1978; Hart, 1981; Safford, 1989).

### Infant and Toddler Programs

Early childhood programs preparing teachers for the youngest age group have a responsibility to include in the knowledge base pedagogy that is specific to the unique demands of infants and toddlers. Merely understanding growth and development is not sufficient. Personnel working with infants and toddlers must be knowledgeable about health care, health practices, nutritional needs, interaction and experiences to nurture development, and working collaboratively with parents (Cataldo, 1982; Dittman, 1984; Honig & Lally, 1981; Weisner, 1982; White, 1975, 1988; Willis & Ricciuti, 1975).

### Health, Nutrition, and Safety

Teachers' responsibilities for health, nutrition, and safety are greater during the early childhood years than at any other point in the child's school years. The beginner gains the essentials for responding in an informed manner from a knowledge base that includes information related to maintaining a healthy classroom environment, procedures to follow with health-related problems (such as infectious diseases), plans for nutritional needs of children, development of safety procedures, and plans for health and nutrition education for young children. The vulnerability of young children and the prevailing health conditions of society heighten the needs for teacher education to address these issues (Decker & Decker, 1988; Kendrick, Kaufmann, & Messenger, 1988).

## Assessment and Evaluation Processes and Procedures

Assessment is not an appendage to an early childhood program. It is a system of collecting information, analyzing it, and making decisions about the progress of children, which is carefully planned within the context of the program goals. The knowledge base should emphasize how to select or develop appropriate assessment tools—both informal (such as observation) and formal (standardized tests, for example)— how to analyze the information, how to interpret test data, how to use information to guide practice, and how to communicate information to parents.

Program evaluation complements the assessment process. The evaluation knowledge base provides an understanding of ongoing assessments of daily and long-range plans related to program goals, physical environment, teacher-child interactions, and teacher-parent relations.

A comprehensive profile of the needs of the children and the program will require multiple ways of collecting and recording information, such as

1. observational checklists of child-child, adult-child, and child-environment interactions;
2. logs or journals of planned experiences and children's responses;
3. interviews with children and parents;
4. accumulation of children's work;
5. videotaping classroom actions;
6. anecdotal recording of children's experiences;
7. rating the classroom environment in relation to the program's goals (Harms & Clifford, 1980).

Beginning teachers must feel confident in collecting data and objectifying information in order to avoid having standardized tests become the only accountability measure (Cartwright & Cartwright, 1984; Cohen & Stern, 1983; Decker & Decker, 1988; Meisels, 1985; Peck, McCaig, & Sapp, 1988; Spodek, Saracho, & Davis, 1987).

## Legal Rights and Responsibilities

Teachers have rights, but they also have responsibilities for the care and protection of children. Programs are governed by statutory laws, with states having authority over education as long as federal rights are protected. The knowledge base should include information regarding terms of employment, discipline of children, injuries to children, reporting of suspected child abuse, and regulations about transportation of children, as these relate to teachers' responsibilities (Fischer, Schimmel, & Kelly, 1987; McCarthy & Cambron-McCabe, 1987). Ignorance of the law cannot be used as a defense.

Additionally, teachers have to make judgments in situations where there are no judicial guidelines. Reasonable and fair policies and practices guide teachers in these circumstances. Thoughtfully planned policies that are regularly reviewed provide a way of responding in troublesome circumstances. Teachers must be capable of meeting these responsibilities.

## Professionalism and Ethics

Throughout this chapter the focus has been on the knowledge base for *beginning* teachers, but a basic program is not enough to sustain a teacher throughout a professional career even if no new research findings are added to the information base. Learning to teach is a career-long process. Katz (1983) identifies four stages of a teacher's development: survival, consolidation, renewal, and maturity. She proposes that, just as we assist beginners in accepting the first stage, we be resourceful in helping them achieve each of the subsequent stages. We must inspire teachers to find ways to participate in knowledge-enhancing activities, to think about the aims of education, and to engage in personal growth experiences. During clinical experiences and student teaching, students should have an opportunity to participate in a set of professional development activities with teachers.

The act of teaching affects others. In carrying out this act teachers draw upon their knowledge of the teaching and learning process and at the same time make judgments that may be either covertly or overtly influenced by their personal values. This places teaching in the realm of a moral or ethical enterprise. Teachers are expected to have an awareness of ethical questions embedded in school practices or curriculum content and an understanding of parent values and implications for school–home relations. How will preservice teachers acquire the understandings needed to respond in an ethical manner? Rest (1986) found that moral dilemma discussions were more effective than seminars in developing a sense of ethical practice. Teacher education is challenged to pay more attention to the development of ethical practitioners (Reeck, 1982; Schon, 1987). Ethical concerns need not be constraints, but should serve to clarify each individual's cherished ideals.

## CLINICAL EXPERIENCES AND STUDENT TEACHING

The knowledge base for teachers consists of *content knowledge*, which provides facts, principles, concepts, and understandings, and *clinical knowledge*, which guides performance. Acquisition of the clinical skill of observing enables a student to draw upon content knowledge and carry out clinical performances such as reflecting, analyzing, assessing, planning, managing, communicating, and evaluating. Through these processes, teachers acquire the information needed to create and maintain a developmentally appropriate learning environment that engages children in productive learning experiences.

### Nature of Clinical Experiences

The ability to objectively observe a classroom action must be developed before other clinical tasks can be performed effectively. Initial experiences in developing observational skills should begin early in the student's program of study and should be focused, simple, and recorded. Each level of observation should become more complex and develop skills for observing for different purposes, for example, observing the nature of teacher–child interactions, the learning environment, parent–teacher interactions, or a child's problem-solving processes. All observations should be accompanied by discussion, reflective thinking, and feedback to facilitate the students' ability to objectify their observational skills and develop their concept of teaching (Bolin, 1988).

Clinical experiences should be continual; they should include exceptional and culturally diverse populations, a variety of settings, and age ranges that reflect the scope of preparation; and they should move from observation to increasingly more responsible roles, thereby developing the skills that will enable students to assume full responsibility for instruction. "Course-specific" models of clinical experience—that is, clinical experience in conjunction with a designated course such as parent involvement, curriculum, or special needs—tend to be more focused and effective in developing the ability to assess, analyze, plan, manage, communicate, and evaluate. This is especially true when the students engage in reflective discourse that probes the premises of their actions (Freeland, 1988; Sarason, Davidson, & Blatt, 1986).

## Student Teaching

Student teaching should be viewed as an experience when students organize their content and clinical knowledge, draw upon their clinical skills and views of teaching, and develop a personal style of practice that is workable, defensible, and ethical. This view moves student teaching away from the apprenticeship model, which implies learning the art of teaching as demonstrated by the cooperating teacher.

Questions about the effectiveness of the student teaching experience, the impact of the cooperating teacher on the socialization of the student teacher, the effect of prestudent teaching clinical experiences, the compatibility of cooperating teachers' philosophy with the teacher education program, and the intellectual and personal maturity of the candidates have been examined in student teaching research (Bunting, 1988; Copeland, 1980; Tabachnick & Zeichner, 1984). Data from these studies have not revealed specific factors that seem to be most influential in the occupational socialization process, even though these factors appear to have the most influence.

Because the needs of learners, the nature of learning, and the learning environment are dramatically different for the infant-toddler, preprimary, and primary age clusters, the student teaching experience for early childhood students should include experiences with at least two of the three age groups. This experience should be accompanied by a seminar that encourages students to examine compatibility of their practices with research, to reflect on alternatives for teaching or guiding behavior, and to consider strategies they would implement in their own classroom. Reflective thinking about one's practices and their implications is the trademark of effective teachers.

## CONCLUSION

Teaching is a complex process. Preparing students to become teachers is equally complex. A teacher education program must be a carefully planned set of experiences that bring together general studies, additional subject-matter content, child development, the teacher education knowledge base, clinical experiences, and student teaching. Important strands of knowledge and skills must be interwoven throughout the program with increasing levels of complexity.

Effective teacher education programs encourage reflective thinking and problem solving, and provide numerous opportunities for students to discuss issues, raise questions, and test ideas. Each student must form his or her personal concept of teaching based on the knowledge and clinical experiences that meet the test of defensible practice. To accomplish this, teacher educators must demonstrate the kind of behaviors they expect students to practice with children. We must create conditions for learning that are conducive to developing the desired outcomes.

Also, teacher educators must develop collaborative efforts with schools and centers providing clinical experiences and student teaching. Collaborative engagements between teacher educators and cooperating teachers, where each will learn from the other, lead to a unified perspective about the field experience. A supportive, well-planned experience enables students to focus attention on assuming the complex role of teaching and minimizes the confusion associated with attempting to meet two diverse sets of expectations.

Identifying the components of the knowledge base is one part of the process of preparing early childhood teachers. The effectiveness of that process will depend on the nature of the teacher education program, how adult learners are viewed, and the type of relationship that is built with schools and centers cooperating in the field experiences.

## REFERENCES

Allen, K. E. (1980). *Mainstreaming in early childhood education*. New York: Delmar.

Becher, R. M. (1985). Parent involvement and reading achievement: A review of research. *Childhood Education, 62*(1), 44-50.

Becker, J. (Ed.). (1979). *Schooling for a global age*. New York: McGraw-Hill.

Bergen, D. (1987). *Play as a medium for learning and development*. Portsmouth, NH: Heinemann.

Berman, B. (1982). How children learn math: Rediscovering manipulatives. *Curriculum Review, 21*, 192-96.

Bolin, F. (1988). Helping student teachers think about teaching. *Journal of Teacher Education, 39*, 48-54.

Brittain, W. L. (1979). *Creativity, art, and the young child*. New York: Macmillan.

Bunting, C. (1988). Cooperating teachers and the changing views of teacher candidates. *Journal of Teacher Education, 39*(2), 42-46.

Carlin, A., & Sund, R. B. (1980). *Teaching science through discovery*. Columbus, OH: Merrill.

Carpenter, J. (1986). *Creating the world: Poetry, art, and children*. Seattle: University of Washington Press.

Cartwright, C. A., & Cartwright, G. P. (1984). *Developing observational skills* (2nd ed.). New York: McGraw-Hill.

Cataldo, C. (1982). *Infant and toddler programs: A guide to very early childhood education*. Reading: Addison-Wesley.

Cataldo, C. (1987). *Parent education for early childhood*. New York: Teachers College Press.

Clark, C. M., & Peterson, P. L. (1986). Teachers' thought processes. In M. C. Wittrock (Ed.), *Handbook of research on teaching* (3rd ed., pp. 255-96). New York: Macmillan.

Cohen, D. H., & Stern, V. (1983). *Observing and recording behavior of young children* (3rd ed.). New York: Teachers College Press.

Copeland, W. (1980). Student teachers and cooperating teachers: An ecological relationship. *Theory Into Practice, 18,* 194-99.

Decker, C., & Decker, J. (1988). *Planning and administering early childhood programs* (4th ed.). Columbus, OH: Merrill.

Dittman, L. (1984). *The infants we care for*. Washington, DC: National Association for the Education of Young Children.

Egbert, R. (1984). The role of research in teacher education. In R. Egbert & M. Kluender (Eds.), *Using research to improve teacher education*. Lincoln: Clearinghouse on Teacher Education, University of Nebraska.

Eisner, E. (1982). *Cognition and curriculum: A basis for deciding what to learn*. New York: Longman.

Fallen, N., & McGovern, J. (Eds.). (1978). *Young children with special needs*. Columbus, OH: Merrill.

Fein, G., & Rivkin, M. (Eds.). (1986). *The young child at play: Reviews of research* (Vol. 4). Washington, DC: National Association for the Education of Young Children.

Ferreiro, E., & Teberosky, A. (1982). *Literacy before schooling*. Portsmouth, NH: Heinemann.

Fischer, L., Schimmel, D., & Kelly, C. (1987). *Teachers and the law* (2nd ed.). New York: Longman.

Forman, G., & Kaden, M. (1987). Research on science education for young children. In C. Seefeldt (Ed.), *Early childhood curriculum: A review of current research* (pp. 141-64). New York: Teachers College Press.

Freeland, K. (1988). A collaborative effort in field experiences. *The Teacher Educator, 24*(2), 22-26.

Frost, J., & Sunderlin, S. (1985). *When children play*. Wheaton, MD: Association for Childhood Education International.

Genishi, C. (1987). Acquiring language and communicative competence. In C.

Seefeldt (Ed.), *Early childhood curriculum: A review of current research* (pp. 75-106). New York: Teachers College Press.

Ginsburg, H. (Ed.). (1983). *The development of mathematical thinking.* New York: Academic Press.

Goodman, K. (1986). *What's whole in whole language?* Portsmouth, NH: Heinemann.

Gottfried, A. (1983). Research in review. Intrinsic motivation in young children. *Young Children, 39*(1), 64-73.

Hall, N. (1987). *The emergence of literacy.* Portsmouth, NH: Heinemann.

Harms, T., & Clifford, R. (1980). *Early Childhood Environment Rating Scale.* New York: Teachers College Press.

Harste, J., Woodward, V., & Burke, C. (1984). *Language stories and literacy lessons.* Portsmouth, NH: Heinemann.

Hart, V. (1981). *Mainstreaming children with special needs.* New York: Longman.

Henderson, J. (1988). A curriculum response to the knowledge base reform movement. *Journal of Teacher Education, 39,* 13-17.

Hill, J., Yinger, R. J., & Robbins. (1981, April). Instructional planning in a developmental preschool. Paper presented at the annual meeting of the American Educational Research Association, Los Angeles.

Holt, B. (1977). *Science with young children.* Washington, DC: National Association for the Education of Young Children.

Honig, A. (1982). Parent involvement in early childhood education. In B. Spodek (Ed.), *Handbook of research in early childhood education* (pp. 426-55). New York: Free Press.

Honig, A., & Lally, J. R. (1981). *Infant care giving: A design for training.* Syracuse: Syracuse University Press.

Hymes, J. L., Jr. (1988, Spring). A teaching credential for the under-six years, *Notes and Comments,* Occasional Paper #3. Carmel, CA: Hacienda Press.

Johnson, J., Christie, M., & Yawkey, T. (1987). *Play and early childhood development.* Glenview: Scott Foresman.

Kamii, C. (1982). *Number in preschool and kindergarten.* Washington, DC: National Association for the Education of Young Children.

Kamii, C. (1985). *Young children reinvent arithmetic.* New York: Teachers College Press.

Kamii, C. (1986). Cognitive learning and development. In B. Spodek (Ed.), *Today's kindergarten* (pp. 67-90). New York: Teachers College Press.

Katz, L. (1983). The education of preprimary teachers. In L. Katz (Ed.), *Current topics in early childhood education* (Vol. 5, pp. 209-28). Norwood, NJ: Ablex.

Kendall, E. (1983). *Diversity in the classroom.* New York: Teachers College Press.

Kendrick, A., Kaufmann, R., & Messenger, K. (1988). *Healthy young children: A manual for programs.* Washington, DC: National Association for the Education of Young Children.

Lasky, L., & Mukerji, R. (1980). *Art: Basic for young children.* Washington, DC: National Association for the Education of Young Children.

Leeper, S., Witherspoon, R., & Day, B. (1984). *Good schools for young children* (5th ed.). New York: Macmillan.

Loughlin, C., & Suina, J. (1982). *The learning environment.* New York: Teachers College Press.

Lyons, P., Robbins, A., & Smith, A. (1983). *Involving parents: A handbook for participation schools.* Ypsilanti, MI: High Scope.

Marzollo, J. (1987). *The new kindergarten: Full-day, child-centered, academic.* New York: Harper & Row.

McCarthy, M., & Cambron-McCabe, N. (1987). *Public school law: Teachers' and students' rights.* Boston: Allyn & Bacon.

McCracken, J. B. (1987). *More than 1, 2, 3: The real basics of mathematics.* Washington, DC: National Association for the Education of Young Children.

McDonald, D. (1979). *Music in our lives.* Washington, DC: National Association for the Education of Young Children.

McIntyre, M. (1984). *Early childhood and science.* Washington, DC: National Science Teachers Association.

Meisels, S. (1985). *Developmental screening in early childhood.* Washington, DC: National Association for the Education of Young Children.

Monighan-Nourot, P., Scales, B., Van Hoorn, J., & Almy, M. (1987). *Looking at children's play.* New York: Teachers College Press.

Newman, J. (1985). *Whole language: Theory in use.* Portsmouth, NH: Heinemann.

Peck, J. T., McCaig, G., & Sapp, M. E. (1988). *Kindergarten policies: What is best for children?* Washington, DC: National Association for the Education of Young Children.

Philips, S. U. (1983). *The invisible culture: Communication in the classroom and community of the Warm Spring Indian Reservation.* New York: Longman.

Powell, D. R. (1986). Research in review. Parent education and support programs. *Young Children, 41*(3), 47–53.

Ramsey, P. G. (1987). *Teaching and learning in a diverse world.* New York: Teachers College Press.

Reeck, D. (1982). *Ethics for the profession.* Minneapolis: Augsburg.

Rest, J. (1986). *Moral development: Advances in theory and research.* New York: Praeger.

Rogers, C., & Sawyers, J. (1988). *Play in the lives of children.* Washington, DC: National Association for the Education of Young Children.

Ryan, F. (1980). *The social studies sourcebook.* Boston: Allyn & Bacon.

Safford, P. (1989). *Integrated teaching in early childhood.* White Plains, NY: Longman.

Saracho, O. N. (1986). Play and young children's learning. In B. Spodek (Ed.), *Today's kindergarten.* New York: Teachers College Press.

Saracho, O. N., & Spodek, B. (1983). *Understanding the multicultural experience in early childhood education*. Washington, DC: National Association for the Education of Young Children.

Sarason, S., Davidson, K., & Blatt, B. (1986). *The preparation of teachers* (rev. ed.). Cambridge, MA: Brookline Books.

Scardamalia, M., & Bereiter, C. (1989). Conceptions of teaching and approaches to core problems. In M. C. Reynolds (Ed.), *Knowledge base for the beginning teacher* (pp. 37-46). New York: Pergamon Press.

Schickedanz, J. (1986). *More than ABCs*. Washington, DC: National Association for the Education of Young Children.

Schön, D. (1983). *The reflective practitioner*. New York: Basic Books.

Schön, D. (1987). *Educating the reflective practitioner*. San Francisco: Jossey-Bass.

Seefeldt, C. (1984). *Social studies for the preschool-primary child* (2nd ed.). Columbus, OH: Merrill.

Shulman, L. (1986). Those who understand: Knowledge growth in teaching. *Educational Researcher, 15*(2), 8-9.

Smith, B. O. (1980). *A design for a school of pedagogy*. Washington, DC: U. S. Government Printing Office.

Spodek, B. (1988). Implicit theories of early childhood teachers: Foundations for professional behavior. In B. Spodek, O. Saracho, & D. Peters (Eds.), *Professionalism and the early childhood practitioner* (pp. 161-72). New York: Teachers College Press.

Spodek, B., Saracho, O., & Davis, M. (1987). *Foundations of early childhood education*. Englewood Cliffs, NJ: Prentice-Hall.

Tabachnick, B. R., & Zeichner, K. M. (1984). The impact of the student teaching experience on the development of teacher perspectives. *Journal of Teacher Education, 35*(6), 28-36.

Veenman, S. (1984). Perceived problems of beginning teachers. *Review of Educational Research, 54*(2), 143-78.

Weber, E. (1984). *Ideas influencing early childhood education: A theoretical analysis*. New York: Teachers College Press.

Weisner, M. S. (1982). *Group care and education of infants and toddlers*. St. Louis, MO: Mosby.

White, B. (1975). *The first three years of life*. Englewood Cliffs, NJ: Prentice-Hall.

White, B. (1988). *Educating the infant and toddler*. Lexington, MA: Lexington Books.

Willis, A., & Ricciuti, H. (1975). *A good beginning for babies: Guidelines for group care*. Washington, DC: National Association for the Education of Young Children.

Yonemura, M. (1986). *A teacher at work: Professional development and the early childhood educator*. New York: Teachers College Press.

CHAPTER 6

# Early Childhood Teacher Preparation in Cross-Cultural Perspective

Olivia N. Saracho
Bernard Spodek

Too often teacher educators look at programs in their own country and assume that they represent the total range of possible alternatives. Yet the way teacher education is organized and implemented in other countries can be far different from what is familiar to those of a single country. The purpose of this chapter is to look at how early childhood teachers are prepared in several countries, both developed and developing. These countries have traditions different from our own in the areas of early childhood education and teacher education, though they have all been influenced by American early childhood education theories and practices.

One of the problems with cross-national comparisons is that, just as the systems of early childhood education differ greatly, the systems of teacher training also differ greatly, making comparisons difficult. In addition, it is not always possible to gather comparable information from each source. The rewards of such comparisons, however, far overshadow the difficulties. Looking at early childhood teacher education within different countries and cultures allows us to better understand our own and to realize that there are many possible conceptions of an early childhood teacher, many possible goals of teacher training programs, and many possible ways of achieving common goals.

The other chapters in this volume deal with teacher education in the United States. Teacher education in other countries is presented in this chapter to provide a comparison that will allow the reader to create a context in which to gain a better understanding of what happens in this country. It is important to realize that what is done in one country is not the only approach to teacher education. Alternative approaches are possible and can be found elsewhere, especially in countries with different educational traditions.

The Republic of Korea, People's Republic of China, Australia, and Israel are studied in this chapter. The section on China is derived from previously published material, while material on the other countries was solicited from specific knowledgeable informants. Specific questions were raised relating to the preparation of early childhood education personnel, as follows:

1. How is early childhood education defined?
2. How long is the teacher training program?
3. At what level is training conducted?
4. Is the training of early childhood teachers different from that of primary or secondary teachers?
5. What is the prescribed content of the program?
6. What proportion of the program is dedicated to each of the components?
7. Where are the field experiences and teaching practice generally done?
8. How are standards set for the teacher preparation program?
9. What have been the most interesting developments in the preparation of teachers in your country?
10. What would you consider to be the most pressing problems that need to be addressed?
11. Are there any other considerations that are worth mentioning in relation to the preparation of early childhood personnel?

The information collected is not totally comparable, since both the style of presentation and the level of specificity varied from one source to another. The material is presented as fully as possible by country, followed by a comparison with the United States. Since the other chapters in this volume deal with early childhood teacher education in the United States, no separate section on the United States is provided in this chapter.

## REPUBLIC OF KOREA

In Korea,[1] early childhood education is considered education before elementary school, that is, for children under seven years of age.

Early childhood education institutions have included kindergartens and Saemaul nursery schools since 1982. In addition, private nursery schools and day care and family day care programs have developed in response to Korean family needs.

Children can enter kindergarten at age 4 and stay until they reach elementary school age. Kindergartens offer half-day programs, and there are both private and public kindergartens. The Saemaul nursery school is unique to Korea; its objective is to expand educational opportunities for low income family children. Children from three to six years of age are accepted in these half-day or full-day preschool programs. While the government wishes the Saemaul nursery schools to operate as child care centers, they are presently functioning more like kindergartens.

Some experimental nursery schools for prekindergarten children operate as university-affiliated schools. They typically serve three- to four-year-old children in half-day programs. Presently, the care of working mothers' children and those from low-income families is receiving considerable national attention. Some businesses are establishing child care centers in the workplace and many family day care centers are being created. In addition, the Ministry of Health and Social Affairs is planning to expand all-day child-care centers. With this increase in child care centers, standards for qualification and preparation of child caregivers are being widely debated. As noted, early childhood education is currently undergoing change in Korea and is becoming more diversified.

## Early Childhood Teacher Training Programs

Teacher training for kindergarten and Saemaul nursery school is conducted in both four-year colleges and universities and two-year junior colleges in Korea, with most early childhood teachers graduating from two-year programs. In 1986, the four-year course training programs (including post-graduate courses) produced about 730 kindergarten teachers, while the two-year programs produced about 6,680 kindergarten teachers. The four-year programs have been established in three national universities and fourteen private universities and other colleges (such as seminaries). The two-year programs are found in three national vocational junior colleges or universities, fifty-one private colleges, and one National Air and Correspondence University. Teacher training is also being offered in graduate schools of education, but these programs do not lead to teacher certification.

The preparation of early childhood teachers in Korea takes place in early childhood education departments of colleges and universities, but the programs are different from those that prepare elementary school teachers. In addition, while early childhood education majors do their student teaching in public or private kindergartens, elementary education majors student teach only in the public elementary schools. Teachers are prepared as either elementary (grades 1-6) or kindergarten (ages 3-5) teachers in Korea; programs and certificates for kindergarten through third grade (K-3) or for nursery school through third grade (N-3) are not available. Graduates in elementary education, however, receive both the elementary school and the kindergarten teachers certificate.

## Program Content

The content and requirements for early childhood teacher training differ between the four-year programs and the two-year programs. The typical four-year university program consists of at least 140 credits or semester hours, including general education (42 credits); foundations (18 credits); the major area (59 credits), including child development, psychology, and early childhood education courses; and the minor area (21 credits).

The typical two-year junior college program consists of at least 90 credits or semester hours, including general education (20 credits); foundations (16 credits); major courses (48 credits), including child development, psychology, and early childhood education methods courses; and electives (6 credits). There are also differences in teaching practice between the two types of teacher education institutions. As mentioned before, early childhood education majors in national universities or national junior colleges do their teaching practice in public or private kindergartens. Early childhood education students in private colleges (universities) or junior colleges usually practice teach only in private kindergartens.

## General Standards

The general standards for teacher preparation in Korea are established by the Education Laws and Enforcement Ordinances of the Ministry of Education. The qualifications for early childhood personnel (teacher, director, assistant teacher), the program's organization (including curriculum and credit requirements) and curriculum, the length of the college's or university's school terms and school year, and the number of students enrolled are all covered by these Education Laws and Enforcement Ordinances, which are enforced within each educational institution. Standards for early childhood personnel vary with the position (director, elementary school teacher, kindergarten teacher, and assistant teacher). Both first-grade and second-grade teachers certificates are offered, each requiring different levels of preparation.

### Recent Developments in the Preparation of Teachers

Among recent developments in the preparation of teachers in Korea is the increased importance being given to teaching practice in teacher education. Legally one month of student teaching in one setting is required, but this is now thought to be inadequate. Most college students are currently being provided with longer and more diverse field experiences. For example, in four-year colleges, one day a week of observation is being required in the term before student teaching. Other classes require additional field work and observation.

With the increased importance being placed on professionalism in early childhood education, there is a trend toward improving the quality of teacher education. The availability of in-service teacher education has also increased. Continuing education institutes have been established in four-year colleges, which provide one-year early childhood education courses for parents as well as for kindergarten directors and teachers.

While many kindergarten teachers were prepared in two-year junior colleges, currently many early childhood educators are concluding that four-year colleges provide better preparation. As a result, there is a movement toward amending the Education Laws and increasing the qualifications for kindergarten teachers. With the rise in the number of child care centers, the requirements and teacher training for child center teachers are also being debated. There is also a feeling that early childhood education courses should prepare teachers for N–3 or K–3. At present early childhood teachers can teach only in kindergartens.

### Pressing Problems in the Preparation of Teachers

The most pressing problems that need to be addressed include the need for changes in the qualifications or standards of early childhood personnel, including teachers and directors. According to the current

Education Law, graduates of four-year colleges and universities and of two-year junior colleges are equally qualified as kindergarten teachers. In addition, teachers who hold an elementary school license are automatically considered to be qualified as kindergarten teachers.

The qualifications for kindergarten directors are also being seen as inadequate. The rule states that a "person with high education and moral standards" can become a director. Therefore, persons without any early childhood education background or experience can become kindergarten directors. In fact, in 1986, only 729 of the 1,111 public and private kindergarten directors (65.6%) were qualified in early childhood education.

The present early childhood teacher education program does not consider the need for articulation between kindergarten and lower grades of elementary school. The curriculum for early childhood teachers and that for elementary school teachers are completely separate, and there is a lack of communication between early childhood teachers and elementary school teachers. The establishment of either K–3 or N–3 teacher preparation programs, it is felt, could alleviate these problems.

Opportunities for field experiences that allow students to apply the theories they learn in courses to actual practical situations before student teaching are scarce. Such opportunities are slowly being increased in teacher education programs; however, theory and practice are still not integrated. Four weeks of student teaching is not sufficient in a teacher preparation program. It represents only 1.4 percent of the four-year program and 2.5 percent of the two-year program. In addition, in some colleges and junior colleges, many of the professors teaching in the early childhood teacher education program do not have a background in early childhood education.

Internship programs for beginning teachers are also being suggested. Presently, it is common for newly employed and prepared teachers to immediately be given total responsibility for a class. There are no career ladders by which assistant teachers could become regular early childhood teachers after acquiring the necessary experience. Rather, assistant teachers are unqualified persons who are responsible for simple clerical work. An internship system could help new teachers acquire experience as assistant teachers and then assume responsibility for their own class.

There is currently an oversupply of qualified kindergarten teachers, and the supply is increasing. The number of students who graduate from early childhood education programs in colleges and junior colleges far exceeds the number of positions available. Qualified persons are not being hired as teachers, and salaries continue to remain low for kindergarten teachers. Fifty-four percent of the public kindergarten teachers are employed as full-time lecturers. Their salaries are lower than those of teachers, and they do not receive the same benefits as teachers. While compensation for public kindergarten teachers is generally based on a fixed standard, owners of private kindergartens determine the salary that their teachers receive, and it is generally lower than salaries in the public schools. Nevertheless the work of the early childhood teacher is heavy.

It is difficult to prepare well-qualified teachers within a two-year junior college program, yet most kindergarten teachers, as noted above, are prepared in these programs. Some experts believe that the junior college courses should be extended to four years or students should be obligated to transfer to four-year colleges.

Increasingly, there is a belief that early childhood education needs to be acknowledged as a profession. Most people regard kindergarten teachers as inferior to teachers at higher levels of education. The impression that early childhood education requires only talent in singing or dancing must be corrected. In addition, there is a need for research into teacher education. Recently, the Korean government has paid some attention to research in early childhood education, but more research needs to be done in the area of teacher preparation as well as in the area of child development, curriculum, and methodology.

## PEOPLE'S REPUBLIC OF CHINA

Kindergartens in China[2] are full-day programs that operate six days a week and serve young children from ages three to six. Nursery schools, on the other hand, serve children under age three. Kindergartens are considered educational institutions; nurseries, however, are not. Kindergartens may be sponsored by the local school authorities, by factories and other work units, or by neighborhoods and communities. Although there is local autonomy in relation to education, the State Education Commission suggests a kindergarten curriculum for the entire nation.

### Kindergarten Teacher Education

Normal schools, parallel to academic secondary or middle schools, prepare teachers for kindergartens and primary schools. Normal universities train secondary school and normal school teachers. Students in these universities are graduates of academic middle schools and, although they may become kindergarten teacher educators, do not have any kindergarten preparation or teaching experiences themselves.

While most kindergarten teachers are trained in kindergarten normal schools, some are prepared in primary normal schools or the kindergarten training classes in vocational middle schools. The normal school program combines general high school education and teacher training. The State Education Commission establishes the program, including the subjects to be taught and the number of hours devoted to each subject, though it is possible to diverge from the program. There are no elective subjects offered. In 1986, the number of hours in the general curriculum was reduced; however, no parallel increase was made in other components of the curriculum.

The kindergarten normal school program consists of general education, pedagogy, teaching practice, and the arts. Usually the content in general education is "professionalized" so that the science course includes health and hygiene in the kindergarten setting and the language course becomes a language arts course.

Pedagogy consists of courses in child psychology, preschool education, and methods of teaching language, arithmetic, science, music, dance, and hygiene. These are taught through lectures, with nationally published textbooks as the main resource. The arts, an essential component of the kindergarten normal school program, include painting, singing, dancing, and playing a musical instrument (for example, piano, pump organ, or accordion). Students are usually trained in adult performance skills rather than in skills for working with young children.

Teaching practice consists of observing children in schools, performing in simulated teaching situations, and student teaching. Student teaching occurs in the last four weeks of the program. Students observe "model" teachers demonstrate lessons, perform in simulations, prepare kindergarten lessons (complete with teaching aids), and teach their fellow students, who act the part of children.

## Problems in the Preparation of Kindergarten Teachers

There are a number of problems related to the preparation of kindergarten teachers in China. Some of the problems stem from the lack of resources in a developing country with a large population. Educational policies established during the Cultural Revolution also contributed to problems. The most pressing problems are discussed below.

*The Lack of Training Resources.* There has been a rapid expansion of kindergarten education in China since 1949, but kindergarten teacher training has not kept up. As a result most kindergarten teachers are not well prepared. Recently, there has been an increase in the number of kindergarten normal schools as well as kindergarten training classes in vocational schools. In-service training is also provided to upgrade the training of existing teachers. Normal university students go to the provinces and offer training courses during their school vacations. Remote teacher training, using television and videotapes, is being developed.

*Recruitment of Kindergarten Teachers.* More applicants are needed for the kindergarten normal schools. Trained kindergarten teachers are able to work near home, a distinct advantage, but they earn low salaries and do not have access to a university education, including normal universities. Thus the field is not considered very attractive for students seeking a higher education and improved status.

In addition, admission to kindergarten normal school is almost tantamount to graduation. Students' achievement is assessed, but students are not failed or dismissed. All graduates become kindergarten teachers regardless of their competence.

## Changing Practices in Early Childhood Teacher Education

Changes were taking place in the preparation of kindergarten teachers at the time of a 1986 survey. These included changes in the selection and recruitment of students and in the method of teaching, including seeking ways of augmenting lectures.

Several normal schools were becoming more flexible, giving students stipends according to the quality of their work, and offering bonuses to teachers of good students. Schools were creating alternative ways for students to meet requirements and were also retaining poor students.

Many of the instructors in Chinese normal schools do not have experience in teaching young children. General education and performance instructors have been trained as specialists in their own field. Pedagogy teachers who teach in normal schools have graduated from academic middle schools. Their contact with young children consists of a four-week student teaching experience in their senior year at the normal school. Even though they know about education from textbooks, they do not have the practical knowledge that is acquired from teaching children in the classroom.

## AUSTRALIA

In Australia,[3] early childhood education refers to programs for children under eight years of age. These programs may be in public schools or they may be run by other authorities. In most of Australia, compulsory school attendance begins at age 6, although in Queensland and South Australia primary education begins at age 5. Educational institutions or classes prior to grade 1 may be called preschools, kindergartens, or reception classes; these terms mean different things in different states.

### Early Childhood Teacher Education Programs

Australian teacher training programs for early childhood and primary school teachers tend to be three-year diploma of teaching programs. It is possible to add a fourth year—usually after at least one year of teaching—to obtain a bachelors degree. In some states, the fourth year can be undertaken through full-time study immediately following the completion of the diploma course. The diploma of teaching–early childhood programs are designed for teachers of children from birth to eight years, birth to five years, or three to eight years.

Individuals with a bachelors degree in a field other than education may take a one-year, full-time graduate diploma course. These graduate diploma courses in early childhood education were developed in the 1980s at many colleges of advanced education (CAEs) or universities. Two-year associate diploma programs prepare practitioners for work in child care. These diplomas are not accepted as the equivalent of a diploma of teaching.

Diplomas of teaching are typically offered within a CAE, though they may be offered also by a university (for example, in Western Australia and in Tasmania). Presently, early childhood teacher education courses are being transferred from the CAEs to universities throughout Australia as part of a major restructuring of higher education. Both colleges and universities offer the opportunity to upgrade from a diploma to a degree, though there are restricted numbers of places available in universities for these programs. Teachers holding primary or secondary school teaching qualifications can extend their qualifications to include teaching of children under five years of age. Technical and Further Education Colleges (TAFE's) offer short courses for teacher assistants as well as two-year associate diploma courses for child care teachers. Colleges of advanced education and some universities also offer two-year associate diplomas.

An early childhood teacher is expected to have undertaken a substantial amount of study in child development and in the use of observational skills designed for providing a curriculum that responds to children and family needs.

## Program Content

The content of early childhood teacher training programs varies by institution. All early childhood education courses have to be reviewed by college or university faculty representing a range of specializations. Employers of teachers also influence program content by their representation on course advisory committees or course assessment bodies. They may also give preference to hiring graduates of programs with particular content.

Programs include general education, professional studies, and field experiences and practice. The proportions of the program dedicated to each component vary by institution. When early childhood education is part of a primary program, child development and early childhood studies may constitute as little as 8 percent of the program. In programs that are specifically tailored to early childhood education, child development and family studies are commonly the major area of study. Up to 13 percent of the program may be in the area of child development, with curriculum and teaching accounting for another 7 percent.

## Field Experiences and Teaching Practices

Students in early childhood education programs usually spend between 70 and 100 days in supervised practice teaching placements. They also spend time observing in other educational and community settings used by families. Such field experiences allow students to learn about the community settings used by young children and the skills for effective work in these settings. The need to increase opportunities for field work in such settings is currently under discussion.

## General Standards

Standards are set for teacher preparation in teacher training institutions through a system of program development, advisory, and assessment committees. The committees include external members representing employers, professional associations, and the community, as well as internal members representing staff involved in teaching the program. State-level accrediting bodies oversee and approve programs for colleges of advanced education but not for universities. A national register of accredited programs is maintained by the Australian Council of Tertiary Awards. Employers exercise a right of veto concerning whether they will employ a program's graduates.

## Recent Developments in the Preparation of Teachers

There have recently been a series of changes in where early childhood teachers will be prepared. Until the early 1970s, most early childhood education teachers were prepared in kindergarten teachers colleges in the capital cities of the various states. These colleges were gradually amalgamated into larger colleges of advanced education as a result of federal policies. In the late 1980s federal government policies were redesigned to create even larger institutions—reducing the number of colleges and universities from 64 to fewer than 40.

As a result of the incorporation of early childhood teacher preparation into multipurpose colleges and universities, there has been a growth in the number of programs preparing early childhood teachers. There are courses now available at different levels—associate diploma, diploma, and bachelors degree—with a major in early childhood education. A few institutions offer masters level courses as well. This is a marked change from the early 1970s, when the three-year diploma from a kindergarten teachers college was the only recognized qualification in the field.

## Pressing Problems in the Preparation of Teachers

Among the problems that need to be addressed include the increased diversification in the settings where early childhood students practice. Programs must be designed to help students develop more varied skills associated with planning and implementing a curriculum for a specific group of children and their families.

## ISRAEL

In Israel[4] early childhood education is defined as the education of children in kindergartens (ages 3 to 6 years) and child care centers (ages 3 months to 3 years).

### Teacher Training Program

Early childhood teacher preparation programs can be either three or four years in length, depending on whether a bachelors of science degree is obtained. There are also one- and two-year training programs for child caregivers. The teacher preparation programs are offered by colleges and/or universities, while the child caregiver programs are offered by technical schools or colleges. While a university education is required of primary or secondary teachers, it is not required of early childhood teachers.

### Program Content

The content of the teacher preparation program includes a core of academic studies plus weekly field experiences from the first year, including specific observation assignments. Teaching practice is also required every year. The field experiences and teaching practice generally occur in supervised kindergartens with good model teachers.

There are national professional standards for the teacher preparation program in addition to specific requirements set by individual colleges.

### Recent Developments in the Preparation of Teachers

The most interesting developments in the preparation of teachers in Israel include the change from preparing teachers for kindergarten teaching only to preparing teachers to work with children three to eight years old. Currently, early childhood teachers are also being prepared to work with children from birth to six or eight years of age. There is currently a great demand for early childhood teachers, and in-service training courses are being expanded. This has led to the development and use of regional pedagogic centers as ongoing training and resource centers.

## Pressing Problems in the Preparation of Teachers

The most pressing problems in early childhood teacher preparation include the need to upgrade the qualifications of teachers of young children, especially those in day care centers. These centers must ensure the children's needs for individual care and attention, while meeting working parents' expectations for a longer school day.

There is also a need to update teachers on current research and developments, especially in relation to programs for developing cognitive skills in infants and toddlers, cultural enrichment programs (art, music, literature), science and technology programs (computers), and programs for enhancing parent–teacher cooperation.

## CONCLUSION

There are a number of similarities among these countries and with the United States in regard to the preparation of early childhood teachers. As in the United States, all of these countries, with the exception of China, differentiate among preparing kindergarten teachers, child care workers, and elementary school teachers. In China, the distinction is related only to age, since the kindergarten also functions as a child care center; in the other countries, the distinction is related to the institutions.

China is also different from the rest of the countries in terms of the level at which kindergarten teachers are prepared. There, kindergarten (and primary) teachers are prepared at the secondary school level, while in the other countries studied, these teachers are prepared at the post-secondary school level. Thus, a prospective teacher in China enters a teacher preparatory program after completion of middle school, the equivalent of an American junior high school. There is a possibility for students in a small number of kindergarten teacher education programs to continue their education through a two-year normal college. China also differs from the other countries in allowing individuals without teaching experience to staff teacher education programs. This creates a problem by limiting what is taught in teacher preparation classes to abstract, textbook-oriented material.

In the United States, certified teachers in early childhood education must complete at least a four-year bachelors degree program. This is not the case in the countries presented in this chapter. Kindergarten teachers in Korea may complete either a two-year or a four-year, post-secondary teacher preparation program; the majority of teachers are graduates of two-year programs. In Australia and Israel, the alternatives are three-year or four-year, post-secondary programs. However, there is clearly a movement in the direction of requiring four-year teacher education programs in these countries. Problems of the selection and recruitment of students to become early childhood teachers are shared by all the countries presented here. Concerns about the content of the teacher education program are also shared. This is especially the case in regard to the need for increased field experiences and teaching practice, which are very limited in both Australia and Korea. In Korea, the limitations on teaching practice are mostly a matter of tradition. In Australia, however, the limitations on practice reflect financial constraints, since cooperating personnel are paid for working with teacher trainees. Thus, increasing the amount of time devoted to teaching practice significantly increases the cost of teacher preparation programs there. It should be noted that the programs in the other countries are becoming more like those in the United States.

At present, no country other than the United States is moving in the direction of requiring post-bachelors degree education as part of the preparation of early childhood teachers. The call for the other reforms in teacher education, such as those coming from the Holmes Group and the Carnegie Forum (see Chapter 10), in the United States also is not being heard in these countries.

The quality of an early childhood program is highly dependent on the quality of the teachers who staff the program. Teacher education programs, to a great extent, determine the quality of the teachers. As countries, including the United States, work to improve their teacher education programs, we should see improvements in the programs that serve young children. The relationship is indirect, however. There is not a direct correlation between outcomes in teacher education programs and outcomes in children's programs.

This move to improve early childhood education and the preparation of its practitioners is an international phenomenon. While improvements will not be consistent from country to country, the trend is consistent. It is heartening to see nations throughout the world working to improve programs to prepare teachers of young children, and to deal with the pressing problems and the various issues that exist in early childhood education and the preparation of early childhood teachers.

## NOTES

*Acknowledgment:* We would like to thank Ms. Gail Halliwell, Senior Lecturer, School of Early Childhood Studies, Brisbane College of Advanced Education, Brisbane, Queensland, Australia; Dr. Ki-sook Lee, Professor of Early Childhood Education, Department of Education, Ehwa Women's University, Seoul, Korea; Dr. Rina Michalowitz, Head, Division of Preschool Education, Israel Ministry of Education and Culture, Tel Aviv, Israel; and Ms. Barbara Piscitelli, Lecturer, School of Early Childhood Studies, Brisbane College of Advanced Education, Brisbane, Queensland, Australia for their help in providing information that became the basis for much of this chapter.

1. This section is based upon material provided by Professor Ki-sook Lee, Ehwa Women's University, Seoul, Korea.
2. This section is based upon material in Spodek, B. (1989), Recent developments in the preparation of early childhood teachers in the People's Republic of China, *Childhood Education, 65,* 268–73, and Spodek, B. (1988), Reform of Chinese kindergartens: The preparation of kindergarten teachers, *Early Child Development and Care, 38,* 103–17.
3. This section is based upon material provided by Gail Halliwell, with the help of Barbara Piscitelli, School of Early Childhood Studies, Brisbane College of Advanced Education, Brisbane, Queensland, Australia.
4. This section is based upon material provided by Dr. Rina Michalowitz, Head, Division of Preschool Education, Israel Ministry of Education and Culture, Tel Aviv, Israel.

## REFERENCES

Spodek, B. (1988). Reform of Chinese kindergartens: The preparation of kindergarten teachers. *Early Child Development and Care, 38,* 103–17.

Spodek, B. (1989). Recent developments in the preparation of early childhood teachers in the People's Republic of China. *Childhood Education, 65,* 268–73.

CHAPTER 7

# Research Horizons and the Quest for a Knowledge Base in Early Childhood Teacher Education

Daniel J. Ott
Kenneth M. Zeichner
Gary Glen Price

In this chapter we examine the findings and methodologies of recent research on teaching and teacher education, and we discuss the implications of this work for the preparation of early childhood teachers. We claim that there are three major domains of research on teaching and teacher education that could potentially inform early childhood teacher education. These are (1) studies of teacher preparation programs, (2) studies on learning to teach, and (3) studies to identify the knowledge bases that teachers use. Each of these domains is described below, but the space devoted to them is by no means equal. The first (studies of teacher preparation programs) has until now dominated the research literature, and it is amply reviewed in other chapters of this volume. The second and third are gaining momentum; for that reason, both legitimately deserve attention in a chapter concerned with research horizons in teacher education. We concentrate on the third.

## Studies of Teacher Preparation

Studies of teacher preparation involve

1. the substance of preservice teacher education programs;
2. how they are organized;

3. how they are implemented; and
4. the relative effectiveness of different methods of preparation.

While this literature has provided us with some limited information about how teacher preparation programs are organized in different institutional settings (for example, American Association of Colleges of Teacher Education, 1987, 1988; Saracho & Spodek, Chapter 6, this volume), it has told us virtually nothing about the character, quality, or implementation of programs, or about the relative effectiveness of different program patterns and structures (Zeichner, 1988). The consensus is that very little empirical research specifically on teacher preparation (and of a kind that could inform policy decisions and program development efforts) has been accumulated to date (Feiman-Nemser, 1990; Katz, 1984; Lanier, 1986).

## Studies on Learning to Teach

A second domain of research that can potentially inform the preparation of early childhood educators is the developing body of research on *learning to teach* (e.g., Carter, 1990; Feiman-Nemser, 1983; Zeichner & Gore, 1990). This research examines the total array of factors affecting the development of teachers. As such, it treats teacher preparation programs as merely one factor among an assortment of factors. The conception of teacher education is thus broadened to include the sundry processes by which teachers learn to teach—and the sundry contexts in which those processes go on. Research on learning to teach was heralded by Doyle (1985) as legitimately part of inquiry in teacher education. This broadened conception of research on teacher education has also been embraced by the Office of Educational Research and Improvement (OERI) of the U.S. Department of Education, which has decided in the next cycle of federally funded research and development centers to broaden the mission of the existing *teacher education* center to one that focuses on *learning to teach*.

Research on learning to teach aims to improve, first, our understanding of the ways in which teachers learn to teach and, second, our understanding of the individual and social factors that affect the various ways that teachers learn. Improved understanding of this kind may enable us to create conditions—in teacher preparation programs and in the workplace—that will support the development of particular kinds of teachers. This broad view of the processes involved in learning to teach may be especially appropriate for early childhood education, given the fact that the majority of teachers at this level have had no preservice teacher education (Katz, 1984).

## A Knowledge Base for Teachers

The third domain of research that can potentially contribute to the preparation of early childhood educators concerns the *knowledge base* needed by teachers. This emphasis on knowledge departs from the process-product era of teacher education research, in which processes (characteristics of teacher education programs) were correlated with products ("good outcomes" in program participants). "Good outcomes" are now presumed to depend on knowledge structures that teachers possess and deploy. It is not a question of *whether* knowledge structures are important; it is a question of *which* knowledge structures are important. Knowledge structures are presumed to be important because, in diverse contexts, cognitive science has amassed persuasive evidence that experts differ from novices primarily in the knowledge structures they possess and deploy.

As Kliebard (1973) documented, efforts to identify and legitimate a knowledge base essential for teachers have continued throughout the twentieth century; opinions about which sources of knowledge are most relevant to teaching have waxed and waned in popularity over the years. In discussions of what teachers need to know, early childhood education has consistently been distinguishable from other teaching fields because it has placed a greater emphasis on child psychology (both child development and child learning). The early childhood education community has historically emphasized studies of children (their learning and their development) as the source of the knowledge needed by teachers (for example, Kirkpatrick, 1923); as Silin (1987) has noted, it has displayed little attention to studies of teachers and teaching.

The elementary and secondary teacher education communities, on the other hand, have emphasized studies of teaching—studies of the characteristics of "good" teachers, studies to identify effective teaching practices, studies of teachers' cognitions, and studies of the differences between expert teachers' and novice teachers' cognitions (Berliner, 1986; Dunkin, 1988). Only recently has the elementary and secondary teacher education literature begun to emphasize studies of pupil learning and the learning of particular subjects as a foundation for teacher preparation (Shulman, 1986).

Some of the recent efforts to identify a knowledge base for teacher education are examined below. First, we consider the idea of constructing a knowledge base as a general approach to education. Second, we examine it as an approach specific to a particular kind of education: teacher education. Here we will examine the general strategy of identifying a knowledge base and its potential for improving teacher preparation. This discussion, while not unique to early childhood teacher education, is potentially applicable to it. Third, we examine several recent attempts to assert a knowledge base specifically for early childhood teaching.

Following a discussion of several recent attempts to assert a knowledge base for early childhood training and teaching in general, we discuss research that needs to be conducted to support efforts to improve early childhood teacher education. One of the major points that we make is the need for a body of teacher education research focused specifically on early childhood educators—on their preservice preparation and on sundry other processes by which they learn to teach. We question the reliance on research concerning the preparation of elementary and secondary teachers for guidance in preparing early childhood teachers.

## OVERVIEW AND CRITICISM OF KNOWLEDGE BASES IN GENERAL

The decision to approach teacher education in terms of an identified knowledge base clearly departs from the process-product era of teacher education research, as noted earlier. The zeitgeist is one that celebrates knowledge bases: Knowledge-base-ism is here. Cognitive science has succeeded in persuading many scholars—not just those concerned with education—to pay heed to the enabling influence of well-conceived, well-organized prior knowledge and the disabling influence of misconceived, badly organized prior knowledge. This represents two steps beyond the behavioristic analysis of skill training, such as the micro-teaching once advocated in teacher education (Callenbach & Gall, 1969). First, it is a step from behavior to cognition, thereby heeding such things as the thought processes of teachers (Clark & Peterson, 1986). Moreover, beyond that it is a step in specificity to one particular class of cognitive constructs: the structures by which knowledge is organized and represented. In his history of the cognitive revolution, Gardner (1985) claimed that "the major accomplishment of cognitive science has been the clear demonstration of the validity of positing a level of mental representation: a set of constructs that can be invoked for the explanation of cognitive phenomena" (pp. 383–84).

## Changes in Students' Representations

A corollary of the emphasis on knowledge structures is that a central purpose of educators—including teacher educators—should be to induce changes in students' mental representations. Greeno (1976, 1987) has described this as a "knowledge structure program," in which cognitive models have been treated as instructional objectives. As Hatano and Inagaki (1987) have claimed, "one of the major goals of education is the acquisition of a well-organized body of knowledge" (p. 27).

This appreciation for the importance of mental representations is a departure from the recent past, which treated lack of knowledge as a problem but underestimated the inertial impediment created by misconceptions. Previously held conceptions can actively interfere with new understanding, as exemplified by the refractoriness of *naive concepts* in science education (Hewson & Posner, 1984; Posner, Strike, Hewson, & Gertzog, 1984). As Romberg and Tufte (1987) put it, "What we learn, and in fact what we are capable of learning, depends on the mental models each of us has developed" (p. 77). This new truism about the inertia of prior knowledge gives new insight to John Locke's (1699/1964) reference to the tutor's task as being one of laying foundations.

## The Expert as a Point of Reference

Efforts to define knowledge bases presuppose not only that mental representations are important and that teacher educators should seek to provoke changes in them, but also that teacher educators know which representations to target. Those representations that typify novices are targeted as the ones that should be changed, and representations that typify experts are targeted as goals. Novices' representations are to be replaced with experts' representations; experts are thus treated as a normative source. This could be called a *think-as-experts-think curriculum*.

# THE KNOWLEDGE BASE FOR TEACHING AND TEACHER EDUCATION IN GENERAL

All teacher education is a form of advocacy. Each program is related to the educational ideology held by a particular teacher educator or teacher preparation institution, even though this relationship may not be made explicit. There is no such thing as a value-free teacher education, just as there is no such thing as a value-free education for children (Katz, 1974; Spodek, 1988).

Throughout the twentieth century, efforts have been made to assert a view, often based on research, of the knowledge, skills, and dispositions needed by teachers. Liston and Zeichner (1990) have identified four distinct traditions of reform that have been associated with these efforts to improve teacher education. The *academic tradition* has emphasized the importance of teachers' general education and their education in particular subjects. The *social efficiency tradition* has stressed efforts to construct a teacher education curriculum based on studies of the thoughts and actions of effective teachers. The *developmentalist tradition*, on the other hand, has its roots in studies of children (their learning and development) and has emphasized the need for teachers to be well informed about the theoretical and practical elements of child development. Finally, the *social reconstructionist tradition* has viewed teaching and teacher education as critical elements in the movement toward a more just society and has emphasized teachers' roles as agents for social reform.

Liston and Zeichner (1990) argue that all attempts to propose a knowledge base for teaching and teacher education and to improve teacher preparation programs in the United States during this century have reflected particular patterns of resonance with these various reform traditions. Sometimes the biases and prejudices within a particular vision of the knowledge base are clearly discernable — as they were in the case of the competency-based teacher education reform movement of the 1960s and 1970s. That movement reflected an almost exclusive focus on the development of specific behavioral patterns suggested by studies of teacher effectiveness (Gage & Winne, 1975). At other times, however, recommendations from adherents of various traditions are lumped together without a clearly articulated vision of the priorities for teaching and teacher education among the assumptions and commitments emanating from the various traditions. Such is the case in *Knowledge Base for the Beginning Teacher* (Reynolds, 1989), which was sponsored by the American Association of Colleges for Teacher Education (AACTE).

Ideological insularity continues to be one of the most serious impediments to the improvement of teacher education in the United States (see Spodek, 1988; Zeichner, 1983). The common pattern has been and continues to be for various subcommunities of teacher educators to operate with relative independence of one another. There continues to be very little cross-fertilization of ideas across traditions of practice, as members of the various subcommunities typically read, discuss, and debate work only within a particular tradition. However, this insularity among teacher educators will not be remedied by the indiscriminate lumping together of ideas (about what teachers need to know and to be able to do) from a wide variety of intellectual bases and traditions of practice. Ideological evenhandedness in teacher education does justice to no tradition. Any viable vision of teacher education needs to be coherent, and this requirement of coherence is incompatible with an unrefereed concatenation of competing ideologies.

To be practical, any plan for teacher education must set priorities among issues — if not also among competing traditions. What is needed for the preparation of early childhood teachers as well as for teachers generally is the specification of a knowledge base that flows from and is articulated with a reasoned educational and social philosophy that take clear positions with regard to the kinds of teachers, schools, and society we should be working toward. Existing efforts to specify a knowledge base for teaching and teacher education within the elementary and secondary teacher education community have not done this very well.

Even if we could come to the point of identifying knowledge bases for teaching and teacher education — knowledge bases that were closely articulated with a clearly expressed educational and social philosophy and mutually enriched by debate and discussion across traditions — we imagine there would still remain some serious limitations to the strategy as a means of improving teacher education. One of the most serious limitations of the knowledge base path of reform is that it does not address the ways in which the knowledge, skills, and dispositions that teachers need can best be developed through deliberate teacher education interventions. This insufficiency was noted by Greeno (1978), who stated that *models of knowledge*, which detail the knowledge that underlies performance, do not suffice as *models of learning*, because they do not detail the transitions through which novices pass en route to expertise.

There have been expert/novice studies that recognize that models of experts do not necessarily suggest processes of transition from novice to expert (Berliner, 1986; Carter, 1990). Prior to the emergence of such studies, most expressions of a knowledge base for teaching and teacher education relied exclusively on models of experts for determining the best ways to prepare novices. Recently the focus has shifted (correctly, in our view) to identifying the knowledge, skills, and dispositions needed by beginning teachers. Unless expressions of the knowledge base are supported, however, by a body of research that can identify how particular opportunities for teacher learning created in teacher preparation programs are related to the development of specific teacher capabilities, we as teacher educators are left with a huge gap.

There are various possibilities for moving from the expression of a knowledge base to the development of particular capabilities among teachers. One could argue that the substance of a knowledge base like that concatenated in the Reynolds (1989) volume ought to form the *content* of teacher education programs. Historically, knowledge base producers have typically expected official endorsement. But, in actuality, formalized knowledge bases have heretofore had little impact on teacher education programs.

One could alternatively argue that the substance of a knowledge base ought to serve as a guide for the ways in which teacher education programs are organized and delivered. This has seldom happened. If, for example, we are told that students actively construct knowledge and that their preconceptions often play an important role in blocking growth from novice to expert, then it seems we should make use of this knowledge in the way in which we conduct our teacher education programs.

Whatever position or positions one chooses to support regarding the links between the expression of a knowledge base for teaching and the conduct of teacher education, it is clear that the expression of the knowledge base needs to be supplemented by explicit arguments about its uses to educate teachers.

Another likely limitation of the strategy of identifying a knowledge base for teaching as a means of improving teacher education is related to the generalizability of the knowledge base. Do its merits generalize across different levels of schooling, different subject areas, and different types of work environments?

One of the earliest attempts within the elementary and secondary teacher education community to identify a knowledge base was *The Commonwealth Teacher Training Study* (Charters & Waples, 1929). It specified different capabilities for teachers at different levels of schooling, including early childhood education. Most subsequent attempts to articulate a knowledge base for teaching and teacher education, including the recent AACTE document (Reynolds, 1989), have treated their proposals as relevant for all teachers. This view has led to some curious claims that the knowledge, skills, and dispositions needed by kindergarten teachers are the same as those needed by high school physics teachers.

Although it may be true up to a certain point that there is a common knowledge base for teachers regardless of the level of schooling at which they work, it seems to us that it is easy to take this argument too far. The preparation of early childhood teachers needs to be informed, at least in part, by efforts to identify what early childhood educators in particular need to know and be able to do in different types of early childhood work environments. Indeed, expert/novice differences found to date are not in domain-general knowledge, but in knowledge specific to the target domain. Experts in one domain are often average or even below average in other domains. As Glaser (1986) put it, "Expertise seems to be very specific. Expertise in one domain is no guarantee of expertise in other areas" (p. 922). In light of that, it would seem prudent to include in a knowledge base for early childhood educators things that are especially germane to this field. We will now examine a few recent efforts within the early childhood education community to do just this.

## THE KNOWLEDGE BASE FOR EARLY CHILDHOOD EDUCATORS

Interest in what may be formally termed the knowledge base for early childhood educators (KBECE) has recently received increased professional attention (Spodek, Saracho, & Peters, 1988). To advance the professional status of early childhood educators, it has been recommended that the field "identify the body of knowledge, specify the reliable principals, and develop a consensus as to the best available practices that will serve as a basis for professional practice in early childhood education" (Katz, 1987, p. 11). Various expressions of what should be included in the KBECE, as enunciated by members and organizations in the early childhood community, will be examined here.

The practice of early childhood educators has always been informed by a broadly conceived knowledge base. Often informal and implicit, this knowledge base has historically been linked to various degrees of folk wisdom and science; as Kamii (1985) states, "common sense, trial and error, and opinions called philosophies." The current challenge, however, is to formally identify the knowledge base that will establish explicit standards by which professional early childhood educators will be judged. Such a challenge presents difficulties that are unique to the field of early childhood education (Katz, 1984; Spodek & Davis, 1982). Elkind (1986, 1987, 1988a, 1988b) has frequently argued that educational programs devised for school-age children have been inappropriately applied to the education of young children. His polemical statements are often cited by representatives of the early childhood community and others who seek to establish the need for a KBECE.

The diversity of roles among early childhood educators makes it difficult to identify a singular knowledge base for the field. The title of "early childhood educator" itself is not clearly understood. The Hostetler and Klugman (1982) survey of National Association for the Education of Young Children (NAEYC) members reveals 19 separate job titles related to "early childhood educator," each of which can claim individual historical movements (primary school, kindergarten, preschool, preschool/handicapped, nursery school, infant, day care, and so on). Seefeldt's (1988) examination of early childhood teacher certification guidelines also suggests that the multidisciplinary nature of the field, the diversity of early childhood settings, and the broad age range of early childhood (birth through age 8) render the establishment of a KBECE problematic. Although there has been increased interest in describing exactly what it is that teachers of young children do when they teach, there is no consensus in the field as to what "effective teaching" is (Ade, 1982; Caldwell, 1983; Feeny & Chun, 1985; Kamii, 1985; Katz, 1984; Medlin, 1984; Nall, 1982; Silin, 1985).

These difficulties notwithstanding, it is acknowledged that only when early childhood educators can clearly articulate the basis for their beliefs and practices will they be able to increase public understanding and support (Lay-Dopyera & Dopyera, 1987). It can be argued that any "state of the art" knowledge base directed toward elementary or secondary teachers may not be appropriate for early childhood educators (Jorde, 1986; Silin, 1985; Spodek & Davis, 1982; Takanishi, 1981). The KBECE, which will serve as a basis for professional practice in early childhood education, must clearly reflect the unique and dynamic nature of the early childhood educator's work. It needs to be sensitive to the different contexts in which early childhood educators work.

*What knowledge should be included in a KBECE?* Characteristic of the field in general, answers to this question are notable by their great diversity. Understanding the theoretical foundations of early childhood education is thought to be a crucial component of the KBECE, yet early childhood teacher educators have traditionally felt defensive about their inclusion. Katz (1987) suggests that teacher preparation programs, which have typically emphasized practical "survival" skills, should be designed to include more study of theory, research, history, and philosophy. Almy (1984) in the foreword to Weber's *Ideas Influencing Early Childhood Education*, provides the rationale for theoretical and historical study in early childhood teacher education programs: " . . . a perspective on the past provides a keener awareness of the multiple possibilities for the instruction and guidance of children and a firmer sense of the reasons for emphasizing some possibilities and ignoring others"

(p. x). She further emphasizes that a theoretical understanding of early childhood education provides for a more informed evaluation of current trends. Although the degree of understanding of theoretical foundations that is necessary to practice in the field has not been established, it is assumed that a greater familiarity results in a greater likelihood of effectiveness (Ade, 1982).

By all accounts, a clear understanding of the early childhood research base should be included in the KBECE. Many organizational endorsements of a research-based KBECE have appeared as officially sanctioned position papers, and these are currently being digested by the early childhood community. Most visible among these is NAEYC's *Early Childhood Teacher Education Guidelines for Four- and Five-Year Programs* (1982) and *Developmentally Appropriate Practice in Early Childhood Programs Serving Children from Birth Through Age 8* (Bredekamp, 1987). Asserting that the quality of early childhood programs is influenced by the degree to which practices are informed by knowledge of child development research, the largest professional organization of early childhood educators has issued what it claims to be a "consensus of experts" about how young children learn, how best to teach them, and how best to prepare early childhood educators. NAEYC's influential statements describe specific, developmentally appropriate practices, and they provide the supporting child development research base. By also identifying inappropriate practices, these position papers in effect suggest: "Do this, but also protect children from that" (Bredekamp & Shepard, 1989, p. 14). Spodek (1989) argues that developmental appropriateness alone should not guide early childhood educators' practice or, for that matter, the KBECE. He suggests that moral and ethical considerations inform practitioners as well.

Other position papers advanced by smaller yet significant early childhood organizations clearly articulate their desire to influence the KBECE. The National Black Child Development Institute (NBCDI), for example, addresses the vital importance of maintaining a racially and ethnically representative staff that is culturally sensitive to the developmental needs of preschool-age children. Its publication, *SAFEGUARDS: Guidelines for Establishing Programs for Four-Year-Olds in the Public Schools* (NBCDI, 1987), suggests that the KBECE should include emphasis on parent education and involvement. Similar position statements published by the International Reading Association (1985), the Association for Childhood Education International (Moyer, Egertson, & Isenberg, 1987), the Minnesota Early Childhood Teacher Educators, Kindergarten Task Force (1986), and the Southern Association on Children Under Six (1984, 1985, 1986a, 1986b) represent a small portion of the early childhood organizations that are formally attempting to shape the nature of early childhood programs and the KBECE. Although these position papers represent strongly and honorably held values and beliefs about what is good for children, they are not designed to persuade a skeptic. As Spodek (1986) put it, "Such value statements are important, but they are not adequate bases for developing new program proposals or for testing the validity of proposed programs" (p. ix). A KBECE that we "know to be true" and that "we know to be good for children" is called for.

The knowledge bases found in publications like those by Seefeldt (1987) and Katz (1986) address research and theory in the curriculum content area. As Seefeldt (1987, p. vii) stated in her Preface, the research and theory presented in her edited volume provide "a rich resource for educators to draw on as they determine directions for the curriculum." It appears that works such as these are a helpful start to a KBECE. Silin (1986), however, believes that the KBECE needs to reflect more than the psychological perspective that has been the cornerstone of early childhood education. Understanding that the field is "defined as much by what it attends to as by what it resists recognizing," Silin (1987, p. 616), whose views resonate with the social reconstructionist tradition mentioned early in this chapter, suggests that the KBECE expand to include a sociopolitical analysis of early childhood education.

Silin (1985) further suggests that a relevant knowledge base needs to be grounded in the work of early childhood educators. Teachers need to be major players in the formation of the KBECE so as to understand the development as well as the implementation of curricula. The distance between research (researcher) and practice (teacher) is also a concern of Takanishi (1981). She warns that, so long as the research community neglects teachers' view of their work, the distance between researchers and early childhood educators will remain. Teachers' research into their own classroom practices such as is now being carried out in the Teacher Research Network (Chattin-McNichols & Loeffler, 1989) has an important role to play in the building of a knowledge base for early childhood teacher education.

Further democratization of the process of formulating a knowledge base for early childhood teacher education along these lines does not necessarily undermine efforts to professionalize the role of early childhood educator (Spodek, Saracho, & Peters, 1988). Efforts to restrict the contributions to this knowledge base to university-conducted research deny the value of the knowledge that is embedded in teachers' actions (Schön, 1983). Such restrictions also limit teachers' access to some forms of knowledge and deliberation that are appropriate for understanding educational practice (Liston & Zeichner, 1987). As Silin (1985) has demonstrated, these restrictions prevent teachers from achieving real power.

Noncurricular areas might also warrant inclusion in the KBECE. Resonating with the National Black Child Development Institute, proposals by Almy (1985) and Caldwell (1983) point to the need for more advocacy training. They suggest that those who work with young children develop skills in forming coalitions with parents, legislators, and other groups. In this way they could proactively move the salient issues of children and early childhood educators forward. Lombardi (1986) notes that such skills should be formally initiated and practiced during preservice training in order to build the future early childhood educator's confidence and motivation to advocate.

The importance of collegiality in early childhood settings has also surfaced as an issue among teachers of young children (Benham, Miller, & Kontos, 1988; Chattin-McNichols & Loeffler, 1989; Jorde-Bloom, 1988a, 1988b; Klass & Nall, 1989). Martin (1985), responding to mounting tensions in her kindergarten, expresses the importance of professional validation: "I think it might not be possible for me to remain in such a stressful job if I did not have the support of a group of colleagues with whom I meet regularly to reflect on children and teaching" (p. 320).

The first-year kindergarten teacher in the Clandinin (1989) case study found that the professional support he was offered was limited to "skills." His voice eloquently argues the importance of both professional and personal collegial support.

> You need somebody to talk to. When you desperately need it then it's not there. . . . What do you do in the week, like last week you can't find, when you say to Carrie (student) at the end of the week, I think I need a hug and she comes and gives you a hug and you realize that you really did need that hug. . . . Where do you find it when you really need it? (pp. 139-40)

## NEEDED RESEARCH IN EARLY CHILDHOOD TEACHER EDUCATION

Early childhood educators must base their practices on more than folklore. Moreover, if a widely acceptable KBECE is formally adopted by the early childhood community, we should seriously consider how it can be utilized most appropriately. How will it inform the significant number of early childhood educators who practice without the benefit of preservice teacher preparation programs? Can it or should it be used to evaluate or certify early childhood educators and their programs? If so, how? Inasmuch as it represents a step toward "professionalism," is it thereby destined to become distinctly esoteric and exclusive? Or, following our child-centered traditions, would children benefit from a publicly accessible, less esoteric knowledge base?

One thing that we know very clearly from the extant research literature in teacher education is that formally organized preservice teacher education programs are only one among many influences on how teachers learn to teach (Feiman-Nemser, 1983; Zeichner & Gore, 1990). Other influences on teacher learning include the experiences that prospective teachers have prior to and apart from their participation in formal teacher preparation programs, and the character and quality of the workplaces in which they eventually teach. Despite this knowledge about the limited impact of preservice teacher education, we know very little about what goes on in different teacher preparation programs. We also know very little about how prospective teachers are affected by participation in different kinds of teacher preparation experiences (National Center for Research in Teacher Education [NCRTE], 1988b). If we think about ways in which research can support and guide efforts to improve the education of early childhood teachers, then one of our most urgent needs is for the development of a research literature, within the early childhood teacher education community, that focuses specifically on how early childhood teachers learn to teach and on the contribution of different varieties of formal teacher education experiences to particular kinds of teacher learning.

We have already expressed our reservations about relying on expressions of a knowledge base for teaching to guide program development and policy making. The expression of a knowledge base by itself does not address critical questions related to the delivery of the knowledge to prospective teachers. There is a variety of influences on teacher learning. Also, the dynamic quality of teacher education programs often results in a lived reality for programs that differs in significant ways from the formal program curriculum and intentions of teacher educators (Tabachnick, 1989). Research therefore needs to provide us with information about what prospective early childhood educators are taught, and what they learn under different conditions of teacher education. In-depth studies of the lived reality of teacher education programs and detailed case studies of the processes of learning to teach, as experienced by specific early childhood educators, are needed.

Examples of this kind of research, which is needed to inform early childhood teacher education, are Howey and Zimpher's (1989) case studies of six diverse teacher preparation programs in the midwest, and the National Center for Research on Teacher Education's case studies of teacher preparation and teacher learning (NCRTE, 1988a). One could argue that the early childhood teacher education community should make use of this research from the elementary and secondary literature. We concur with this view up to a certain point.

Early childhood teacher educators can indeed benefit from recent studies that illuminate such things as the mis-educative aspects of particular kinds of clinical experiences (for example, Feiman-Nemser & Buchmann, 1987); the character and quality of particular ways of organizing teacher education programs (NCRTE, 1988b); and the relative effectiveness of different strategies for altering prospective teachers' conceptions (for example, Zeichner, 1987). But this literature, although exemplary in many respects, fails to address the particular conditions of early childhood teaching. Consequently, characteristics of exemplary teacher preparation programs for early childhood teachers may not match those found for elementary and secondary teachers.

There are characteristics unique to the preparation of early childhood educators. Katz (1987), while acknowledging that the education of preprimary teachers shares some of the same problems as the education of elementary and secondary teachers, identifies some unique ones, such as (1) the great diversity in the employment settings served by early childhood teacher education programs (and the resultant ambiguity over the appropriate goals and content for programs serving such diverse needs), and (2) the low pay for members of the occupation (which is related to the large proportion of uncertified personnel and volunteers in preprimary educational settings).

If knowledge-base-ism is here to stay, the early childhood community has at its disposal a rich diversity of resources with which to build its knowledge base. A narrowly defined prescription of "what works" is in the best interest of neither children nor early childhood educators. We would argue that a knowledge base for early childhood education must reflect and accommodate the diversity that exists in the field.

## REFERENCES

Ade, W. (1982). Professionalism and its implications for the field of early childhood education. *Young Children*, 37(3), 25–32.

Almy, M. (1984). Foreword. In E. Weber (Ed.), *Ideas influencing early childhood education* (pp. ix–xi). New York: Teachers College Press.

Almy, M. (1985). New challenges for teacher education: Facing political and economic realities. *Young Children, 40*(6), 10–11.

American Association of Colleges of Teacher Education. (1987). *Teaching teachers: Facts and figures*. Washington, DC: AACTE.

American Association of Colleges for Teacher Education. (1988). *RATE II – Teaching teachers: Facts and figures*. Washington, DC: AACTE.

Benham, N., Miller, T., & Kontos, S. (1988). Pinpointing staff training needs in child care centers. *Young Children, 43*(4), 9–16.

Berliner, D. (1986). In pursuit of the expert pedagogue. *Educational Researcher, 15*(7), 5–13.

Bredekamp, S. (Ed.). (1987). *Developmentally appropriate practice in early childhood programs serving children from birth through age 8*. Washington, DC: National Association for the Education of Young Children.

Bredekamp, S., & Shepard, L. (1989). How best to protect children from inappropriate school expectations, practices, and policies. *Young Children, 44*(3), 14–24.

Caldwell, B. (1983). How can we educate the American public about the child care profession? *Young Children, 38*(3), 11–17.

Callenbach, W., & Gall, M. D. (1969). Micro-teaching versus conventional methods in training elementary intern teachers. *Review of Educational Research, 63*, 136–41.

Carter, K. (1990). Learning to teach. In W. R. Houston (Ed.), *Handbook of research on teacher education* (pp. 291–310). New York: Macmillan.

Charters, W. W., & Waples, D. (1929). *The Commonwealth teacher training study*. Chicago: University of Chicago Press.

Chattin-McNichols, J., & Loeffler, M. (1989). Teachers as researchers: The first cycle of the Teachers' Research Network. *Young Children, 44*(5), 20–27.

Clandinin, J. (1989). Developing rhythm in teaching: The narrative study of a beginning teacher's personal practical knowledge of classrooms. *Curriculum Inquiry, 19*(2), 121–42.

Clark, C. M., & Peterson, P. L. (1986). Teachers' thought processes. In M. C. Wittrock (Ed.), *Handbook of research on teaching* (3rd ed., pp. 255–96). New York: Macmillan.

Doyle, W. (1985). Learning to teach: An emerging direction in research on preservice teacher education. *Journal of Teacher Education, 36*(1), 31–32.

Dunkin, M. (1988). *Recent trends in research on teaching and teacher education*. Paper presented at the First Asia-Pacific Conference on Teacher Education, Bangkok, Thailand.

Elkind, D. (1986). Formal education and early childhood education: An essential difference. *Phi Delta Kappan, 67*(9), 631–36.

Elkind, D. (1987). Readiness for kindergarten. *Young Children, 42*(3), 2.

Elkind, D. (1988a). Educating the very young: A call for clear thinking. *NEA Today, 6*(6), 22–27.

Elkind, D. (1988b). The "miseducation" of young children. *Education Week, 7*(19), 15–16.

Feeny, S., & Chun, R. (1985). Effective teachers of young children. *Young Children, 41*(1), 47-52.

Feiman-Nemser, S. (1983). Learning to teach. In L. Shulman & G. Sykes (Eds.), *Handbook of teaching and policy* (pp. 150-170). New York: Longman.

Feiman-Nemser, S. (1990). Teacher preparation: Structural and conceptual alternatives. In W. R. Houston (Ed.), *Handbook of research on teacher education* (pp. 212-233). New York: Macmillan.

Feiman-Nemser, S., & Buchmann, M. (1987). When is student teaching teacher education? *Teaching and Teacher Education, 3,* 255-73.

Gage, N., & Winne, P. (1975). Performance-based teacher education. In K. Ryan (Ed.), *Teacher education* (pp. 146-172). Chicago: University of Chicago Press.

Gardner, H. (1985). *The mind's new science: A history of the cognitive revolution.* New York: Basic Books.

Glaser, R. (1986). On the nature of expertise. In F. Klix & Hagendorf (Eds.), *Human memory and cognitive capabilities* (pp. 73-96). New York: Elsevier.

Greeno, J. G. (1976). Cognitive objectives of instruction: Theory of knowledge for solving problems and answering questions. In D. Klahr (Ed.), *Cognition and instruction* (pp. 123-59). Hillsdale, NJ: Erlbaum.

Greeno, J. G. (1978). A study of problem solving. In R. Glaser (Ed.), *Advances in instructional psychology* (Vol. 1, pp. 13-75). Hillsdale, NJ: Erlbaum.

Greeno, J. G. (1987). Mathematical cognition: Accomplishments and challenges in research. In T. A. Romberg & D. M. Stewart (Eds.), *The monitoring of school mathematics: Background papers* (Vol. 2, *Implications from psychology: Outcomes of instruction*, pp. 3-26). Madison: Wisconsin Center for Education Research.

Hatano, G., & Inagaki, K. (1987). A theory of motivation for comprehension and its application to mathematics education. In T. A. Romberg & D. Stewart (Eds.), *The monitoring of school mathematics: Background papers* (Vol. 2, *Implications from psychology: Outcomes of instruction*, pp. 27-46). Madison: Wisconsin Center for Education Research.

Hewson, P. W., & Posner, G. J. (1984). The use of schema theory in the design of instructional materials: A physics example. *Instructional Science, 13,* 119-39.

Hostetler, L., & Klugman, E. (1982). Early childhood job titles: One step toward professional status. *Young Children, 37*(6), 13-22.

Howey, K., & Zimpher, N. (1989). *Profiles of preservice teacher education.* Albany: State University of New York Press.

International Reading Association. (1985). *Literacy development and pre-first grade.* Newark, DE: International Reading Association.

Jorde, P. (1986). Early childhood education: Issues and trends. *The Educational Forum, 50*(2), 171-81.

Jorde-Bloom, P. (1988a). *Professional orientation and structural components of*

*early childhood programs: A social-ecological perspective*. Paper presented at the Annual Meeting of the American Educational Research Association. New Orleans, April.
Jorde-Bloom, P. (1988b). Assess the climate of your center: Use the Early Childhood Work Environment Survey. *Day Care and Early Education, 15*(4), 9-11.
Kamii, C. (1985). Leading primary education toward excellence. *Young Children, 40*(5), 3-9.
Katz, L. (1974). Issues and problems in teacher education. In B. Spodek (Ed.), *Teacher education*. Washington, DC: National Association of Education for Young Children.
Katz, L. (1984). The education of preprimary teachers. In L. Katz (Ed.), *Current topics in early childhood education* (Vol. 5, pp. 209-28). Norwood, NJ.: Ablex.
Katz, L. (1986). *Implications of recent research for the preschool and kindergarten curriculum*. ERIC Document Reproduction Service ED 274 463.
Katz, L. (1987). The nature of professions: Where is early childhood education? In L. Katz & K. Steiner (Eds.), *Current topics in early childhood education* (Vol. 7, pp. 1-16). Norwood, NJ.: Ablex.
Kirkpatrick, E. A. (1923). *Fundamentals of child study*. New York: Macmillan.
Klass, C., & Nall, S. (1989). Accessible professional development: A community-based program for early childhood educators. *Childhood Education, 65*(4), 224-27.
Kliebard, H. (1973). The question in teacher education. In D. McCarty (Ed.), *New perspectives in teacher education* (pp. 8-24). San Francisco: Jossey-Bass.
Lanier, J. (1986). Research on teacher education. In M. C. Wittrock (Ed.), *Handbook of research on teaching* (3rd ed., pp. 527-569). New York: Macmillan.
Lay-Dopyera, M., & Dopyera, J. (1987). Strategies for teaching. In C. Seefeldt (Ed.), *The early childhood curriculum: A review of current research* (pp. 13-33). New York: Teachers College Press.
Liston, D., & Zeichner, K. (1987). Reflective teacher education and moral deliberation. *Journal of Teacher Education, 38*(6), 2-8.
Liston, D., & Zeichner, K. (1990). *Teacher education and the conditions of schooling*. New York: Routledge.
Locke, J. (1964). *Some thoughts concerning education* (F. W. Garforth, Ed.). Woodbury, NY: Barron's Educational Series. (Abridged and edited version reprinted from Locke's 4th ed., 1699)
Lombardi, J. (1986). Training for public policy and advocacy: An emerging topic in teacher education. *Young Children, 41*(4), 65-69.
Martin, A. (1985). Back to kindergarten basics. *Harvard Educational Review, 55*(3), 318-20.
Medlin, D. S. (1984). Teacher training and the improvement of public education. *American Education, 20*(6), 5-7.

Minnesota Early Childhood Teacher Educators, Kindergarten Task Force. (1986). *Kindergarten excellence: Knowledge and competencies of kindergarten teachers.* St. Paul: Minnesota Department of Education.

Moyer, J., Egertson, H., & Isenberg, J. (1987). The child centered kindergarten. *Childhood Education, 63*(4), 235-42.

Nall, S. W. (1982). Bridging the gap: Preschool to kindergarten. *Childhood Education, 58*(8), 107-10.

National Association for the Education of Young Children. (1982). *Early childhood teacher education guidelines for four- and five-year programs.* Washington, DC: NAEYC.

National Black Child Development Institute. (1987). SAFEGUARDS: *Guidelines for Establishing Programs for Four-Year-Olds in the Public Schools.* Washington, DC: The National Black Child Development Institute, Inc.

National Center for Research in Teacher Education. (1988a). *Dialogues in teacher education.* East Lansing, MI: NCRTE.

National Center for Research on Teacher Education. (1988b). Teacher education and learning to teach: A research agenda. *Journal of Teacher Education, 39*(6), 27-32.

Posner, G. J., Strike, K. A, Hewson, P. W., & Gertzog, W. A. (1984). Accommodation of a scientific conception: Towards a theory of conceptual change. *Science Education, 66,* 211-27.

Reynolds, M. C. (Ed.). (1989). *Knowledge base for the beginning teacher.* New York: Pergamon Press.

Romberg, T. A., & Tufte, F. W. (1987). Mathematics curriculum engineering: Some suggestions from cognitive science. In T. A. Romberg & D. Stewart (Eds.), *The monitoring of school mathematics: Background papers* (Vol. 2, *Implications from psychology: Outcomes of instruction,* pp. 71-108). Madison: Wisconsin Center for Education Research.

Schön, D. (1983). *The reflective practitioner.* San Francisco: Jossey-Bass.

Seefeldt, C. (Ed.). (1987). *The early childhood curriculum: A review of current research.* New York: Teachers College Press.

Seefeldt, C. (1988). Teacher certification and program accreditation in early childhood education. *Elementary School Journal, 89*(2), 241-51.

Shulman, L. S. (1986). Paradigms and research programs in the study of teaching. In M. C. Wittrock (Ed.), *Handbook of research on teaching* (3rd ed., pp. 3-36). New York: Macmillan.

Silin, J. G. (1985). Authority as knowledge. *Young Children, 40*(3), 41-46.

Silin, J. G. (1986). Psychology, politics, and the discourse of early childhood educators. *Teachers College Record, 87*(4), 611-17.

Silin, J. G. (1987). The early childhood educator's knowledge base: A reconsideration. In L. Katz & K. Steiner (Eds.), *Current topics in early childhood education* (Vol. 7, pp. 17-31). Norwood, NJ: Ablex.

Southern Association on Children Under Six. (1984). *Position Statement on Developmentally Appropriate Educational Experiences for Kindergarten.* ERIC Document Reproduction Service ED 272 272.

Southern Association on Children Under Six. (1985). *Position Statement on Quality Four Year Old Programs in Public Schools.* ERIC Document Reproduction Service ED 272 272.

Southern Association on Children Under Six. (1986a). *Position Statement on Supporting Parents.* ERIC Document Reproduction Service ED 272 272.

Southern Association on Children Under Six. (1986b). *Position Statement on Quality Child Care.* ERIC Document Reproduction Service ED 272 272.

Spodek, B. (1986). Introduction. In B. Spodek (Ed.), *Today's kindergarten. Exploring the knowledge base: Expanding the curriculum.* New York: Teachers College Press.

Spodek, B. (1988). Implicit theories of early childhood teachers: Foundations for professional behavior. In B. Spodek, O. N. Saracho, & D. L. Peters (Eds.), *Professionalism and the early childhood practitioner* (pp. 161–72). New York: Teachers College Press.

Spodek, B. (1989). Conceptualizing today's kindergarten curriculum. *The Elementary School Journal, 89*(2), 203–12.

Spodek, B., & Davis, M. (1982). A study of programs to prepare early childhood personnel. *Journal of Teacher Education, 33*(2), 42–45.

Spodek, B., Saracho, O. N., & Peters, D. L. (Eds.). (1988). *Professionalism and the early childhood practitioner.* New York: Teachers College Press.

Tabachnick, B. R. (1989). Needed for teacher education: Naturalistic research that is culturally responsive. *Teaching and Teacher Education, 5*(2), 155–63.

Takanishi, R. (1981). Early childhood education and research: The changing relationship. *Theory Into Practice, 20*(2), 86–93.

Zeichner, K. (1983). Alternative paradigms of teacher education. *Journal of Teacher Education, 34,* 3–9.

Zeichner, K. (1987). Preparing reflective teachers. *International Journal of Educational Research, 11*(5), 565–76.

Zeichner, K. (1988). *Understanding the character and quality of the academic and professional components of teacher education.* East Lansing, MI: National Center for Research on Teacher Education.

Zeichner, K., & Gore, J. (1990). Teacher socialization. In W. R. Houston (Ed.), *Handbook of research on teacher education* (pp. 329–348). New York: Macmillan.

CHAPTER 8

# Setting and Maintaining Professional Standards

## Susan Bredekamp

The primary goal of the nation's largest organization of early childhood educators, the National Association for the Education of Young Children (NAEYC), is to improve professional practice in programs for young children, from birth through age 8. Founded in 1926 as the National Association for Nursery Education, the first 50 years of the NAEYC's efforts were directed primarily at providing resources for teachers, such as books and a professional journal, and opportunities for sharing expertise through national conferences and a network of state and local affiliate groups. Since 1980, however, NAEYC has established itself as the standard-setting organization for the early childhood profession. The adoption of *Early Childhood Teacher Education Guidelines for Four- and Five-Year Programs* (NAEYC, 1982) was the first major attempt by NAEYC to specify standards for professional preparation. The association has since adopted guidelines for associate degree programs (NAEYC, 1985) and guidelines for advanced degrees in early childhood education (NAEYC, 1990).

During this unprecedented wave of standard setting, NAEYC also established standards for professional practice, including criteria and procedures for a national accreditation system for early childhood centers and schools (NAEYC, 1984a) and standards for developmentally appropriate practice in programs serving children from birth through age 8 (Bredekamp, 1987).

These activities have provided a rare opportunity to observe and compare trends in actual practice in programs for young children with the standards established for early childhood teacher preparation by state and national agencies, and professional organizations. The picture that emerges is complex, but the lessons learned are instructive as the early childhood profession continues to struggle to define itself in the 1990s and beyond.

In this chapter the roles of state and national agencies relevant to setting and maintaining professional standards are described. At the state level, certification and licensing are addressed. National agencies addressed include the Council for Early Childhood Professional Recognition and the National Board for Professional Teaching Standards. Then the role of professional associations is described. An overview of the activity of the National Council for the Accreditation of Teacher Education (NCATE) is provided. The chapter concludes with a detailed description of NAEYC's involvement in setting and maintaining standards for early childhood professional preparation and practice.

## THE ROLE OF STATE AND NATIONAL AGENCIES

### State Certification and Licensing

Undoubtedly the most influential standard setters are state agencies, which establish regulatory standards that carry the weight of legal enforcement. The classic early childhood dichotomy between care and education is clearly reflected in the division of responsibility between state agencies, with state departments of education setting standards for certification of teachers for public schools, who presumably are educators, and state social service agencies or health departments establishing standards for personnel in child care centers and/or preschools, whose role is perceived as caregiving. This false dichotomy of care and education is being challenged (Elkind, 1988; Kagan, 1988), but continues to present a barrier to improving the status and compensation of early childhood teachers. Of course, perception of roles is not the only barrier to improving status and compensation. Other barriers include program sponsorship, with public school teachers generally earning more than private school teachers, and the age level of children served, with teachers of older children often earning more than teachers of younger children.

If these two separate systems share anything in common, it is probably the enormous variability in standards among different states. Cooper and Eisenhart describe early childhood teacher certification in various states in Chapter 10; a complete discussion will not be repeated here. Suffice it to say that only half the states offer specialized certification for early childhood teachers, and among those 24 states, 9 different definitions of the scope of the early childhood certificate are used (McCarthy, 1988). Only three states, Illinois, New Hampshire, and Vermont, use NAEYC's definition of early childhood as birth through age 8.

All state teacher certification requires a baccalaureate degree as a minimum qualification. With little or no distinction in most states between the degree in elementary education and that in early childhood education, the profession is rightly concerned that the distinctive learning and developmental characteristics of young children are being sadly neglected in teacher preparation programs. State certification standards must begin to reflect the reality that more than half the states now provide public school-sponsored prekindergartens for four-year-olds and even three-year-olds in some cases (Marx & Seligson, 1988). Some school systems will not permit uncertified teachers in these classrooms, thus running the risk of positions being filled by certified but unqualified individuals. In other cases, where there is a shortage of teachers with early childhood teaching certificates, emergency certificates may be offered or teachers may be hired who meet state child care licensing criteria. Thus, we face a variety of situations, including programs staffed by qualified, but uncertified, teachers, or unqualified, uncertified teachers. Attention to the enormous variability in state certification is certainly needed and has been identified as a priority for NAEYC action in the future (NAEYC Colloquium, 1988). In 1989, the Association of Teacher Educators (ATE) appointed a Commission on Early Childhood, whose first priority is to work on a joint position statement with NAEYC on early childhood certification. The ATE Commission is proceeding with work on the position statement, which should be available in late 1990. We will discuss the impact of state certification more fully later in describing the role of NCATE.

Rivaling the diversity of state certification standards is the diversity of state licensing requirements for personnel in child care programs (Morgan, 1987). State standards for "group leaders" vary from California's maximum qualification of 12 semester hour credits of early childhood or child development courses to Alabama's minimal regulation that the individual be 16 years of age and able to read and write. If NAEYC's accreditation criteria were met, individuals responsible for the care and education of a group of children would have at least a Child Development Associate (CDA) credential or an associate degree in early childhood education or child development. While more than 40 states list the CDA credential as a means for complying with licensing standards, all those states list other options as well. No states come close to requiring the equivalent of an associate degree (which NAEYC's standards define as incorporating 30 semester hours of professional course work, including at least 300 hours of supervised field experience).

The role of state licensing is presumably to establish a minimum standard for legal operation, but the existence of such low qualifications tends to affect the maximum level that programs are capable of providing. NAEYC accreditation sets relatively high standards for children's programs, but decisions are based on substantial compliance, with the greatest weight given to the observed interactions among staff and children and the appropriateness of the curriculum. Among programs achieving NAEYC accreditation, which are self-selected, the weakest component of the program is invariably staff qualifications (Bredekamp & Apple, 1986).

To date, the impact of state agencies in setting and maintaining standards has been to support the artificial distinction between care and education in early childhood programs, to perpetuate confusion in defining professional roles and functions of early childhood teachers, and to maintain the lower status and levels of compensation of early childhood practitioners.

## The Impact of National Agencies

Since states function relatively autonomously in providing education and social service, there is naturally a lesser role for national agencies in influencing standards. Nevertheless, several national endeavors have had considerable impact on the field and new agencies will undoubtedly emerge in the future. The two most influential national agencies are closely linked—the national Head Start Bureau and the Council for Early Childhood Professional Recognition, the private, nonprofit agency created by NAEYC to administer the CDA National Credentialing Program. Head Start has played a role in standard setting since it first promulgated the Head Start Performance Standards. The CDA competencies and the credentialing program were developed with considerable financial support from the federal government, which continues to underwrite a portion of the program's operations. Head Start's standard-setting role continues. For example, its most recent mandate is that by 1992 every Head Start classroom will be staffed by a qualified teacher who has a degree in early childhood education or child development (either associate or baccalaureate) or a CDA credential.

The Council for Early Childhood Professional Recognition plans to implement a new training model for early childhood professional preparation in the 1990s. That model, which would lead to the acquisition of the competence required of a CDA, will be equivalent to nine to twelve semester hours of study, a considerable increase over the current CDA training requirement of three training experiences (each of which could be a workshop) and over the amount of training required by state licensing.

The child care debate in the 101st Congress may create a new national agency; the formation of a task group to advise on model standards is a provision of the Act for Better Child Care. Among the areas of greatest concern in the proposed national standards are training of child care personnel.

A new national agency has recently arrived on the education scene, the National Board for Professional Teaching Standards, that will influence standards for early childhood education. Growing out of the recommendations of the Carnegie Forum on Education and the Economy (1986), the National Board plans to develop standards and instruments for national teacher certification comparable to board certification currently available in other professions, such as medicine, law, and accounting. The National Board's position is that states license teachers to practice at a minimal level of qualification, but it is the role of the teaching profession to set standards and verify performance of master teachers (Tucker & Mandel, 1986). The National Board is in its infancy and has the daunting task of developing assessment procedures that are valid, reliable, credible, fair, efficient, and affordable. Its initial work has been to develop policy statements that define generically what teachers need to know and be able to do. These early efforts appear heartening in that the National Board has given more attention to knowledge of child development and learning than is usually apparent in documents that apply to secondary and elementary education, although their emphasis on subject matter to be taught reflects a lack of understanding and sensitivity to the early childhood educator's point of view. However, the Board's initial policies and perspectives indicate that early childhood, which is defined as prekindergarten through grade 3, is among the fields for which it intends to develop certificates (National Board for Professional Teaching Standards, 1989). The National Board represents a major attempt to professionalize the broader field of education, and early childhood education needs to be represented in its work.

## THE ROLE OF PROFESSIONAL ASSOCIATIONS

In the area of standard setting, professional organizations speak louder and carry a much smaller stick than state and national agencies. Professional associations tend to set goal standards to which the field will hopefully aspire. In the United States, professional associations have tended to rely on accreditation as a means to implement and maintain their standards (Christensen, 1985). Unlike licensing, accreditation lacks the clout of legal enforcement, but has the benefit of serving as a positive incentive by offering recognition to institutions that voluntarily meet standards higher than the minimal requirements. Additional benefits accrue to accredited institutions, such as eligibility for third party payments, transferability of credits, and other reciprocal agreements. The professional accrediting body for teacher education is the National Council for Accreditation of Teacher Education. NAEYC is an associate member of NCATE, representing the specialty area of early childhood education. NAEYC has worked with NCATE for the last 10 years toward the goal of improving early childhood teacher education programs. An examination of NCATE's activity relevant to setting standards for early childhood education is followed by a description of NAEYC's experiences in accreditation.

## NCATE's Influence on Early Childhood Education

NCATE's standards and procedures have undergone extensive revisions during the 1980s. The effect for specialty areas such as early childhood education has been mixed. In some ways the influence of specialty area guidelines has increased, while in other ways it seems to have diminished.

NAEYC joined NCATE initially at the request of some association members who, as teacher educators in NCATE-accredited institutions, were required to show how their programs used guidelines of the national professional association. In fact, it was in response to requests such as these that NAEYC initiated development of teacher education guidelines in the first place (Bredekamp, in press; Seefeldt, 1988). Faculty also found the need to justify elements of their programs in times of budget reappraisal and retrenchment, and the guidelines were intended to provide assistance. One of NAEYC's first tasks after joining NCATE was to successfully petition for separate listing for early childhood education programs in NCATE's Annual List of Accredited Programs. The separate listing is an important recognition that early childhood and elementary education are not identical fields of endeavor and preparation.

The curriculum standards of NAEYC's *Teacher Education Guidelines* were among the first sets of professional preparation standards approved by NCATE in 1982. Since then, institutions seeking NCATE accreditation have been required to submit a description of their early childhood program to NAEYC for review against its standards, a process known as folio review. The significance of folio review in the NCATE process has evolved over time. Under the redesign of NCATE that is now in place, institutions are required to submit folios for programs for which NCATE-approved curriculum standards exist, as a precondition for accreditation. The appropriate professional association reviews the folio and reports whether the program is in compliance with the specialty standards. If the program is found to be in noncompliance, it may choose to submit a rejoinder or submit to a site visit to obtain a positive review.

The statements of compliance are one form of information that is used to determine if the institution meets one of NCATE's standards (Standard 2.4). Compliance with that standard is used by the Board of Examiners, which visits the institution, and the Unit Accreditation Board, which makes the accreditation decision. In short, an early childhood education program (or a mathematics education or science education program, for that matter) could be found not to comply with the specialty guidelines but the institution's teacher education unit could still be accredited. Less likely but certainly possible, a program could be found in compliance with national specialty guidelines, while the overall unit was not found to be accreditable. Teacher education programs in accredited teacher education units that are in compliance with specialty guidelines will be identified in the Annual List by a special notation.

NCATE and NAEYC operate under the assumption that the existence of approved guidelines helps to improve programs as they seek to demonstrate compliance, and that the potential for achieving notation in the Annual List as being in compliance with national professional standards motivates faculty and administrators to meet national standards.

A new development in the redesigned NCATE process is the State Recognition System, the impact of which is not yet known at the time of this writing. The purpose of the State Recognition System was to improve coordination and lessen duplication in accreditation of teacher education. Under the NCATE redesign, states have four options for collaborative relationships with NCATE, ranging from using NCATE's system for state accreditation of teacher education to the state's system being recognized by NCATE. If NCATE recognizes a state under one of the options, the institutions in that state are not required to submit to folio review by the specialty associations. Instead, as part of the process of state recognition, the professional associations review the state's certification standards in their specialty area and advise the state and NCATE on the degree of congruence between the state standards and the professional standards. To date, NAEYC has had the opportunity to review certification standards from several states and, not surprisingly, has found very little congruence between state standards and NAEYC's guidelines. In fact, only one state, Illinois, has been found to have standards that are reasonably congruent with NAEYC's. Nevertheless, most of the states reviewed have been recognized by NCATE, and, therefore, institutions in those states will not participate in folio review unless they voluntarily choose to do so in the hope of being noted in the Annual List.

Depending on whether one is inclined to optimism or pessimism, the predicted impact of NCATE's State Recognition System will vary. On the one hand, it provides a previously unavailable opportunity to communicate with state certification agencies about the strengths and weaknesses of their standards for early childhood education. On the other hand, it could undermine the entire system of folio review if sufficient numbers of states achieve recognition, programs in those states do not submit to review, and the Annual List notation system becomes a meaningless distinction.

NCATE's sphere of influence tends to be limited to colleges of education, many of which have traditionally defined education as K–12. The preparation of teachers to work with younger children has often been the purview of child development programs, which may or may not be affiliated with colleges of education and, therefore, are less likely to be associated with NCATE. In addition, not all institutions that prepare teachers, under whatever auspices, choose to be affiliated with NCATE. Similarly, teachers in child care centers are more likely to be prepared in two-year community college or vocational education programs. Although NAEYC developed guidelines for such programs, there is no mechanism for evaluating compliance. Associate degree programs in early childhood education have no accrediting body comparable to NCATE; some faculty in two-year programs have, in fact, petitioned NAEYC to act as such a body on their behalf. Despite these limitations, NAEYC continues to participate with NCATE because NCATE currently provides the only vehicle for applying the association's guidelines in the evaluation of teacher education programs and because it also provides opportunities for communication and liaison with professional associations representing other areas of education. For example, NAEYC recently participated on an NCATE-appointed task force to develop guidelines for elementary education.

## Lessons from NAEYC's Experiences

Although the role of NAEYC has been discussed throughout this chapter, what remains is to present what has been learned from NAEYC's experiences in setting and maintaining standards for teacher education and to identify issues and questions that need to be resolved in the future. A summary of what has been learned from reviewing the descriptions of approximately 200 early childhood teacher education programs for compliance with NAEYC's guidelines follows.

A major frustration of NAEYC members who serve as folio reviewers is that the project is only a review of documents. Their legitimate concern is that programs can present themselves well on paper and not actually provide adequate preparation of teachers. This criticism is inherent in all paper reviews, but what is perhaps of greater concern is the pattern of weaknesses that can be observed by reviewing documents only.

The most obvious pattern is that very few programs that NAEYC reviews define early childhood according to its definition of birth through age 8. When the *Teacher Education Guidelines* were first developed, there was concern that preparation to work with children of such a broad age span is an unrealistic expectation of a four-year program (Bredekamp, in press). However, opinions were equally strong that NAEYC should not compromise on its definition of early childhood. Defining early childhood as birth through age 8 makes sense not only developmentally, but also politically. If early childhood educators are to have any influence on the content and experiences provided in the primary grades, the birth through age 8 definition must be maintained. In applying the guidelines during folio review, a compromise is made — programs are required to provide a broad base of knowledge of the developmental period (birth through age 8), and specific preparation for working with children in two of the three periods represented in that age span (infant-toddler, preschool-kindergarten, and primary). Thus, the integrity of the definition of early childhood is maintained, while recognizing the difficulty of designing a program to prepare teachers to serve children across the entire range of ages.

It is safe to say that certification standards are the tail that wags the teacher education dog. Folios inevitably begin with a statement about the scope of the state's certification and proceed from there. Many states, for example, Washington, offer only an early childhood endorsement on an elementary certificate. Therefore, institutions in those states inevitably juggle program requirements to find sufficient hours to adequately prepare early childhood teachers within the constraints of an endorsement only. Approximately one-third of the programs reviewed by NAEYC have been endorsements on kindergarten through grade 6 or grade 8 certificates. In some cases, early childhood endorsements require only two courses and a kindergarten student teaching placement. In some states, such as Georgia, early childhood certification is for kindergarten through fourth grade. Often institutions in states with K–4 certification offer early childhood programs in which students may or may not student teach at the kindergarten level; even if they do, students graduate as early childhood majors having had no course work or field experience directly related to teaching children younger than age 5.

Most of the programs reviewed by NAEYC define early childhood as kindergarten through grade 3 or preschool through grade 3. These programs are more likely to be found in compliance with NAEYC's guidelines, and yet patterns of weaknesses can be identified. Most commonly, these programs do not provide field experiences with diverse age groups and in diverse settings, as the guidelines call for. There is simply insufficient exposure to the teaching and caregiving responsibilities of full-day child care. Virtually no attention is given to the important role of routines as learning experiences, and very little content is presented on health, safety, and nutrition. Despite the diversity of settings that young children now occupy, public school kindergartens and primary grade classrooms remain the most common student teaching placements. It is extremely rare for an early childhood program seeking NCATE accreditation to offer any course work, much less field experience, relevant to working with infants and toddlers, which is the fastest growing age group in child care.

Other common weaknesses in early childhood teacher preparation programs are a lack of preparation and opportunities for practice in working with families. Since many of the programs are essentially elementary education programs, and the elementary school as an institution has not been open to family participation, the omission is not surprising. However, the tradition of parents as partners in early childhood education requires sound preparation in the knowledge and skills required for working with diverse families.

A consistent weakness in early childhood teacher education programs, including those that are primarily K–3, remains a lack of methods courses specifically designed to prepare teachers to teach young children in ways that are appropriate for their age and developmental level. Methods courses in general stress teaching strategies that are more appropriate for older children. For instance, there is little recognition that young children learn best through play in a classroom that is structured for child-initiated activity. Instead, there is undue emphasis on teaching practices that are almost exclusively teacher-directed and that emphasize a behavioristic approach to teaching and learning rather than a more appropriate, constructivist-interactionist approach. For example, designers of reading courses have been slow to acknowledge the research on emerging literacy. One syllabus reviewed for a course on classroom management surveyed 17 different discipline models with no indication of prioritization or value of any one technique for developing social competence in young children.

Another almost universally common weakness, perhaps more representative of society's weakness than the field's, is an appalling lack of attention to cultural diversity. When multicultural education is addressed at all, it is usually limited to a cursory examination of holiday celebrations or artifacts from different cultures. Perhaps more destructive is the tendency to see cultural diversity as a deficit that must be "handled" like other special needs rather than respected and promoted as a strength. Finally, there is essentially no recognition of the importance of the role of teachers in helping children overcome the biases that are so prevalent in American society (Derman-Sparks, 1989).

Another concern that teacher preparation programs will need to address in the future is the integration of early childhood and special education preparation. This will become more important with the implementation of Public Law 99-457 requiring services for children under the age of 3 who have handicapping conditions. The traditional dichotomies between special education and early childhood education and between preparation for work with infants-toddlers and older children no longer apply.

A final concern that has emerged from reviewing early childhood program folios is the lack of adequate standards for qualified faculty. NAEYC's role in reviewing folios does not extend to reviewing faculty vitae, but is limited to reviewing curricula. It must rely on the NCATE Board of Examiners to determine compliance with standards for faculty. Nevertheless, faculty qualifications can often be inferred from folios, and alarming trends have been seen. For example, too often one or perhaps two qualified early childhood faculty teach all the available courses. Sometimes it is apparent, judging from syllabi and textbooks, that the faculty are not current in the field. For example, one syllabus listed as an objective for students that they become familiar with a variety of curriculum models and listed the models studied in Planned Variation Head Start in the early 1970s. When university teacher preparation programs are no more current than this, it becomes less difficult to understand how inappropriate teaching practices persist in primary schools and trickle down to younger and younger children (Bredekamp & Shepard, 1989). Perhaps the new guidelines for advanced degrees in early childhood education, jointly endorsed by NAEYC and the National Association of Early Childhood Teacher Educators (NAEYC, 1990), can provide a standard for faculty qualifications. But unless NCATE chooses to firmly enforce standards for faculty qualifications, it is highly possible that "early childhood" courses and student teaching will be conducted by faculty without adequate professional qualifications. A related concern is whether faculty have had relevant teaching experience. Conducting child development research is certainly an important qualification for supervising dissertations, but by itself does not constitute adequate qualification for preparing undergraduates to become classroom teachers.

This summary of observed trends in weaknesses in teacher education programs seeking NCATE accreditation does not purport to describe the entire field of early childhood teacher preparation. But it is of interest to compare these findings with trends in the weaknesses found in early childhood programs seeking NAEYC accreditation (Bredekamp, 1989; Bredekamp & Apple, 1986). For example, the two criteria for NAEYC accreditation that are most frequently not met are those that address appropriate hand-washing and cultural diversity. This finding is not surprising in light of the minuscule attention paid to these topics by teacher education programs. A related weakness is the way routine transitions are handled. Too often routines are handled rigidly, with all children expected to participate and little room for individualization. Of greater concern is the lack of understanding of the importance of child-initiated rather than teacher-directed activity. It is hard to believe that programs get as far as an on-site visit in the accreditation process without their teachers knowing that a morning of teacher-directed activity followed by an afternoon of free play does not constitute a balance of teacher-directed and child-initiated activity. But this is believable in light of the content of some "early childhood" teacher education methods courses.

One of the most frequently observed trends in NAEYC's experience in accrediting early childhood centers and schools has been that if there is one weak classroom or program area in an otherwise good center, it is inevitably the toddler or, less frequently, the infant group. The vulnerability of these age groups makes inappropriate or poor practice particularly disturbing. But the complete omission of infants and toddlers from teacher preparation programs makes it hardly surprising. This situation cannot remain uncorrected. Among the children's programs to be accredited in the first two years of operation of the center accreditation program, more than half served toddlers and almost one-fourth served infants (Recken, 1989).

## CONCLUSION

The findings from NAEYC's experience reviewing teacher education folios and accrediting programs for children are presented not to denigrate teacher education or the state of early childhood practice, but to challenge the field to work toward greater consistency between the knowledge base and practice. As developmentalists, early childhood educators should not be dismayed by the realization that standard setting is also a developmental process. Like so many other phenomena, standard setting tends to function on a pendulum swing from generality to specificity and back again. The *Teacher Education Guidelines* were NAEYC's first attempt to obtain broad consensus for a major position statement. As a result, they are almost too general to be really useful in guiding program development. Each subsequent set of standards developed has been slightly more specific and therefore more potentially valuable in influencing practice, with the developmentally appropriate practice statements the most specific to date. With greater clarity (in the form of accreditation standards and appropriate practice guidelines) about what it is that we are preparing teachers to do, it may be time to re-examine the teacher education guidelines and revise them for even greater clarity and specificity. There is also a need to provide examples of models of successful implementation in which teachers are prepared for the full age span of birth through age 8, or the objective is achieved through other means.

Continuing its role of standard setter for the profession, NAEYC's current projects include development of a Code of Ethical Conduct (Feeney & Kipnis, 1989), guidelines for appropriate curriculum and assessment, and a re-examination of the existing position statement on nomenclature (NAEYC, 1984b), which has been less influential than its other attempts at standard setting (Spodek & Saracho, 1988). The goal of the latter project is to develop a model for early childhood professional development that would define professional categories and designate preservice and in-service qualifications for each. Such a model would have potential application in establishing various career ladders and staffing patterns. It will be a challenging task to accomplish given the economic and philosophical dilemmas facing the field (Spodek, Saracho, & Peters, 1988; Willer, 1988).

Setting and maintaining standards for professional preparation and practice are important indicators of the increased professionalism of early childhood education (Friedson, 1983; Spodek et al., 1988; Vollmer & Mills, 1966). NAEYC has contributed a great deal to this process by establishing important position statements and guidelines for practice. Currently, the most influential of these sets of standards are the curriculum guidelines for teacher education in four- and five-year programs and the accreditation criteria for early childhood centers. The greater influence of these standards lies in the fact that procedures exist for outside evaluation and verification of compliance. Nevertheless, in both instances, decisions are based on substantial compliance because current practice is far from congruent with the goal standards of the profession. As the need for qualified early childhood teachers increases, it is imperative that the early childhood profession obtain greater consensus about its expectations for professional preparation and practice. The best place to start is usually at the beginning, and teacher education is where it all begins.

## REFERENCES

Bredekamp, S. (Ed.). (1987). *Developmentally appropriate practice in early childhood programs serving children from birth through age 8*. Washington, DC: National Association for the Education of Young Children.

Bredekamp, S. (1989). Measuring quality through a national accreditation system for early childhood programs. Paper presented at the Annual Meeting of the American Educational Research Association, San Francisco.

Bredekamp, S. (in press). The development and application of professional standards for early childhood education. In S. Kilmer (Ed.), *Current topics in early education and day care*.

Bredekamp, S., & Apple, P. (1986). How early childhood programs get accredited: An analysis of accreditation decisions. *Young Children, 42*(1), 34–38.

Bredekamp, S., & Shepard, L. (1989). How best to protect children from inappropriate school expectations, practices, and policies. *Young Children, 44*(3), 14–24.

Carnegie Forum on Eduction and the Economy. (1986). *A nation prepared: Teachers for the 21st century*. New York: Carnegie Forum.

Christensen, D. (1985). NCATE: The continuing quest for excellence. *Action in Teacher Education, 6,* 17–22.

Derman-Sparks, L. (1989). *Anti-bias curriculum: Tools for empowering young children*. Washington, DC: National Association for the Education of Young Children.

Elkind, D. (1988). Early childhood education on its own terms. In S. Kagan & E. Zigler (Eds.), *Early schooling: The great debate*. New Haven: Yale University Press.

Feeney, S., & Kipnis, K. (1989). NAEYC code of ethical conduct and statement of commitment. *Young Children, 45*(1), 24–29.

Friedson, E. (1983). The theory of professions: State of the art. In R. Dingwall & P. Lewis (Eds.), *The sociology of the professions* (pp. 19–37). New York: St. Martin's Press.

Kagan, S. L. (1988). Current reforms in early childhood education: Are we addressing the issues? *Young Children, 43*(2), 27–32.

Marx, F., & Seligson, M. (1988). *The public school early childhood study.* New York: Bank Street College of Education.

McCarthy, J. (1988). *Early childhood teacher certification requirements.* Washington, DC: National Association for the Education of Young Children.

Morgan, G. (1987). *National state of child care regulation 1986.* Watertown, MA: Work/Family Directions.

National Association for the Education of Young Children. (1982). *Early childhood teacher education guidelines for four- and five-year programs.* Washington, DC: Author.

National Association for the Education of Young Children. (1984a). *Accreditation criteria and procedures of the National Academy of Early Childhood Programs.* Washington, DC: Author.

National Association for the Education of Young Children. (1984b). Position statement on nomenclature, salaries, benefits, and the status of the early childhood profession. *Young Children, 40*(1), 52–55.

National Association for the Education of Young Children. (1985). *Guidelines for early childhood education programs in associate-degree granting institutions.* Washington, DC: Author.

National Association for the Education of Young Children. (1990). *Early childhood teacher education guidelines: Basic and advanced.* Washington, DC: Author.

NAEYC Colloquium. (1988). Early childhood teacher education: Traditions and trends. *Young Children, 44*(1), 53–57.

National Board for Professional Teaching Standards. (1989). *Initial policies and perspectives of the National Board for Professional Teaching Standards.* Detroit, MI: Author.

Recken, R. (1989). Accreditation update: Who gets accredited? *Young Children, 44*(2), 11–12.

Seefeldt, C. (1988). Teacher certification and program accreditation in early childhood education. *Elementary School Journal, 89*(2), 241–51.

Spodek, B., & Saracho, O. (1988). Professionalism in early childhood education. In B. Spodek, O. Saracho, & D. Peters (Eds.), *Professionalism and the early childhood practitioner* (pp. 59–74). New York: Teachers College Press.

Spodek, B., Saracho, O., & Peters, D. (1988). Professionalizing the field: The tasks ahead. In B. Spodek, O. Saracho, & D. Peters (Eds.), *Professionalism and the early childhood practitioner* (pp. 3–9). New York: Teachers College Press.

Tucker, M., & Mandel, D. (1986). The Carnegie Report: A call for redesigning the schools. *Phi Delta Kappan, 67*(5), 24–27.

Vollmer, H., & Mills, D. (1966). *Professionalization.* Englewood Cliffs, NJ: Prentice-Hall.

Willer, B. (1988). *The growing crisis in child care: Quality, compensation, and affordability in early childhood programs.* Washington, DC: National Association for the Education of Young Children.

CHAPTER 9

# Issues in the Recruitment, Selection, and Retention of Early Childhood Teachers

## Barbara T. Bowman

The publication of *A Nation at Risk* in 1983 riveted public attention on the "failures" of American schools, and a new educational reform movement began. The "crisis in education" was on the short list of catastrophes of such varied interest groups as the Committee for Economic Development (1987), the Carnegie Forum (1986), the National Black Child Development Institute (1985), and the American Council on Education (1988a). It has been of concern to both critics and defenders of the educational establishment.

The reasons given for the "crisis" vary: low productivity and falling quality standards of American workers; the decline in international competitiveness of the United States; the potential for major social upheaval as the population is increasingly poor, minority, and undereducated; the loss of uniform cultural standards — particularly in literacy; the failure to achieve educational equity for minorities since the Brown decision in 1954; and the challenge of new technologies have all been cited as causes for alarm. Schools are identified as the culprit in creating the crisis and as the means to rectify it. Public scrutiny of schools has led to a number of new initiatives designed to improve educational outcomes for American children.

### EARLY CHILDHOOD EDUCATION

Early childhood education has been in the forefront of recommendations for school improvement. The National Association for the Education of Young Children includes the years from birth to age 8 — including preschool, primary grades, and day care—as the accepted definition of this period. Infant-toddler interventions and parent education have become popular strategies for enhancing the development of young children. Preschool education has been proposed to prevent later educational failure, particularly for children who have traditionally not done well in school—poor children, children with disabilities, children from families with social and mental health problems. Reform of primary education and better quality day care have also been recommended as measures to improve the health and educational achievement of young children. The National Association of School Boards of Education (NASBE, 1988) has pointed to inappropriate school curriculum; retention and failure policies; overreliance on worksheets and standardized tests; poor transition between grades; and inadequate coordination with day care as contributing to children's poor school performance.

## Teacher Training

Many recommendations, programs, and policies have fixed on teacher preparation—the handmaiden of public education—as a major factor in school improvement. Teacher education programs have been criticized for enrolling the least capable candidates (from the bottom one-quarter of high school and college students), weighting programs heavily with methods courses as opposed to more intellectually challenging subject-matter content, and graduating too few minorities (Quisenberry, 1987).

In response to these criticisms, teacher preparation programs are undergoing re-examination and change. One group of institutions, Project 30, a consortium of colleges and universities—including Ivy League schools and historic black colleges and universities—is considering "the knowledge and values that teachers must have to be educated persons; knowledge of the subject to be taught; teaching ability; the role of race, ethnicity, and sex in the curriculum; and the shortage of minority-group members in the teaching profession" (Thirty Colleges to Participate in Project, 1988, p. A15).

One of the most prestigious of the reform groups, the Holmes Group—a consortium of research institutions organized in 1986 and expanded in 1987—has been working to implement a number of innovations in teacher education. It has recommended that teacher preparation programs place greater emphasis on the liberal arts and sciences, provide students with a strong background in a major area of study, and make professional education curriculum more "comprehensive and intellectually demanding," and more relevant to the needs of prospective teachers (Watkins, 1989, p. A1). See Cooper and Eisenhart (Chapter 10, this volume) for a discussion of the Holmes Group's work.

The recently formed National Board for Professional Teaching Standards, sponsored by the Carnegie Foundation, has as its central purpose the development of a national system to certify teachers. Its task is to identify the knowledge, skills, and dispositions necessary for effective practice, to involve teachers in setting standards of practice, and to improve the assessment of teacher qualifications (Certifying and Rewarding Teaching Excellence, 1989).

Most reform efforts have focused on strengthening training standards, identifying and assessing effective practice qualities and behaviors, encouraging greater emphasis on general education and discipline area knowledge, and increasing minority participation in teaching careers.

## A Shortage of Teachers

A serious shortage of teachers is predicted for the near future unless present trends in teacher education change (Hart, 1987). The importance to colleges and universities of recruiting, selecting, and retaining potential teachers is illustrated by the attention these activities currently receive at professional meetings, in journals, and among university faculty. Liberal arts and science graduates are being actively recruited, and strategies for attracting undergraduates, even during high school, are being devised (Haberman, 1988).

Teacher enrollment dipped sharply in the 1970s and has recovered only gradually since 1983. In 1988, 8.8% of students were interested in elementary or secondary school teaching, up from 4.7% in 1982. This small gain in interest will not lead to enrolling sufficient students to meet the projected need for new teachers (American Council on Education, 1988b).

Despite the expected increase in the demand for teachers, teaching is not favored as a career among students. The reasons for the decreased interest in teaching include an oversupply of teachers in the 1970s, lower status and salaries of teachers compared with other professions, and greater opportunities for women in nontraditional fields. The disfavor of teaching as a career choice extends to parents, who would prefer their children *not* to grow up to be teachers. In 1969, 75% of parents liked the idea of their children teaching school, but by 1983 this number had shrunk to 45% (Andrew, Parks, & Nelson, 1985).

While the number of students selecting education as a career may have diminished, the number of those seeking early childhood education courses and programs has not, as witnessed by the increase in such courses and programs offered by colleges and universities. The demand for early childhood courses is propelled by the need for early childhood teachers and the gradual increase in training requirements in state child care standards. In many sections of the country the need for teachers is outstripping the supply (Whitebook & Granger, 1989).

A number of factors contribute to the shortage of early childhood teachers. First, many early childhood teachers do not remain in teaching very long. High turnover, changes in job positions, and short tenure are characteristic of the early childhood field, particularly in day care. In New York City in 1988, 27% of positions in publicly funded day care were unfilled, and 67% of the directors of these centers indicated difficulty finding personnel to fill positions. It is unclear which teachers are leaving the field and why (Whitebook & Granter, 1989), but low salaries, poor working conditions, low status, and minimum state educational requirements for child care staff are generally considered responsible for the instability in early childhood staffs (Phillips, 1988). It is likely that many early childhood professionals work for a few years and then leave the field for better paying and more prestigious work, thus increasing the annual need for new trained teachers.

The second factor in creating a shortage is the rapid increase in the number of organized programs for young children. Although poor pay, status, and working conditions tend to limit the number of degreed teachers in day care centers and community-sponsored preschools such as Head Start, the proliferation of these programs has fueled the need for professionally trained personnel.

The third source of demand is from the public schools. Prior to 1980, eight states served preschool-age children. This number had risen to 26 by 1987 (Marx & Seligson, 1988), and many communities have had too few certified teachers to meet the need for them in preschool and early childhood special education programs. Many of these programs have drawn certified and certifiable teachers from public and private day care and Head Start into the higher paying school positions, creating serious shortages of four-year college graduates in those centers.

The demand for early childhood teachers with four-year degrees is expected to expand through the end of the century. The United States Bureau of Labor Statistics projects a growth rate of approximately 40 percent in the next 10 years (Whitebook, 1986). However, if salaries, working conditions, and respect for the profession do not improve, the number of prospective teachers is apt to be seriously compromised as students disdain early childhood education as a career choice.

## EARLY CHILDHOOD TEACHER EDUCATION

Many of the problems affecting teacher education in general are mirrored in programs for early childhood teachers. Training standards for early childhood teachers are even more lax than those for elementary and high school teachers. While all states have requirements for teaching certificates for kindergarten and primary grade teachers, many do not have special ones for preschool teachers, and outside of public schools—in day care centers, nursery schools, and other preschool programs—there are usually few educational standards for teachers of young children. Many states require only a high school certificate as preparation for working in the field.

Although large numbers of early childhood teachers have a professional degree reflecting a four-year college program, these are obtained in a variety of departments in colleges and universities. Phillips (1988) has listed 21 departments offering courses for early childhood caregivers and teachers: early childhood education, home economics, elementary education, family and child studies, family and environmental resources, child care, child development, allied health, occupational home economics, social sciences, health occupations, education, human development, teacher education, behavioral sciences, vocational arts, psychology, human ecology, public service, family and consumer education, and education and family day care. The requirements for admission to and graduation from these programs are enormously varied, and except for students trained in education departments, graduates are usually not eligible for teaching certificates. Noncertified teachers work primarily in nursery schools, Head Start, and day care centers.

Kindergarten and primary grade teachers are required to meet state certification standards. Nineteen states have certification standards that include preschool, three have certificates that extend from birth to grade 3 (age 8), and nine certify teachers for preschool and primary grades. The remainder of the states have no special preschool certification (Phillips, 1988). See Cooper and Eisenhart (Chapter 10, this volume) for a list of state requirements.

### General vs. Professional Education

One of the great controversies in teacher education is the appropriate balance between general and subject area courses and those devoted to professional issues and methods. The rationale for a strong general education and subject-matter emphasis is that children can learn only what teachers themselves know. Implicit in this perspective is the belief that "how to teach," or pedagogy, is less amenable to serious inquiry than the liberal arts and sciences. Spodek and Saracho (1982) found 59 percent of students' programs were in general education, but that proportion has probably increased under pressure from reform groups.

The appropriate balance between general and professional education is even more contentious in early childhood teacher education than at other levels. Should teachers of young children concentrate on the traditional disciplines—mathematics, sciences, literature, and history—or should they concentrate on knowledge more specific to working with young children? Research has associated desirable outcomes for children with teachers trained solely in child development and early childhood education (Ruopp, Travers, Glantz, & Coelen, 1979). These studies suggest that specific information about children and how they learn and how to teach them is a more important underpinning for professional practice than general knowledge.

On the other hand, Berk (1985) reported that teachers with at least two years of college were more apt to display the teaching behaviors associated with better children's programs—more verbal interaction, indirect guidance, encouragement, and direction—than were high school graduates, thus demonstrating "the relevance of broad higher educational foundations for the practical endeavor of providing developmentally stimulating caregiving experiences for young children and for fostering the integration of caregiver child-oriented attitudes with behavior" (p. 127). The National Association for the Education of Young Children (1982) recommended that general education account for at least 50 percent of an early childhood teacher education program.

Most four-year colleges and universities require satisfactory performance in general education courses before admission to a teacher preparation program. This is a problem for many early childhood teachers who begin their collegiate education following a career path of work and study. Teachers and caregivers may enter the field with little or no higher education, but are motivated and encouraged by their work with children to enroll in college programs while continuing to work (Phillips, 1988). Professional course content is rarely integrated with the liberal arts and sciences, and courses in pedagogy usually are taken after the completion of the required general education courses. This means that during the first two years of college, when career-oriented students are interested in professional courses, they are expected to confine their studies to general education. Students who do take professional courses at the junior college level often must repeat them in senior college since professional courses may not be transferable. Employed two-year college students, who are the most vulnerable both financially and academically, are not encouraged through their professional interests to remain in school and often must take extra credits in order to meet four-year degree graduation requirements (Haberman, 1988).

Joint planning and guaranteed admission agreements between senior and junior colleges can help alleviate their problems (Haberman, 1988), but frequently students are caught in the web of conflicting requirements and overlapping offerings as they seek to achieve a professional education. The Education Commission of the States has organized a national panel of policy makers to consider the specific problem of helping minority students, who are most likely to begin higher education in two-year colleges, to make the transition to four-year institutions (Update on Minority Groups, 1989).

## Admission Criteria

*Early Childhood Teacher Education Guidelines* (NAEYC, 1982) list as a standard for four- and five-year teacher education programs that "where specific standards for admission are applied, they are relevant to the work the candidate is preparing to do" (p. 14). Definitions of desirable teacher qualities should therefore be related to the conceptualization of teachers' professional activities.

Who makes a good early childhood teacher? The answer to this question seems to swing back and forth between "anyone" and "only the best and the brightest." In the 1870s, the "female nature" was all that was considered necessary to teach kindergarten (Hewes, 1988). The history of elementary education offers evidence that teacher candidates have generally been "unpromising." Teachers of young children were young (often in their teens), relatively uneducated compared with other professionals, and often ignorant of professional education. Teachers were held in low esteem and their salaries reflected this. The slow acceptance of a baccalaureate level education for elementary teachers, combining both general and professional courses, has been achieved only in the last 50 years (Warren, 1985).

Bloom (1985) studied the qualities most often associated with the first teachers of talented adults. During the early stages in the acquisition of high level skills, he found the best qualities in first teachers to be more social than cognitive or technical. He discovered that the first teachers in his study liked children, made learning "pleasant and rewarding" to the children by using play activities, and set high standards for their students using positive reinforcement (p. 514). In addition, the teachers' relationships with the children's families were friendly, and they enlisted parental cooperation to monitor children's performance at home.

Clark (1988) describes teaching as "complex, uncertain, and dilemma-riddled" (p. 10) and questions whether student teachers are aware of the "artistry" and "demandingness" of classroom teaching (p. 11). Clark's list of desirable teacher attributes includes such characteristics as the ability to plan and reflect, to tolerate ambiguity and uncertainty, to think for themselves, and to make and correct inferences about pupil performance and appropriate teaching techniques.

The Holmes report, according to Phillip Jackson (1987), implicitly described classroom teachers as clinicians driven by a science of pedagogy. He said, "The improvement of teaching, in this view, consists of establishing the linkages between teachers' actions (causes) on the one hand and student outcomes (effects) on the other" (p. 387). Jackson complained that this is a poor model for teachers because it suggests that we have greater scientific knowledge about teaching than we actually have and it leads to undervaluing qualities like thoughtfulness and commitment in teachers (p. 389). Bolster (1985) echoed this concern and contended the failure of the science of pedagogy to provide appropriate direction for classroom teaching was due to using a cause and effect model for research. Instead, he advocated a "process" model that captures the unfolding of learning within the culture of the classroom. These two models, teacher as technician and teacher as observer-participant in the mini-culture of a classroom, lead to somewhat different definitions of the career of teaching and different personality and value attributes of desirable candidates.

Carlson (1987) described teachers as both agents of oppression and oppressed workers, and believed that school reform based either on more accountability to the bureaucracies or on greater respect and professionalism will not "reform" education. Using a critical theories argument, he contended that the only hope for improving education, particularly for those children currently underachieving, is to have radical teachers. Accordingly, he viewed political radicalism as a desirable characteristic in teachers.

Despite the inability to resolve the issue of what makes a good early childhood teacher, programs generally have established preadmission standards. Spodek and Saracho (1982) list the criteria most frequently used for admission to conventional teacher education programs as grade point average, personal interviews, secondary school grades, standardized test scores, and secondary school class rank. Since 1983, some programs have raised their standards and attempted to attract students of higher intellectual and academic standing as future teachers. This has led to considerable discord, particularly over the use of standardized tests as the sole or a heavily weighted criterion for admission.

Until 1979, only Tennessee used a test of basic skills as a criterion for admission to a teacher education program. In the early part of the century, when teachers had only high school educations, it was common to require them to pass basic skills tests. However, as more teachers matriculated in four-year college programs, the number of states requiring such tests diminished, and colleges and universities were given the responsibility for ascertaining the skills of student teachers. The pressure to test teachers was revived in the 1970s, and currently, under pressure from the reform movement, 48 states require some form of teacher competency tests. Many colleges and universities use basic skills portions of such tests as the criterion for admission into the teacher education program (U.S. Department of Education, 1987).

Teacher testing is based on the assumption that test scores reflect teacher quality. This belief is shared by legislators, businesspeople, and the public at large, who find test results a quick and efficient way to evaluate quality in programs and in people. Critics opposed to testing give the following reasons: It encourages faculty to "teach to the test," thus restricting curricula; there is little evidence that teachers who score higher will be better teachers; school administrators report no correlation between performance on written tests or grade point averages and teaching ability (Spodek & Saracho 1982); tests are barriers to teaching careers for minorities.

Haberman (1988) wrote, "Universities are notorious for confusing entrance and exit criteria" (p. 16). He suggested that the screening and testing currently done are analogous to the approaches followed by schools of fine arts, which want people to arrive already skilled in the content the schools are supposed to teach.

Screening potential teachers of young children for desirable personal, social, academic, and intellectual characteristics will remain controversial as long as the characteristics of effective teachers and the tests and procedures used to assess these qualities are in question.

## Retention of Student Teachers

Professional education usually consists of three sets of requirements: an academic program focusing on the historical, psychological, and sociological foundations of education; methods courses and laboratories that illustrate the organization and presentation of content material for children; and a series of practicum experiences in schools and social agencies, culminating in student teaching lasting 6 to 12 weeks.

Techniques to assess teacher candidates on these components are limited (Spodek & Saracho, 1982). Standardized tests, grades in major courses (B or above is generally required), and observation of student teaching are the primary ways teacher training institutions evaluate potential teachers. In 48 states teachers also must pass a competency test before being certified to teach. The emphasis on testing has increased in recent years, in response to the demand for more qualified teachers.

Criticisms of these tests abound. The Educational Testing Service, makers of the popular National Teachers Examination used by 30 states to qualify teachers, responded to the criticism of its multiple choice, paper and pencil tests with a totally new assessment strategy. It will include an essential skills component to be given to sophomores before entry into teacher education programs, a professional skills part to be given at the completion of the teacher education degree program, and a classroom performance review to follow practice teaching. The new process will make use of computer simulations, interactive video, portfolio development, and classroom observations as well as paper and pencil tests (Fields, 1988). The use of multiple sources of evidence to assess teachers is supported by the Association of Teacher Educators (1985), which recommended classroom observations, portfolios, interviews, peer references, parent evaluation, self-evaluation, and written tests to evaluate teachers.

Some students withdraw from teacher education programs before completion. Clark (1988), in summarizing the research on teacher thinking, pointed out that students come to teacher education programs with ideas, attitudes, and beliefs that affect how they understand the task of teaching. While there seems to be little evidence to determine whether the differences in approach support or hinder students' performance, undoubtedly personal style preferences play a role in the satisfaction of students with their education and their acceptance of the philosophy and practices recommended by their teacher training program. To what extent these preconceptions distort or fit with the teacher education program in which the student is enrolled undoubtedly affects the satisfaction of the student. Similarly, philosophical and personality differences between students and faculty may contribute to student dissatisfaction and encourage withdrawal from the program.

Retention of students in teacher education programs is also affected by the cost of education. College tuitions have risen dramatically since 1983, and the low salaries in early childhood education and minimal educational requirements characteristic of the field make the investment in college less attractive. In addition, the recommendations of school reform groups, such as the Holmes Group, have led some institutions to extend teacher education into a five-year program. This has obvious implications for impoverished students and makes teachers' salaries less attractive in relation to tuition costs.

## BARRIERS TO RECRUITING AND RETAINING MINORITY TEACHERS

Probably the most serious and explosive issue in education today is how to respond to the educational needs of poor and minority communities. It is estimated that by the year 2000, 25 million new workers will be needed in the United States and that white males can account for only 15 percent of this number (Haberman, 1988). Continuation of current trends of school failure among some minority groups will severely jeopardize the work force participation of millions of citizens. Early childhood education is equally concerned with these problems. Alexander and Entwistle (1988) have pointed out that school failure is predictable by the end of the primary grades, making early childhood a critical time for achievement. In addition, preschool interventions have been shown to have long-term effects on children's social and educational futures, placing them in the forefront of the struggle for educational equity (Berrueta-Clement et al., 1984).

The question of how schools can achieve excellence and racial and cultural equity has been debated strenuously over the past 25 years. Many educators, professional groups, and public policy makers believe that one way of improving schools is to have teaching staffs that reflect the racial and cultural diversity of the United States. It is argued that having teachers of every ethnic, racial, and cultural background offers opportunities for all children to see representatives of their own and other groups in the status roles of teachers and principals. Having minority people in leadership roles can provide powerful motivation for their children to achieve in school. Yet since the 1960s, the effort to increase the number of minority teachers has waxed and waned. In 1988, fewer minority students were preparing for careers in education than in the past (American Council on Education, 1988b).

The label "minority" refers to racial, cultural, and cultural/linguistic groups that are outside of the mainstream of American life—African-Americans, Hispanics (Mainland Puerto Rican, Mexican-American, Central and South American), Native Americans, and Asian-Americans. Differences in social class, geography, family values and preferences, and individual differences all create variations within each group in terms of their participation in the mainstream. Asians, for instance, may be recent Laotians, or Vietnamese immigrants, or third generation Chinese and Japanese citizens. Spanish speaking people may be illegal aliens just arrived from Mexico or Central or South America, Cuban emigrants, or Puerto Rican citizens. Whether they are newly arrived or have been American citizens for many generations, whether they are rich or poor, educated or not, these groups experience greater difficulty participating in mainstream institutions than others do. Poor African-Americans, Native Americans, and Hispanics are the least represented among teaching professionals. They are least likely to have access to careers in teaching because of poor elementary and secondary school preparation and/or indifferent and racist attitudes in colleges and universities.

The pool of minority teachers is growing smaller in relation to the population. While minorities constitute 26% of the American schoolchildren, they are less than 12.5% of the teachers. By 1990 minorities will have grown to 30% of the child population, and the percentage of teachers will have shrunk to 5% (Whitehurst, Witty, & Wiggins, 1988). Graduates from the historic black colleges declined by 37% between 1981–82 and 1985–86, and Laredo State University, which serves a predominantly Mexican-American student body, reports that the number of students in its elementary and secondary teacher preparation program dropped from 162 in 1984 to 95 in 1985 due to the introduction of qualifying tests (Fields, 1988).

The decline in African-Americans attending college is all the more dramatic when compared with the increasing number completing high school. The percentage of African-Americans who finished high school has risen sharply since 1970, while the number enrolled in institutions of higher education has decreased since 1976 (Gibbs, 1988). This means that although African-Americans are completing high school at about the same rate as white Americans, they are not moving on to higher education at the same rate. One explanation for this is that the poor quality of high school education available to African-American children ill prepares them for additional education. The high school test scores of school districts serving large numbers of African-American children are well below the national average, as are SAT scores. In addition, the perception of many African-American students is that higher education will not bring them rewards commensurate with their effort. There is evidence for such a perspective: The opportunities and earnings of

African-Americans who have completed college are considerably lower than those of whites with the same education (Ogbu, 1973).

The failure of minorities on qualifying examinations for teaching positions is also a cause for alarm. A survey on the effects of testing on the supply of minority teachers revealed a high failure rate. For instance, in California in 1986–87, 34 percent of African-Americans, and 59 percent of Mexican-Americans passed the test for a teaching credential (Fields, 1988).

Should there be different criteria for teachers from underrepresented groups? In 1943, when integration was not a high social or educational priority, Snyder wrote,

> In some cases there may be a certain justification for relaxing selection standards to ensure the employment of a minimum number of local persons on the assumption that there should be on every teaching staff individuals so thoroughly conversant with local conditions and with the basic community mores that they can help to orient teachers from outside, aid non-residents in avoiding pitfalls into which their lack of familiarity with the community might unwittingly lead them, and serve as interpreters between the community and the non-local teachers when necessary. (p. 142)

This perspective is being advocated today by many educators who are concerned about the diminishing number of minority teachers available to teach in public schools.

There is not universal approval for changing standards to encourage diversity in college enrollees. Many citizens insist that no students should be given preferential treatment in enrollment, and quotas to ensure diversity have been declared unacceptable by the courts. Some educators have been equally adamant that rules should not be bent in order to admit minority students. Such a pristine position flies in the face of the fact that colleges and universities traditionally retained special admission standards for the children of alumni, wealthy contributors, and other groups seen as advantageous to the school or the community.

### Standardized College Entrance Tests

One of the immediate causes of the shortage of minority teachers is the increased use of standardized tests to determine access to teacher education programs and to teaching certificates. Minorities generally perform less well than whites on these tests, and thus their increased use has had a disproportionate effect. Fields (1988) says that "tens of thousands of black, Hispanic, American Indian, and other minority group students have been prevented from entering teacher-education programs in the past few years because they did not pass state-required standardized tests" (Fields, 1988).

In response to a lawsuit charging sex discrimination, in 1989 the U.S. District Court in Manhattan said that the use of SAT scores alone as the basis for awarding scholarships is discriminatory because young women are excluded from consideration due to their lower scores. The judge noted that the scholarships are intended to reward past performance and that the SAT is not a measure of this, since women's high school grades equal or exceed those of men even though women's SAT scores average 60 points lower. This may open the door for minorities to challenge the use of standardized tests as the sole basis for financial assistance and admission into programs.

Is the SAT culturally biased? Holden (1989) asserted that no evidence of race or sex bias has been found in college admission tests and that they predict well first-year college grades. Supporters of testing contend that though certain groups of students—because of their poorer preparation, cultural embeddedness, or biological inadequacies—do less well on these tests, it is not evidence of their bias.

SAT scores reflect the overlap between test criteria and the grading system of colleges and universities. Both are biased toward particular skills and values found more often in one social group than in others; that is, whites, as the dominant group in the society, receive the highest scores on tests and the highest course grades. To the extent other groups share in these skills and values, their scores and grades are also higher. Interestingly, the SAT overpredicts for African-Americans—they actually get lower grades than expected (Holden, 1989). There are several possible reasons for this: It may be the professors, who generally are white, are less able to judge the academic competence of African-Americans and/or undervalue their achievements.

Scores on the SAT also have implications for Asian-American students. Their math scores predict their college performance better than their scores on the verbal section, and they typically have higher math and lower verbal scores than whites. Raising the requirements on the verbal section of the test, as has been suggested, would have a greater effect on them than on whites. For both whites and Asian-Americans, high school grade point average is a better predictor of freshman grades than test scores are (SAT Results Differ, 1989), suggesting that the overlap between the high schools whites and Asians attend and their colleges is greater than that between the test and their colleges.

## State Teacher Examinations

Standardized tests also sharply limit the number of minority students who complete the requirements for teacher certification. Fields (1988) reported that in 19 states where test failures were reported by race, 38,000 African-Americans, Hispanics, Asian-Americans, American Indians, and other minorities did not pass the state examination. The high failure rate of these potential teachers is presumably explained by the poor quality of their general education as well as by the teacher preparation program. Many critics of competency examinations point out that the minorities who fail are the same ones who do poorly on other standardized tests because of their linguistic and cultural differences. While test makers assert that the tests correct for cultural bias, the huge failure rate of minorities sharply limits the number of students who complete teacher education programs.

Haberman (1988) recommended that tutoring and academic support should be provided by programs to ensure that more students are able to pass the tests that now bar their way to careers in teaching. Students can be prepared for norm-referenced standardized tests if faculty counsel and coach them within the context of a trusting relationship (Haberman, 1988, p. 12).

## Financial Assistance

Financial assistance is a barrier to greater participation by minority students in higher education. Cutbacks in student aid made by the Carter and Reagan administrations seem to have had little effect on white enrollment (it has risen slightly), but African-American and Hispanic enrollment has dropped sharply. Minority students tend to be poorer and respond more strongly to financial aid than other students (Jackson, 1988).

The American Council on Education survey results (1988b) show that fewer first-year college students participate in federal aid programs than in the past. This means that students are more dependent on themselves and their families to pay for their education. Since the income of 53 percent of African-American families was under $19,999 in 1985 as compared with only 15 percent of white families, tuition represents a disproportionate burden in the African-American community. According to Gibbs (1988), in view of this financial hardship African-Americans actually show a greater willingness to sacrifice for higher education than whites do.

The decrease in scholarship assistance is particularly discouraging to early childhood education students. Average salaries for teachers in schools accredited by the National Association for the Education of Young Children, schools whose quality is presumably highest, are approximately half of those in public schools (Preschool Salaries Lagging, 1989). This means that minority day care and Head Start teachers have even less income than whites from which to pay tuition and repay student loans.

## Racism

Mason (1988) notes that some of the barriers to African-American enrollment are psychological. Since the mid-1980s the number of racist incidents on largely white college campuses has increased dramatically. Even the traditionally liberal Ivy League colleges have not been immune to such outbreaks. Minority students are often outraged and angry about racist occurrences or depressed and uncomfortable in an environment with which they are not familiar — and in which they are often treated with disdain or paternalism. There are usually few role models and mentors among faculty and graduate students. The more prominent research institutions are particularly apt to have few minority faculty or graduate students and to be unwelcoming to minority students (Olson, 1988).

"Institutional atmosphere" plays a critical role in the recruitment and retention of minority students (Olson, 1988). Smith (1988) recommended increasing the number of African-American faculty in schools of education as a step toward increasing the sensitivity to and encouragement of minority students. He pointed out that in the 1970s, 50 percent of all Ph.D.s were obtained in education, and thus there should be a substantial pool from which to draw faculty, yet there are few African-American faculty in higher education. Berger (1989) noted that at Teachers College, Columbia University, only about 4 percent of the 130 full-time faculty are African-American. To increase the number of minority faculty, colleges and universities will need to recruit more intensely for graduate programs.

Most colleges recruit only the best-prepared minority students to enroll; however, a few institutions are working to expand the pool of potential students. Connecticut College, for instance, is recruiting high school students and their teachers to attend institutes at the college with the faculty. The institutes are designed to help students develop the academic skills necessary for college. In addition, because the students will come in a group from the same school and with their own teachers, their comfort (and presumably their performance) on campus will be enhanced. The president of the college said the students should derive from this experience a feeling of "connectedness" to the college (Hechinger, 1989).

While many of these efforts are expected to expand the pool of prospective minority teachers, they may have a devastating effect on Head Start and day care. As more minority teachers complete college programs, they will probably be less willing to work for the lower pay characteristic of these programs. Unless pay and benefits become more equal, the better-educated teachers may abandon these important jobs.

## MEN IN EARLY CHILDHOOD PROGRAMS

Minority groups are not the only groups underrepresented in early childhood programs. The overwhelming majority of teachers entering elementary education are female (Murnane, Singer, & Willett, 1988), and day care is a female-dominated profession. Men are the underrepresented group of early childhood teachers: In 1985, only 5 percent of early childhood personnel were men (Seifert, 1988).

Many educators, parents, and public policy makers are eager to increase the presence of men in early childhood programs. The call for male teachers has been heard since the early 1940s and is based on a perceived need for more masculine qualities to be part of children's school and/or day care experiences. Advocacy for a greater male presence has increased as the number of children from mother-headed households has risen. It is suggested that males in schools can help compensate for their absence in the home (Seifert, 1988).

There is little research to justify this expectation. The assumption that men would provide a masculine model that would serve to neutralize the overwhelming feminine environment found in early childhood centers has received little support. Most research on gender differences in male and female teachers has not shown sex-specific differences in how teachers work with children (Seifert, 1988; Skeen, Robinson, & Coleman, 1986). The hope that men will help compensate for the absence of fathers in the home has been clouded because of the high turnover in their employment, making enduring relationships between them and children less likely (Robinson, 1979).

Susan B. Anthony identified one possible reason for the small numbers of men choosing elementary education as a career. She said that because women were thought of as incompetent, men selecting teaching as a career "tacitly admitted they had 'no more brains than a woman'" (Warren, 1985, p. 9). Salaries were kept low because the practitioners were women who, with few opportunities to earn more, were willing to work for those salaries. Low salaries continue to be cited as a factor in why so few men select teaching as a career (Robinson, 1979).

During the 1970s the number of men in the field increased steadily, although Robinson (1979) noted a relationship between high unemployment and the number of men working in child care. However, men also drop out of early childhood teaching more often than women, and men in early childhood teaching drop out more often than men in traditionally "masculine professions." Robinson (1988) compared a sample of day care teachers and engineers for two years and found in that short time 70% of the men teachers in the sample left the field of early childhood teaching as compared with 30% of the women teachers and 30% of male engineers. Evidently, men who originally select early childhood education as their profession are less likely to continue in the field than are men who begin engineering careers or women who enter early childhood teaching.

Factors suggested to account for the small number of men entering and remaining in early childhood programs are gender-role traditions in the United States, beliefs that men are unsuited to work with young children, prejudice of female teachers and administrators, and concern about possible sexual molestation of children by men teachers.

## CONCLUSION

Early childhood teacher preparation is in a period of rapid change. The new popularity of early childhood programs and the concomitant emphasis on improving school quality make the training of teachers a high priority. Teacher education institutions must face important issues if they are to meet the challenge. Colleges and universities must find the energy to re-examine and seek change in some traditional practices for the recruitment, selection, and retention of education students.

More rigorous academic standards for entrance into teacher education programs and increased intellectual content in teacher education courses raise questions about the appropriate relationship between the liberal arts and sciences and professional education — between scholarship and teaching — particularly in the early grades. The new emphasis requires that teachers in training be among the most gifted college students in the depth and breadth of their formal education. Will this result in teachers better able to stimulate and support the development of young children?

Will such high standards exclude minorities, thus creating a two-tiered educational system: one largely white with state-certified teachers in public schools, the other heavily minority with uncertified teachers in day care and Head Start? If so, what will the implications of this be for educational success of minority children?

Leaders in the field of early childhood teacher education believe that the most pressing need is to clarify and define what is unique about early childhood education as a discipline (National Association for the Education of Young Children, 1988). This is important because there is so little agreement as to what should be assessed in teacher education. Is too much stress placed on the kind of information that lends itself to paper and pencil tests rather than on the knowledge that underlies effective teaching? Jones (1987) complained that students spend too much time memorizing facts rather than understanding content. She recommended that courses in child development be designed to be personally meaningful so that students are sensitive to their own growth and development as well as that of others. Obviously, assessment of personal meaningfulness does not lend itself to objective measures.

Professional education courses are faulted for not equipping students for the realities of teaching. The problems confronting teachers in schools (cultural differences, working mothers, violence, drugs) require a greater range of knowledge and skills than is traditionally covered in courses in pedagogy. Katz (NAEYC, 1988) questioned whether teacher education programs should prepare students to practice in schools as they exist or to practice "state of the art" education, which may conflict with current school practice. If teacher training institutions continue to provide students with skills and knowledge that are impractical and irrelevant to schools, will new teachers soon drop out of teaching careers despite completion of a training program?

The ways in which the preparation of early childhood teachers should be qualitatively different from that of elementary or secondary teachers must be addressed and defended. Early childhood education demands skills often ignored by teacher education programs, such as working effectively with parents and collaborating with other social service resources in the community.

Does the absence of men in early childhood programs deprive young children of an opportunity to learn and develop? If so, what can be done about it?

What effect will the dramatic increase in the number of early childhood programs have on their quality? Hewes (1988) points out that the increased enrollments in kindergarten led to lower standards for kindergarten teachers. Will the results be similar in the 1990s for preschool education? What teacher training regulations are necessary to guarantee quality in preschool and day care programs?

The current turmoil in teacher education will inevitably lead to some needed changes. But Quisenberry (1987) pointed out that much of what is wrong with early childhood programs cannot be solved in teacher training institutions alone. She cited such factors as the low esteem of the teaching profession, inadequate financial aid, poor pay, and isolation of beginning teachers as also contributing to poor quality of candidates and graduate teachers. State policies, budget problems, demographic shifts, and university politics all conspire to make change more difficult.

Early childhood teacher education is at a critical juncture, and the attempt to improve it will require concerted effort by institutions of higher education, state and federal policy and regulatory agencies, as well as the schools. To what extent these changes will result in greater success for America's schoolchildren remains to be seen.

## REFERENCES

Alexander, K., & Entwistle, D. (1988). *Achievement in the first 2 years of school: Patterns & processes.* Monograph of the Society for Research in Child Development, Vol. 53, No. 2.

American Council on Education. (1988a). *One third of a nation.* Denver, CO: Education Commission of the States.

American Council on Education. (1988b). *Freshman survey results.* Cooperative Institutional Research Program, University of California, Los Angeles.

Andrew, L., Parks, D., & Nelson, L. (1985). Phi Delta Kappa Commission on teacher/faculty morale. In *Administrators' handbook for improving faculty morale.* Bloomington, IN: Phi Delta Kappa.

Association of Teacher Educators. (1985). *Developing career ladders in teaching.* Reston, VA: Association of Teacher Educators.

Berger, J. (1989). Teachers College is pondering new challenges. *New York Times,* January 18, p. A21.

Berk, L. (1985). Relationship of education to child-oriented attitudes, job satis-

faction, and behaviors toward children. *Child Care Quarterly, 14,* 103–29.
Berrueta-Clement, J. R., Schweinhart, L. J., Barnett, W. S., Epstein, A. E., & Weikart, D. P. (1984). *Changed lives: The effects of the Perry Preschool Program on youths through age 19.* Ypsilanti, MI: High Scope Press.
Bloom, B. (1985). *Developing talent in young people.* New York: Ballantine.
Bolster, A. (1985). Toward a more effective model of research on teaching. *Harvard Educational Review, 53,* 294–308.
Carlson, D. (1987). Teachers as political actors: From reproductive theory to the crisis of schooling. *Harvard Educational Review, 57,* 282–308.
Carnegie Forum on Education and the Economy, Task Force on Teaching as a Profession (1986). *A nation prepared: Teachers for the 21st Century.* Washington, DC: Carnegie Forum.
Certifying and Rewarding Teaching Excellence: The National Board for Professional Teaching Standards. (1989, Spring). *Carnegie Quarterly,* 1–9.
Clark, C. (1988). Teacher preparation contributions of research on teacher thinking. *Educational Researcher, 17,* 5–12.
Committee for Economic Development. (1987). *Children in need: Investment strategies for the educationally disadvantaged.* New York: CED.
Fields, C. (1988). Poor test scores bar many minority students from teacher training. *Chronicle of Higher Education,* November 2, p. A1.
Gibbs, J. (1988). *Young, black and male in America.* Dover, MA: Auburn House.
Haberman, M. (1988). Proposals for recruiting minority teachers: Promising practices and attractive detours. (ERIC Document Reproduction Service No. ED 292 760)
Hart, A. (1987). A career ladder's effect on teacher career and work attitudes. *American Educational Research Journal,* 479–503.
Hechinger, F. (1989). About education. *New York Times.* February 1, p. B7.
Hewes, D. (1988, Fall). Kindergarten teacher training in the United States from 1879 to 1920. *National Association of Early Childhood Educators, 9,* 13–17.
Holden, C. (1989). Court ruling rekindles controversy over SATs. *Science, 243,* 885–87.
Hunter, C. (1977). An interpersonal relations and group process approach to effective education for young children. *Journal of School Psychology, 15,* 141–51.
Jackson, G. (1988, September/October). Financial aid and minority access. *Change,* 48–49.
Jackson, P. (1987). Facing our ignorance. *Teachers College Record, 88,* 385–89.
Jones, E. (1987). *Teaching adults: An active learning approach.* Washington, DC: National Association for the Education of Young Children.
Marx, F., & Seligson, M. (1988). *The Public School Early Childhood Study.* New York: Bank Street College of Education.
Murnane, R., Singer, J., & Willet, J. (1988). The career paths of teachers:

Implications for teachers supply and methodological lessons for research. *Educational Researcher, 17*(6), 22-30.
National Association for the Education of Young Children. (1988). Early childhood teacher education: Traditions and trends, an executive summary of colloquium proceedings. *Young Children, 44*(1), 53-57.
National Association for the Education of Young Children. (1982). *Early Childhood Teacher Education Guidelines.* Washington, DC: NAEYC.
National Association of School Boards of Education. (1988). *Right from the start.* Alexandria, VA: NASBE.
National Black Child Development Institute. (1985). *Who bears the burden? Black children in America.* Washington, DC: NBCDI.
Ogbu, J. (1973). *Minority education and caste.* New York: Academic Press.
Olson, C. (1988). Recruiting and retraining minority graduate students: A systems perspective. *Journal of Negro Education, 57,* 31-42.
Phillips, C. (1988). Briefing paper for the National Association of School Boards of Education (Draft). Council for Early Childhood Professional Recognition.
Preschool Salaries Lagging, Says New GAO Report. (1989). *Report on Preschool Programs, 21,* August 30, 181.
Quisenberry, N. (1987). Teacher education: Challenge for the future. *Childhood Education, 63,* 243-47.
Robinson, B. (1979). An update on the status of men in early child care work. *Child Welfare, 58,* 471-77.
Robinson, B. (1988). Vanishing breed: Men in child care programs. *Young Children, 43,* 54-58.
Ruopp, R., Travers, J., Glantz, F., & Coelen, C. (1979). *Children at the center.* (Vol. 1, Final report of the National Day Care Study.) Cambridge, MA: Abt Associates.
SAT Results Differ for Asians and Whites. (1989). *Chronicle of Higher Education.* February 1, p. A1.
Seifert, K. (1988). Men in early childhood education. In B. Spodek, O. N. Saracho, & D. C. Peters (Eds.), *Professionalism and the early childhood practitioner.* New York: Teachers College Press.
Skeen, P., Robinson, B., & Coleman, M. (1986). Gender role attitudes of professional female educators toward men in early childhood education. *Psychological Reports, 59,* 723-30.
Smith, A. W. (1988). Maintaining the pipeline of black teachers for the twenty-first century. *Journal of Negro Education, 57,* 166-77.
Snyder, H. (1943). *Educational inbreeding.* New York: Teachers College Press.
Spodek, B., & Saracho, O. N. (1982). The preparation and certification of early childhood personnel. In B. Spodek (Ed.), *Handbook of research in early childhood education* (pp. 399-425). New York: Free Press.
Thirty Colleges to Participate in Project. (1988). *Chronicle of Higher Education,* November 16, A15.

Update on Minority Groups. (1989). *Chronicle of Higher Education*, January 25, p. 37A.
Warren, D. (1985). Learning from experience: History and teacher education. *Educational Researcher, 14*, 5-12.
Whitebook, M. (1986). The teacher shortage. *Young Children, 41*, 10-11.
Whitebook, M., & Granger, R. (1989). Mommy, who's going to be my teacher today? *Young Children, 44*, 11-15.
Whitehurst, W., Witty, E., & Wiggins, S. (1988). Racial equality: Teaching excellence. In J. Sikula (Ed.), *Action in teacher education: 10th year anniversary issue* (pp. 159-167). Reston, VA: Association of Teacher Educators.
U.S. Department of Education (1987). *What's happening in teacher testing.* Washington, DC: U.S. Government Printing Office.

CHAPTER 10

# The Influence of Recent Educational Reforms on Early Childhood Teacher Education Programs

James M. Cooper
Corinne E. Eisenhart

The 1980s were a period of educational reform of astounding proportions. During the decade state legislatures passed well over 1,000 pieces of educational legislation related to teachers, teaching, and teacher education, a substantial percentage of which have been put into practice. Therefore, teaching has surely been "reformed" if measured by the sheer volume of legislation (Darling-Hammond & Berry, 1988).

Reviewing the reform efforts of the decade, educational policy analysts have identified two "waves" of reform. The first wave, perhaps characterized best by *A Nation At Risk*, published in 1983, called for establishing higher standards in education. This wave of reform activities was based on a belief that our expectations for students, teachers, and schools had eroded over time and that the remedy was to raise our expectations and to enforce higher standards. Thus, legislators, governors, and other educational policy makers implemented legislation and policy that lengthened the school day and year; required students to earn more credits to graduate from high school; increased academic requirements in such subjects as mathematics, science, and foreign languages; required passing competency examinations as a condition for high school graduation; and required licensure examinations for teachers, to name but a few of such policies.

The second wave of educational reform was initiated in 1985 with the publication of reports from the Holmes Group, the Carnegie Forum on Education and the Economy, the National Governors' Association, and the Education Commission of the States, among others. Although these reports differed in a number of ways, they all cited the critical importance of improving the status and power of teachers by "professionalizing" the occupation of teaching. These reports all emphasized that improving education in our nation's elementary and secondary schools was dependent on attracting and retaining good teachers. Increased salaries for teachers were important but not sufficient for improving the quality of the teaching work force. Only by making teaching more attractive and more professional, these reports argued, could capable people be attracted to and retained in teaching. Furthermore, this could not be accomplished without granting teachers and principals more autonomy in making educational decisions—in other words, professionalizing teaching. Frank Newman (1986), President of the Education Commission of the States, characterized the difference between the first and second waves of reform by stating that in the first wave teachers were the objects of change, but in the second wave they had to be the agents of change.

The bargain proposed by the second wave of reformers was greater regulation of teachers through more rigorous preparation, licensure, and selection, in return for deregulation of teaching, that is, fewer rules on what and how to teach. As Darling-Hammond and Berry (1988) point out, this is the bargain that all professions make with society: The profession guarantees the competence of its members in exchange for professional control over work structure and standards of practice.

## RECENT REFORM TRENDS AND EARLY CHILDHOOD TEACHER EDUCATION

Although this chapter examines the influence of the reform efforts on early childhood teacher education programs, most of the reforms are aimed at all levels of education, not specifically the preparation of early childhood teachers. In fact, most of the reform legislation and regulations largely ignore early childhood teacher education. Many of the reforms seem to be intended for secondary school teachers, but have been applied to all teachers, including teachers of special education and early childhood education. Therefore, the reform efforts will be reviewed with respect to their effect on preparing early childhood education teachers and, in particular, their congruence or incongruence with the *Early Childhood Teacher Education Guidelines*, a position statement of the National Association for the Education of Young Children (NAEYC, 1982).

Defining early childhood as "birth through age eight," the guidelines address nine components of programs, including program objectives and standards for each of the components. The curriculum component is most relevant to this topic because it identifies the general areas of knowledge that should be addressed in an early childhood teacher education program. Among these areas are

1. General education that provides knowledge and understanding of the liberal arts; humanities; and social, biological, and physical sciences; and that extends candidates' written and oral communication competence; mathematical skill; and knowledge of the world through study in a range of scholarly disciplines.
2. Professional studies in three essential areas: (a) professional foundations; (b) instructional knowledge of the principles and methods of teaching and learning; and (c) practice in a variety of supervised field experiences.

The standards for the foundations and the instructional knowledge areas call for theoretical and research knowledge and practical skills in

Human development
Historical, philosophical, psychological, and social foundations of early childhood education
Curriculum for teaching young children
Observation and recording of children's behavior
Working with atypical children
Interpersonal communication
Family and community relations
Values and ethics
Comprehension of cultural diversity
Legislation and public policy as it affects children, families, and programs for children

In the practice area, the standards recommend that field work be taken in conjunction with course work in professional foundations and instructional knowledge. Additionally, the guidelines propose that at least 150 hours of student teaching be spent in each of two different settings, serving children of two different age groups, one of which must be infants-toddlers or preprimary-age children.

Before examining the influences of specific reform efforts on early childhood teacher education, it is important to note that the reforms, as implemented across the various states, are often contradictory. It is difficult to identify any of the reforms around which there exists a national consensus. Thus, for example, one state may have placed a cap on the maximum number of credits a prospective teacher may earn in professional education, while another state may have increased the number of credits required in professional education.

Recognizing this lack of a national consensus in implementing reforms, as well as the reformers' use of a secondary model that basically disregarded many unique needs of early childhood teacher education, this chapter examines seven specific reform efforts:

1. abolition of the undergraduate degree in education and the requirement of a liberal arts major;
2. extended programs;
3. maximum caps on professional education hours;
4. extended field experiences and induction period;
5. alternative certification;
6. teacher certification and performance tests;
7. specific vs. broad credentialing.

## Abolition of Undergraduate Education Degree/ Extended Programs/Credit Hour Caps in Education

A widely held perception among the general public and educational policy makers that emerged during the 1980s was that too many teachers had an inadequate understanding of the subjects they were teaching. This perception was formed in part by the poor performances of many prospective teachers on such examinations as the Scholastic Aptitude Test, the National Teacher Examination, and the various basic skills tests that different states required either for entry into teacher education or for state licensure. As policy makers were increasing the standards for high school students and demanding more academic emphasis in the secondary curriculum, similar attention was expected to be given to the teacher education curriculum.

In 1986 both the Holmes Group report, *Tomorrow's Teachers*, and the Carnegie Forum's report, *A Nation Prepared*, recommended abolishing the undergraduate degree in education, requiring a major in the liberal arts, and moving professional education to the graduate level. In fact, California for years had required that the baccalaureate degree be in the liberal arts. By recommending at least a year of graduate work in professional education, followed by a year of supervised internship, both the Holmes Group and the Carnegie Forum recognized that a strong liberal arts background, ample professional training, and lengthy supervised practice were all essential aspects for producing well-educated and well-trained beginning teachers.

While accepting the notion that beginning teachers needed more liberal arts education, policy makers in a number of states were reluctant to require an extra year or two at the graduate level to prepare teachers. Such a requirement would obviously be costly, both for the state and for the student. Furthermore, many states were facing predicted teacher shortages, and policy makers were concerned that requiring an additional year or two of college teacher education would cause enrollments to plummet. Many college and university officials, including large numbers of teacher educators, shared these concerns.

The result in some states, such as Texas, Virginia, and New Jersey, was an emphasis on the liberal arts and subject-matter specialties at the expense of professional education. This was accomplished by abolishing the undergraduate education major, requiring an arts and sciences major, and limiting the number of credit hours that could be earned in education courses as part of the baccalaureate degree. In Texas, no more than 18 credit hours could be taken in education courses, including student teaching and field experiences; in Virginia, a cap of 18 hours in education courses, excluding student teaching and field experiences, was implemented; and in New Jersey, a maximum of 30 credit hours in professional education could be taken. At the same time, advisory boards and education commissions in other states, such as Washington, Connecticut, and New York, endorsed the Holmes Group's and Carnegie Forum's recommendations to move teacher education from the undergraduate to the graduate level.

What are the implications of these reform policies for early childhood teacher education programs? Clearly, the NAEYC guidelines for early childhood teacher education programs suggest extensive work in both the liberal arts and professional education, as well as field experiences in schools and other early childhood settings. However, the NAEYC guidelines do not specify the number of credit hours that are expected in the general education and professional education areas, nor the recommended distribution between them. In fact, except for specifying the number of clock hours required for student teaching experiences, the NAEYC guidelines provide no quantitative expectations for any of the other standards. Nor do the NAEYC guidelines address the issue of whether the degree awarded for early childhood teacher education programs should be from arts and sciences, education, or child development. Thus, recommendations that call for abolishing the undergraduate education major and requiring a liberal arts major are not inimical to the NAEYC guidelines so long as ample room is left in the curriculum for professional education and field experiences. It is only when a baccalaureate degree in arts and sciences is required and credit hours in professional education courses are limited to a number insufficient to meet the NAEYC standards that the authors see a problem.

In Texas, which has imposed an 18-credit-hour cap (including student teaching), undergraduates specializing in early childhood education, as well as bilingual education, special education, reading, or English as a second language, may obtain additional credits in professional education. Students of early childhood education typically take 24 credit hours in pedagogy, foundations, and child development (Vodicka, 1989). Virginia excludes student teaching and other field experiences from its 18-hour cap on professional education courses at the baccalaureate level, while New Jersey includes student teaching and field experiences within its 30-hour cap on professional education courses. It should be noted, however, that in Virginia the 18-hour cap on professional education courses may be exceeded when universities or colleges provide persuasive justification to state officials. Nonetheless, whether an early childhood teacher education program can adequately address the NAEYC guidelines and standards within the caps imposed in Virginia, Texas, and New Jersey is not clear and is probably a matter of judgment.

With the exceptions of human development, which is often taught in psychology courses; family and community relations, which may be taught in sociology; and values and ethics, which are taught in philosophy and religious studies departments, most of the professional foundations and instructional knowledge areas of the NAEYC guidelines are not currently taught in arts and sciences courses. Even for the topics that are taught, their implications for teaching young children are unlikely to be addressed in arts and sciences courses that are not specifically tailored for teaching majors. It is possible, but unlikely, that the professional foundations and instructional knowledge areas of the NAEYC guidelines could be assumed by courses in arts and sciences. A more likely scenario, however, would be that these topics would continue to be taught in departments or schools of education to the extent that the state maximum limitations on hours in professional education would permit, with a less thorough treatment of the topics the probable outcome.

Therefore, as long as teacher education is restricted to a baccalaureate program requiring an arts and sciences major, and the number of hours allowed for professional education is limited, the effect is likely to be deleterious for the abilities of early childhood education teachers to work effectively with young children. However, it appears to the authors that requiring an arts and sciences major at the undergraduate level but uncapping the credit-hour limits on professional education for undergraduate students, or extending professional education to the graduate level, would strengthen the preparation for teachers of young children.

## Extended Field Experiences and Induction Period

Although the prevailing trend is toward de-emphasizing education courses in favor of liberal arts courses, this trend does not include practica and field experiences. In fact, state policies have increased the practical experiences required throughout teacher education programs. For example, the required time spent in field experiences prior to student teaching was increased to 100 hours in Colorado and Wisconsin, and 150 hours in Kentucky (AACTE, 1988). Similarly, student teaching requirements were lengthened, for example, 10 weeks in North Carolina and North Dakota; 12 weeks in Oklahoma, Pennsylvania, South Carolina, Kentucky, and Mississippi; and 14 weeks in New Mexico and Wisconsin (AACTE, 1986).

The direction toward increased field experiences and lengthened student teaching reflects a belief by policy makers, and many teachers, that an individual really learns to teach by experience, not by taking education courses. Supporting this trend is the fact that 16 states have legislated entry-year programs designed to provide beginning teachers with support and assistance during that critical first year of teaching (AACTE, 1987).

The increased requirements for practica and lengthened student teaching being implemented in many states are quite compatible with the NAEYC guidelines for early childhood teacher education programs. These guidelines emphasize the need for field work that includes observation of and participation with children and adults in early childhood settings, including interaction with families as well as children from a variety of cultural and socioeconomic backgrounds. The student teaching guidelines propose a minimum of 150 clock hours spent in each of two different settings, serving children of two different age groups, with one setting involving infants-toddlers or preprimary-age children. Lengthening the student teaching period to between 10 and 14 weeks will enable student teachers to spend two 150-clock-hour experiences with two different age groups of children, whereas earlier requirements of 6 to 8 weeks of student teaching would not provide enough time to meet this standard.

## Alternative Certification

In times of teacher shortages most states have traditionally allowed individuals who wish to teach but have not completed approved teacher education programs to be hired on an "emergency certification" basis. In 1983, 46 states allowed such substandard emergency certification, and 27 permitted certificates to be issued to teachers who did not hold a bachelors degree (Feistritzer, 1984).

As part of the 1980s reforms to improve teacher education and licensure some states developed "alternative certification" programs as a substitute for emergency certificates. These alternative certification programs are designed to attract and prepare teachers from outside the standard teacher education routes. These programs generally enroll individuals with at least a bachelors degree, usually in an arts and sciences discipline, and offer curricular shortcuts and special assistance that lead to a standard teaching credential. An often stated rationale for these alternative programs is that there are many individuals with bachelors degrees in the liberal arts who want to teach but do not want to endure all those "Mickey Mouse" education courses required as part of traditional teacher education programs. Thus, although alternative certification programs may have higher standards than emergency certification procedures, they nonetheless de-emphasize teacher education and legitimize different entries into teaching. The number of states that have implemented alternative routes to certification has increased from eight in 1984 to twenty-three in 1986 (Feistritzer, 1986).

Interestingly, the overwhelming majority of states that have implemented alternative certification programs specify that only secondary teachers and those needed for "shortage areas" (bilingual education, for example) can use the alternative certification route (McKibben, 1988). Of the twenty-one states surveyed by McKibben that have alternative certification routes, only six seemed to permit prospective teachers interested in early childhood licensure to use the alternative route. Follow-up telephone calls to officials at the American Association of Colleges for Teacher Education and the Southern Regional Education Board revealed that of those six states only New Jersey truly allows a shortcut certification route for prospective early childhood teachers. Although alternative certification programs have received a great deal of attention in both the public and professional education press, their applicability to early childhood teacher education seems to be almost nil.

## Teacher Certification and Performance Testing

By 1986, all but four states had mandated teacher competency tests in either basic skills, subject-matter knowledge, or professional knowledge (Darling-Hammond & Berry, 1988), revealing a staunch conviction by state policy makers that many prospective teachers lacked the knowledge and skills necessary for effective teaching. In addition to paper and pencil tests, such as the National Teacher Examinations, 18 states required beginning teachers to undergo on-the-job performance assessments during their first year of teaching (AACTE, 1986).

Paper-and-pencil competency tests do not seem to affect early childhood education teachers any differently than teachers at other educational levels. That is, there is no evidence with which we are familiar indicating that teachers of young children are more or less affected by these competency tests than secondary teachers are. On-the-job performance tests, on the other hand, would seem to favor elementary over secondary teachers because these performance tests tend to be based on behaviors related to teaching basic skills at the elementary grade level. Although these performance assessments are intended to measure generic (as opposed to subject-specific) competencies that cut across grade levels and subject matter, most of the research from which these competencies were derived was conducted in grades 2 through 5, in reading and mathematics. This fact, and the observation that elementary and early childhood teachers usually take more credit hours in education, where these competencies are likely to be addressed, would seem to favor early childhood and elementary teachers over their secondary counterparts.

In Virginia, under the direction of the Beginning Teacher Assistance Program (BTAP), new teachers are assessed on 14 competencies by specially trained observers. Beginning with the first BTAP assessment (Autumn 1985), a greater percentage of elementary teachers have demonstrated the required competencies when compared with secondary teachers. The latest data available (Autumn 1988) indicate that 88% of elementary teachers (K–6) demonstrated at least 12 of the 14 competencies, whereas only 83% of secondary teachers (7–12) demonstrated the same number of competencies. It is interesting to note on this specific assessment upper elementary teachers (4–6) performed slightly higher on BTAP competencies (90%) when compared with their early childhood counterparts (87%) (Caldwell, 1989).

The irony of on-the-job performance tests is that they measure teaching competencies that are likely to be taught in education, not arts and sciences, courses, precisely at a time when some of these same states are placing caps on the maximum number of education hours permitted in teacher education programs. Thus, beginning teachers' access to courses in which they would be taught these teaching competencies is being limited by state policy.

## Specific vs. Broad Credentialing

Prior to the 1980s many states certified teachers along broad categories, such as kindergarten through eighth grade or secondary science, rather than narrower grade ranges or more specific subject-matter specialties. These broad categories were created to give teachers and school systems more flexibility in teaching assignments. During the 1980s, in response to public concern that many teachers were inadequately prepared in the subjects they were teaching, some states began to require more specific credentialing in the subject matter and/or grade level in which the teachers were planning to teach.

At this time considerable variance exists in the licensing of early childhood educators (see Table 10.1). Almost half the states offer neither certification nor endorsement[1] for early childhood education, while 23 states and the District of Columbia have certification identified as "Early Childhood Education" (McCarthy, 1988). The variations among these 23 states range from actual certification in early childhood education to add-on endorsements to elementary education programs, with hybrid combinations in between. McCarthy (1988) reports that seven states have developed certification procedures that recognize a combination of training in both early childhood and special education. This is primarily a result of federal legislation, P.L. 99-457 (1986), which requires the provision of public education for children with special needs by age 3. This legislation amended P.L. 94-142 (1975), the Education for All Handicapped Children Act, which mandated that all children with disabilities be provided with a free appropriate education and related services designed to meet their special needs (Hume, 1987).

Even among states that offer early childhood certification there is a great range in what is meant by "early childhood." The early childhood certificate that covers prekindergarten or nursery to grade 3 is perhaps the most common, with five states sharing this pattern. Virginia, Geor-

**Table 10.1.** Early Childhood Teacher Certification: A National Perspective

|     | State | Range of Applicability | P & P | OTJ |
|-----|-------|------------------------|-------|-----|
| 1.  | Alabama | N-Grade 3 | x | |
| 2.  | Alaska | no | | |
| 3.  | Arizona | no | x | |
| 4.  | Arkansas | no (K endorsement) | x | |
| 5.  | California | no (K endorsement) | x | |
| 6.  | Colorado | 3–8 years | x | |
| 7.  | Connecticut | no | x | |
| 8.  | Delaware | N–K and K–Grade 3 | x | |
| 9.  | Florida | no (K endorsement) | x | x |
| 10. | Georgia | K–Grade 4 | x | x |
| 11. | Hawaii | no | x | |
| 12. | Idaho | no | x | |
| 13. | Illinois | birth–Grade 3 | x | |
| 14. | Indiana | 0–4 years (K–Grade 3) | x | x |
| 15. | Iowa | PreK–K | | |
| 16. | Kansas | 0–4 years | x | |
| 17. | Kentucky | no (K–Grade 4) | x | x |
| 18. | Louisiana | (N–K) | x | |
| 19. | Maine | no | x | x |
| 20. | Maryland | (N–K) | x | |
| 21. | Massachusetts | K–Grade 3 | x | |
| 22. | Michigan | no | | |
| 23. | Minnesota | (PreK–K) | x | |
| 24. | Mississippi | no | x | x |
| 25. | Missouri | N–Grade 3 | x | |
| 26. | Montana | no | x | |
| 27. | Nebraska | birth–K | x | |
| 28. | Nevada | no | x | x |
| 29. | New Hampshire | birth–Grade 3 | x | |
| 30. | New Jersey | (N–K) | x | |
| 31. | New Mexico | no | x | |
| 32. | New York | no | x | x |
| 33. | North Carolina | K–Grade 4 | x | x |
| 34. | North Dakota | no (K endorsement) | x | |
| 35. | Ohio | (PreK–K and K–Grade 3) | | |
| 36. | Oklahoma | N–Grade 2 | x | x |
| 37. | Oregon | no | x | x |

(*continued*)

**Table 10.1.** (*Continued*)

| | | | | |
|---|---|---|---|---|
| 38. Pennsylvania | N-Grade 3 | x | x |
| 39. Rhode Island | N-Grade 2 | x | |
| 40. South Carolina | K-Grade 4 | x | x |
| 41. South Dakota | (N endorsement) | x | x |
| 42. Tennessee | (K-Grade 3) | x | |
| 43. Texas | (Pre K-Grade 3) | x | x |
| 44. Utah | N-Grade 3 | | |
| 45. Vermont | birth-age 8 | x | x |
| 46. Virginia | N-K-Grade 4 | x | x |
| 47. Washington | N-Grade 3 | | x |
| 48. Washington D.C. | N-K | | |
| 49. West Virginia | N-K | x | |
| 50. Wisconsin | (EC and K endorsements) | | |
| 51. Wyoming | K-Grade 3 | x | |

NOTE:  ( ) = Endorsement, not early childhood certification
P & P = Paper and pencil test
OTJ = On-the-job performance test
N = Nursery school
K = Kindergarten

*Sources:* M. P. Burks (1988), *Requirements for certification. 1988-89* (53rd ed.). Chicago: University of Chicago Press, and J. McCarthy (1988, January), *State certification of early childhood teachers: An analysis of the 50 states and the District of Columbia.* (Prepared for NAEYC). Paper presented at the National Association for the Education of Young Children Early Childhood Teacher Education Colloquium, Miami, Florida.

gia, and North Carolina include grade 4 as part of their early childhood certificates. In several states only a preschool certificate is issued under the early childhood heading, with an elementary education certificate needed for kindergarten and beyond.

Although NAEYC cites standards for early childhood teacher certification, the specific boundaries of credentialing are not clear. Since early childhood is defined from birth to age 8, one would assume that the early childhood teacher would be certified to teach children within this age group. However, the skills needed to work with infants and toddlers certainly differ from those needed to teach in a primary classroom. Thus, should there be two distinct areas of early childhood certification: an infant-toddler certificate (birth to age 2) and a preschool-primary certificate (ages 3 to 8)? Would separate certification better meet the developmental needs of young children by enabling teachers to specialize, or would such licensing result in the fragmentation of early childhood education?

Narrow certification may allow early childhood teachers to become more expert in working with an age-specific group of children; however, it could severely limit their employment opportunities (McCarthy, 1988). This, in turn, may adversely affect the enrollments in early childhood teacher education programs (Lamme, McMillin, & Clark, 1983). Additionally, since a preschool-primary certification falls within the parameters of the public school setting, especially with the advent of four-year-old programs, would this result in higher salaries for preschool-primary teachers and less status for infant-toddler teachers? Certainly early childhood certification should ensure a continuity of quality education across the entire span of birth to age 8. McCarthy (1988) maintains that the "scope" of early childhood education is not as important as the "competencies" that are needed by teachers of young children. These competencies are clearly delineated in NAEYC's position statement, *Developmentally Appropriate Practice* (Bredekamp, 1987), and in Chapter 8 of this volume.

In 1982 the National Council for the Accreditation of Teacher Education (NCATE) adopted the NAEYC early childhood certification standards. Ideally, through the NCATE accreditation process, early childhood teacher education programs will become more consistent throughout the nation. This, in turn, could influence not only the scope of early childhood state certification, but the competencies of teachers as well. Nonetheless, the authors see no evidence that national consistency of early childhood teacher education programs and/or certification is likely in the near future.

## INFLUENCE OF THE REFORM MOVEMENT

Has the reform movement influenced early childhood teacher education programs? Certainly there has not been a direct impact. This is due primarily to two issues addressed earlier in this chapter. First, policy makers have almost exclusively used a secondary teacher education model when proposing reform and generally have not addressed the needs of early childhood teacher education. Second, most of the actual reform efforts have been "driven" by the individual state governors and legislators (e.g., development of prekindergarten programs); thus, the outcomes have been nationally inconsistent. As a result, although there have been many legislated "reforms," few have directly affected early childhood teacher education, nor have any proposed reforms received a national mandate.

This lack of a national consensus, especially relating to early childhood teacher education, is clearly evident when comparing the differences in state certification standards. Some states do not distinguish between elementary and early childhood education, and a K–6 category for certification is typically established. Other states consider early childhood to be a subset of elementary education. Thus, N–3 or K–4 certification patterns are evident. Still other states consider early childhood education a unique entity; in these states teachers may obtain a specialized early childhood certification, often extending from infancy to the age of 8. Early childhood is identified more as an age range than a grade level.

Perhaps the central issue that affects the variance in early childhood teacher certification is that of responsibility. At what age does the state accept responsibility for the education of children? In many states, the health, safety, and welfare, but not the education, of preschool children are considered state responsibilities. These states may have strict standards for day care facilities, but the licensure of the day care providers may be lax. Thus, the physical *care* or safety of preschool children is seen as a state responsibility, but their *education* is considered a parental responsibility. Even today, some states do not have mandated kindergarten programs (for example, Alaska, California, and Pennsylvania); in most states, although school systems are required to offer kindergarten, attendance is not compulsory (for example, Arizona, Connecticut, and Virginia).

American society is changing, and this is reflected in our institutions, especially schools. The increase in working mothers, one-parent families, children from poverty homes, and non-English speaking students has spawned an interest in four-year-old programs that are incorporated into public schooling. Many state legislatures have focused on early education as a vehicle to prevent later problems and to propel their statewide reforms of excellence (Kagan & Zigler, 1987). In 1986, one-third of the states provided funds for programs for four-year-olds (Morado, 1986). An appreciable increase in that percentage would most likely result in a great demand for early childhood teachers. Such an exigency would assuredly affect early childhood teacher education and certification requirements. In effect, programs have been created in many states for which no teacher certification exists.

Additionally, school administrators have become more aware of the special skills needed to teach young children. An educator proficient in teaching ten-year-olds may not be effective with four-year-olds. This awareness of the specialized teaching skills of early childhood educators has often resulted in a grassroots movement and a "trickle up" influence.

Teachers of young children have long been "second-class" educators. They have often been paid less and as a result suffered from lower status. However, as states begin to accept a greater responsibility for the education of young children, early childhood specialists will have to meet more rigorous certification standards. This will not happen overnight. But as society evolves, and the education of young children becomes more important, the need for highly educated teachers of young children will become crucial. This will affect the licensure of early childhood teachers, resulting in a bottom-to-top action that should influence the direction of future reform movements.

## NOTES

1. A certification in early childhood education is a license that authorizes an individual to teach children of a specific age or grade range. Although there is variance among the states, certification usually is authorized after completion of a course of study at a college or university and passing of a competency test, such as the National Teacher Examination.

   An endorsement in early childhood education is an addendum to an individual's certification, such as in elementary education. Endorsements in early childhood education are available in some states, but the specific requirements vary. To receive an endorsement an individual may be required to take additional courses, pass a competency examination, or student teach in an early childhood educational setting.

## REFERENCES

American Association of Colleges for Teacher Education. (1986). *Teacher education in the states: A 50-state survey of legislative and administrative actions*. Washington, DC: American Association of Colleges for Teacher Education.

American Association of Colleges for Teacher Education. (1987). *Teacher education policy in the states: A 50-state survey of legislative and administrative actions*. Washington, DC: American Association of Colleges for Teacher Education.

American Association of Colleges for Teacher Education. (1988). *Teacher education in the states: A 50-state survey of legislative and administrative actions*. Washington, DC: American Association of Colleges for Teacher Education.

Bredekamp, S. (Ed.). (1987). *Developmentally appropriate practice in early childhood programs serving children from birth through age 8*, (exp. ed.). Washington, DC: National Association for the Education of Young Children.

Burks, M. P. (1988). *Requirements for certification, 1988-89* (53rd ed.). Chicago: University of Chicago Press.

Caldwell, M. S. (1989, August). Personal communication. University of Virginia, Charlottesville.

Carnegie Forum on Education and the Economy. (1986). *A nation prepared: Teachers for the 21st century.* New York: Carnegie Forum.

Darling-Hammond, L., & Berry, B. (1988). *The evolution of teacher policy.* The RAND Corporation, JRE-01-CSTP.

Education Commission of the States. (1985). State characteristics of kindergarten. *Clearing House Notes* (updated 1989), Denver: ECS.

Feistritzer, E. C. (1984). *The making of a teacher: A report on teacher education and certification.* Washington, DC: National Center for Educational Information.

Feistritzer, E. C. (1986). *Teacher crisis: Myth or reality?* Washington, DC: National Center for Educational Information.

Holmes Group. (1986). *Tomorrow's teachers: A report of the Holmes Group.* East Lansing, MI: Michigan State University.

Hume, M. (1987). *A mandate to educate: The law and handicapped children.* Alexandria, VA: Capitol Publications.

Kagan, S. L., & Zigler, E. F. (Eds.). (1987). *Early schooling: The national debate.* New Haven, CT: Yale University Press.

Lamme, L. L., McMillin, M. R., & Clark, B. H. (1983). Early childhood teacher certification: A national survey. *Journal of Teacher Education, 34*(2), 44-47.

McCarthy, J. (1988, January). *State certification of early childhood teachers: An analysis of the 50 states and the District of Columbia.* Washington, DC: NAEYC.

McKibben, M. D. (1988). Alternative teacher certification programs. *Educational Leadership, 46*(3), 32-35.

Morado, C. (1986). Prekindergarten programs for 4-year-olds: Some key issues. *Young Children, 41*(5), 61-63.

National Association for the Education of Young Children. (1982). *Early childhood teacher education guidelines for four- and five-year programs.* Washington, DC: NAEYC.

Newman, F. (1986). "The states and teacher education: How can the institutions lead the change," speech presented at the annual meeting of the American Association of Colleges for Teacher Education, Chicago, IL, February 26, 1986.

Vodicka, E. (1989, February). Personal communication. Office of Teacher Certification, Austin, Texas.

CHAPTER 11

# Issues in the Preparation of Teachers of Young Children

Lilian G. Katz
Stacie G. Goffin

Teachers of young children have much in common with their colleagues who teach elementary and secondary school children. At all levels of education, teachers seek to help pupils acquire certain knowledge, skills, dispositions, and feelings, although the relative importance of each of these categories of learning may vary with the age of the pupil.

Though the broad, general aims may be similar at all levels, the role of the early childhood teacher varies in many ways from that of teachers at other levels. These variations can be attributed to factors linked to the age and experience of the learners, the particular organizational contexts in which early childhood teachers work, and the distinctions between early childhood and other levels of education.

Similarly, the preparation of early childhood teachers has much in common with the preparation of teachers of older children. The early childhood teacher's role and the context of early childhood education, however, generate unique issues that require consideration in designing early childhood teacher education programs. This chapter seeks to identify the unique aspects of the field of early childhood education that need to be addressed in planning for the preparation of its teachers: the programmatic and policy context of early childhood education and the unique characteristics of young children.

Changes in professional terminology reflect some of the changes in the field of early childhood education concerning its purposes and mission, its sponsors, and clients. For example, in the first edition of the *Handbook of Research on Teaching* (Gage, 1963), the term *nursery education* is used in the title of a chapter on teaching young children (Sears & Dowley, 1963). The term *early childhood education* does not even appear in the index. In the second edition of the same *Handbook* (Travers, 1973), which followed the explosion of early intervention programs in the 1960s, the term *preschool* came into common use. This was followed by adoption of the term *early childhood education* in the third edition of the *Handbook* (Wittrock, 1986).

Even though the term *early childhood education* seems to be in common use at present (as indicated by the title of this volume), its meaning varies in terms of the age span included, the main purposes and functions of the programs, and the suggested qualifications of the staff. Because of the broad scope and nature of programs included in early childhood education, for purposes of this chapter *early childhood education* will refer to group settings deliberately intended to influence the development and learning of children from age 3 to the age when they normally become eligible to enter the first grade. These settings include child care centers, preschools, and kindergarten classes.

## THE CURRENT CONTEXT OF EARLY CHILDHOOD TEACHER EDUCATION

Little research on early childhood teacher education per se has been reported (Katz, 1985). However, like teacher education at the elementary and secondary level, scrutiny of teacher education in the early childhood field has been stimulated by the reform reports of the 1980s. In addition, the current rapid growth of programs for young children is expected to continue until the end of the century, raising many concerns about the supply and quality of teacher personnel (Katz, 1988; McCarthy, 1988).

### RECENT INTEREST IN EARLY CHILDHOOD EDUCATION

The national focus on teacher education has been stimulated by and reflected in the Holmes Group (1986), Carnegie Forum Task Force on Teaching as a Profession (1986), and National Commission on Excellence in Teacher Education (1985) reports. Although focused primarily on elementary and secondary education, these reports also include concerns about early childhood teacher preparation. At the same time, the National Council for Accreditation of Teacher Education (NCATE) has redesigned its national accreditation process to require teacher education programs to conceptualize their primary purposes and theoretical framework (Gollnick & Kunkel, 1986). The efforts of these four groups have stimulated the re-examination of teacher education requirements by many state legislatures and teacher education institutions. Because many early childhood teacher education programs are offered alongside elementary and secondary programs in colleges and schools of education, early childhood programs are also being re-examined in the light of these reports.

As a result of the issues and recommendations found in these reports, early childhood teacher education has been confronted with two fundamental questions: Which is the appropriate academic discipline for early childhood teacher education candidates, and what should early childhood teachers be prepared to teach?

No consensus to these two questions has yet been achieved, for at least two reasons. First, unlike elementary and secondary education, early childhood curriculum is not traditionally or typically content-, subject-, or discipline-oriented. Instead, children's interests are promoted as the hub of an integrated program of studies. Yet Shulman (1987) contends that teaching is content specific. Emphasis in early childhood education on an integrated curriculum suggests that it cannot rely on knowledge of separated disciplines and must frame the education of its teachers within a context different from that of teachers of older children.

Second, although pedagogical knowledge is, of course, an appropriate category of study for early childhood educators, current concern with "developmentally appropriate practice" confounds *what* should be taught in early childhood education with *how* it is taught. Early childhood education needs to more clearly delineate its goals and distinguish its pedagogy from its purposes. Yet, as White and Buka (1987) conclude in their review of early childhood programs, traditions, and policies,

> There have been many conceptions or philosophies of early education during its 200-year history, but it seems safe to say that no substantive, detailed view of the principles and goals that are appropriate for early education has ever won broad acceptance among the public at large, or among early educators themselves. (p. 85)

With respect to elementary education, White and Buka (1987) point out that "there is broad agreement on some basic goals like the proverbial 3 R's." But, even though these agreements are few, they "go far beyond what exists for early education" (White & Buka, 1987, p. 85).

This lack of consensus is also reflected in certification requirements for early childhood teachers. While the preparation of individuals who teach first through third grade is usually obtained in conventional teacher preparation programs in colleges and universities that are governed by state certification requirements, the requirements of teachers of younger children lack such unity. As McCarthy (1988) points out,

> The certification processes which states use to prepare teachers of young children can best be summed up with one word: variety. Patterns vary from actual certification in early childhood education to add-on endorsements to programs in elementary education with additional combinations in between. . . . Even when the terminology is the same, there is no guarantee that the content is equivalent. (p. 2)

The variety of certification requirements among the states reflects variations in the way states define early childhood education and the extent to which they attempt to control the training of teachers who work outside the public school system. Consequently, in many states, certification of child care teachers frequently resides in departments separate from those certifying public school teachers. In some states, nursery school teachers are totally excluded from certification requirements.

## EXPANSION OF EARLY CHILDHOOD EDUCATION

The recent rapid rate of growth in the field of early childhood education can be attributed, in part, to the increasing participation of young children in child care. It is projected that by 1995, two-thirds of children under the age of six will have mothers in the work force (Hofferth & Phillips, 1987). The dramatic growth and public attention to child care programs due to maternal employment has overshadowed the equally dramatic growth of other preschool programs such as private nursery schools, the expansion of preschool services in public schools and of Head Start programs, the growth of early intervention programs for children with special needs, and the now virtually universal availability of kindergarten classes.

These facts highlight not only the expansion of the field, but the diversity of settings, purposes, and sponsorship of programs that all come under the rubric of early childhood education. This diversity impinges in complex ways on the nature and structure of early childhood teacher education programs. Most significantly, it has contributed to a differentiated conceptualization of teacher training. As a result, not only is there considerable diversity in the expectations associated with teacher certification and licensure, but the origins of teacher preparation are also scattered. Whereas the recommendations of the Holmes and Carnegie groups focus on colleges and universities, early childhood teacher preparation frequently consists of in-service programs organized as workshops, summer institutes, high school child development and vocational programs, the Child Development Associate credential, two-year associate degrees, and baccalaureate and fifth-year programs.

It has not been determined whether teachers employed in different settings need the same amount and kinds of training. Should all teachers be expected to master a common core of knowledge and skills? Should candidates be differentially selected into programs that prepare teachers for each of the varieties of settings? A critical, unanswered question is how much an early childhood education practitioner should be required to know about children, content, and pedagogy, to be certified. What is the minimum level of understanding about early childhood education, its purposes, and its clientele below which no early childhood practitioner should be permitted to fall? Furthermore, should the answers to these questions be related to the kind of setting in which practice will occur?

The complexity of answering these questions is further exacerbated by the increasingly diverse characteristics of the children and families being served by early childhood education programs. Changing patterns in the population, and the birth rate of subgroups within it, suggest that early childhood teachers will be working with an increasingly heterogeneous population, some of whom will be "at-risk" due to circumstances rarely addressed by educators (for example, homelessness and drug abuse). Added to this medley of factors affecting the field is the observation by some that the very nature of children is shifting (Zimiles, 1986).

The diversity of currently available teacher preparation options, and the controversy they often generate, reflects the programmatic and policy distinction traditionally made between the care and education of young children. Objection to the suggestion that all early childhood practitioners should meet even minimally similar standards of preparation can be seen in public resistance to even minimal federal standards for child care teachers and the differential standards being proposed for child care vs. preschool teachers, even when both are working in the public school system (Zigler, 1987).

Issues in the preparation of early childhood teachers, therefore, mirror the challenges confronting the field: lack of consistent professional nomenclature, low status of the profession, low salaries, lack of employment benefits, high staff turnover, and the historical and practical distinctions drawn among child care, preschool, and public school programs for young children. Furthermore, these realities are discouraging entrants into the field and contributing to the early exit of those who choose to enter.

Kagan (1988) has condemned the two-tiered system of uneven care and education that has been created by the current fragmented and categorical approach to the provision of early childhood services. This system is being aggravated and reinforced by the multitiered system of teacher preparation programs. Teachers who satisfy state certification requirements seek the better-paid positions in public school settings. Teachers without certification are funneled into employment in lower paying programs such as Head Start and child care centers.

Given the mixture of settings, requirements, and sponsors, it is clear that the field of early childhood education cannot be addressed as a monolithic entity. The issues within the field directly affect the status, growth, and configuration of early childhood teacher education. The inequities, discontinuities, and fragmentation that characterize services for children (Kagan, 1989) can just as easily be applied to early childhood teacher education.

## UNIQUE ASPECTS OF EARLY CHILDHOOD EDUCATION AND THEIR IMPLICATIONS FOR TEACHER PREPARATION

Although the role of teachers of young children overlaps in many ways with the role of teachers of older children, some important aspects are distinctive. These distinctions are linked primarily to the developmental characteristics of the learner and the philosophical framework of early childhood education.

### Wide Scope of Teacher Role

In principle, the younger the child, the wider the range of the child's functioning for which an adult must assume responsibility. Frequent references in the early childhood literature to the "whole child" allude to this aspect of the early childhood teacher's role—namely, that teachers of children aged six or under must respond to and accept responsibility for a variety of emotional, social, physical, and intellectual needs and developmental tasks. Thus, the role of the teacher of young children is wide ranging and suffers from unclear role boundaries (Katz, 1980).

The wide scope of teaching functions with respect to young children and the ambiguities associated with them exacerbate the problem of precisely identifying the knowledge, skills, and dispositions that should be emphasized in the curriculum. Consequently, there is considerable confusion about what teaching competencies should be emphasized in early childhood teacher education programs.

## Diversity of Mission and Ideology

In addition to role ambiguity, early childhood education is characterized by diversity and ambiguity concerning its principal mission, purposes, and goals. Some programs are aimed primarily at socializing children into institutional life, and some are intended to provide enrichment to alleviate the effects of social or economic disadvantage and to intervene into a hazardous environment. Some programs are committed to early academic preparation, while some are dedicated toward the child's development of social and intellectual competence. Some of the leading teacher education programs for early childhood education (for instance, Montessori programs, Bank Street College of Education) are organized around particular ideologies that specify desired goals and methods.

The field of early childhood education, therefore, is marked by strong ideological disputes concerning appropriate goals and teaching methods (Bereiter, 1986; Gersten, 1986; Katz, 1975; Schweinhart et al., 1986a, 1986b). The disagreements center particularly on the extent to which formal instruction is appropriate for young children and the validity of academic outcomes as a legitimate purpose of early childhood education.

The ideological nature of the field poses a dilemma for teacher educators: On the one hand, should the preparation program be organized around a particular coherent approach to early childhood education, or, on the other, should candidates be exposed to all the available competing approaches? Each "horn" of the dilemma has advantages and disadvantages for all involved in teacher preparation. The "coherent approach" would result in candidates receiving similar, or at least concordant, messages from all instructors. They would be likely to perceive a clear message about how to proceed and what is "good" or "bad," "right" or "wrong" in teaching. However, if graduates were employed in settings that adopted other approaches, they might be ill-suited to the work. Furthermore, such a "doctrinaire" approach is antithetical to the norms and ethos of higher education institutions that prize openness to alternative points of view. Indeed, one of the virtues of locating teacher education inside multipurpose (vs. single purpose) institutions is that candidates can be exposed to a range of disciplines, competing ideas, and peers unlike themselves.

The eclectic approach, in which candidates are exposed to competing approaches to early childhood education, might foster recognition that alternative views of appropriate practices exist and must be considered. It would also afford candidates the opportunity to seek out an approach to practice that is most consistent with their own particular proclivities and dispositions. However, given that candidates are likely to be at a stage in their development in which they seek clear, unambiguous guidelines or "tips for teaching," exposure to competing philosophies could become a source of confusion and anxiety. Candidates might also perceive the eclectic approach to be a sign of disorder or chaos in the teacher education curriculum (Katz, 1988), or, conversely, they might perceive all strategies as equally valid. This conclusion could deter prospective teachers from placing their practice within a conceptually coherent framework.

## Vulnerability of the Child

In principle, the younger the learners, the more physically, emotionally, and socially dependent they are on adults. In this sense, age is related to vulnerability to all the potential hazards of the interpersonal and physical environment; therefore, the younger the children, the more critical their need for knowledgeable and qualified teachers. Young children's physical and emotional dependence suggests that teacher preparation must address the provision of safety and the nature and intensity of supervision and vigilance required to safeguard the "whole" child's experience within the setting.

Because the younger the children, the less likely they are to be able to articulate their feelings, needs, desires, confusions, and other needs for assistance, the teacher must be able to infer children's emotional and cognitive status on the basis of their behavior and demeanor, and to interpret their feelings and moods. The less articulate the children, the more important it is that the teacher have the finely developed interactive skills required for probing children's thinking and feelings and for soliciting information from them. This requires being able to discern the particular meanings individual children give their unique experience, in the context of their own family, cultural background, and level of social and cognitive development.

Bowman (1989) asserts that teachers of young children must work within two knowledge systems: the systematic knowledge of human behavior and the implicit knowledge system derived from their own and others' experiences. Teachers can use both sources of knowledge through processes of reflection to ensure that both their subjective reactions and formal knowledge are optimally responsive to children.

Because of the central importance of interactive skills for teachers of young children, clinical experiences that permit students to translate their knowledge of child development and educational purposes into educational practice under close supervision should constitute a central feature of their preparation. Furthermore, in light of the vulnerability of young children, candidates' dispositions to be accepting, warm, nurturant, and patient must be addressed in their preparation (Katz & Raths, 1985).

However, such dispositions are unlikely to be strengthened via instruction or other kinds of didactic approaches. Indeed, it is not clear whether such dispositions can be "taught" at all; it may be that they can only be strengthened (or weakened) if they are present in the candidate. Strengthening a disposition, therefore, is likely to require direct and frequent interactions with teacher educators or an on-site educational leader from the early childhood program (such as a child care director or early childhood supervisor).

## Socialization Focus

Children in the early years are in the process of learning how to manage their impulses and adapt to group living and institutional constraints and demands. This suggests that one of the functions of early childhood teachers is easing the transition from home to an early childhood setting, and helping children to cope with separation anxieties and adjust to the routines of institutional life.

For a large proportion of children, this transition entails entry into a new cultural and linguistic community. A teacher's effectiveness with respect to such transitions may depend on her ability to achieve optimum intimacy and warmth with each child and to provide supportive guidance. In addition, the younger the child, the larger the role adults usually play in fostering the development of peer interactive skills. Candidates, therefore, should also learn techniques for coaching children in effective peer interactions (Mize & Ladd, 1990).

## Teacher-Parent Relations

In principle, the younger the learners, the more directly and emotionally involved their parents are in their daily functioning. This emotionality and involvement are likely to be manifested by frequent informal interaction with teachers over a wide range of issues. Because the scope of the teacher's responsibilities covers the "whole child," the content of interaction may span the full range of concerns about the child's development.

Teachers of young children, unlike primary grade teachers, are frequently asked by parents to advise them on matters of child rearing. Because of unclear role boundaries, some parental resentment, disagreement, and even hostility are likely to enter teacher-parent relationships. According to Becher (1986), teachers have rated teacher-parent relations as a leading source of job-related stress. Early childhood's emphasis on the role of families in children's development requires that early childhood educators be knowledgeable in facilitating parent-teacher interactions.

## Ethical Issues

In principle, the more vulnerable a client is with respect to the practitioner, the more important it is that the power of the practitioner be constrained by an internalized code of ethics. The adoption of a code of ethics by a membership association is one attribute of a profession. In the interest of stimulating the ethical practices and strengthening the professionalism of its members, the National Association for the Education of Young Children has adopted a code of ethics (Feeney & Kipnis, 1989). The code addresses the major ethical concerns confronted by practitioners in terms of responsibilities to children, families, colleagues, employers and employees, and the larger society.

Now that a code of ethics has been adopted, the issue of how it is to be "learned" and enforced will have to be addressed. It is not clear how a code of ethics is internalized. The disposition to behave ethically is also not likely to result from didactic instruction. Teacher education programs may need to develop a common body of prototypical ethical dilemmas for all candidates to study and address as part of their preparation program.

## Curriculum Issues

Traditionally, the early childhood curriculum prior to the primary grades has focused not on academic outcomes but on goals related to many other aspects of children's development and learning. This core derives from the developmental characteristics of young children, which give rise to the field's consistent emphasis on enhancement of children's social-emotional, physical, language, and intellectual development. Furthermore, the younger the children, the more learning is enhanced by direct, firsthand interactive experiences rather than by indirect, secondhand, passive-receptive experiences. In principle, therefore, the younger the child, the more integrated the curriculum should be.

Young children's learning tends to be undifferentiated by subject boundaries. An integrated curriculum is built on the exploration and investigation of worthwhile topics of potential interest to young children, in the course of which language, mathematical, scientific, and social studies and other conceptual systems are introduced and applied. The organization of the curriculum in terms of academic disciplines is appropriate later, when children are old enough to apply well-developed metacognitive skills to the formal study of subjects like language, science, and mathematics. This suggests that prospective teachers of young children need help identifying suitable topics and ways of addressing them so that all major disciplines can be applied to them in an integrated way (Katz & Chard, 1989).

This principle suggests that the younger the child, the greater the proportion of time that should be allocated to informal activities. Such activities can be of three main types: spontaneous play, semi-structured manipulative activities (puzzles, games, creative activities like painting), and project work. The teacher's role during these times is complex; sensitive monitoring of individual and small group behavior and progress, an understanding of children's unique ways of learning, and a strong sense of appropriate learning goals are required.

These curriculum principles suggest that early childhood teachers must be able to capitalize on children's spontaneously expressed interests and on emerging events in the classroom. They must be able to shift scheduled activities and to balance the daily program so that an optimum level of routines is maintained. Implementation of an informal curriculum requires resourcefulness and tolerance for ambiguity on the part of the teacher.

## DEFINING THE ISSUES FOR EARLY CHILDHOOD TEACHER EDUCATION

The characteristics of young children suggest that the major competencies required of teachers are interactive skills. It is through interactive processes that teachers are most likely to uncover children's feelings, needs, and perspectives about a situation. Such interactive skills are unlikely to be acquired solely from direct instruction in formal academic courses. Their development also requires observation of competent teachers, trial and error, and specific feedback from supervisors of student teaching and other practicum experiences.

This view of the teacher's role raises questions concerning whether traditional modes of teacher education can foster nontraditional, open-ended ways of teaching young children. Can candidates learn to teach young children in informal and integrated ways when their training is formal and largely subject specialized? The complex nature of an appropriate curriculum for young children argues that content courses need to address this complexity and that teaching practica should constitute a greater proportion of the total preparation program. While there is, as yet, no empirical basis for determining the most appropriate ratio of practica to content courses, the focus on interactive skills suggests the need to better conceptualize and integrate the clinical component in teacher preparation programs.

The nature of the curriculum for young children also suggests a distinctive interweaving of liberal arts and teacher education. Early childhood educators need a strong liberal arts education, less in the sense of a content specialty than in the sense of being an "educated person." Early childhood educators need to be well informed on many topics in order to be perceptive and responsive to ways of enhancing children's interactions and understandings of their environments. Comprehensive knowledge and understandings can assist in interpreting children's actions and knowing how to extend a child's knowledge and understandings.

Because of the impact of issues within the field of early childhood education on the delivery of early childhood programs, discussions about early childhood teacher education cannot be restricted to a focus on early childhood curriculum. Early childhood teacher education must also address issues of policy.

The quality of early childhood programs is determined by many contextual factors; thus, prospective early childhood educators need to understand that their concern for quality education for young children cannot be limited to their practice within classrooms. Within this context, early childhood teacher educators are in an optimal position to take a leadership role in promoting advocacy on behalf of children, their families, and the early childhood profession. Advocacy needs to be integrated as a vital component of an expanded conceptualization of the early childhood teacher's role (Goffin, 1989b, 1990; Goffin & Lombardi, 1988).

## Case Study Approach to Teacher Preparation

The case study method to professional development may be an appropriate approach to the preparation of early childhood teachers (McAninch, 1989). To develop a case study approach to teacher preparation, the field itself would need to identify the standard predicaments most frequently faced by practitioners (Katz, 1984). The standard predicament is similar to a critical incident in that it depicts a problematic event confronted by teachers.

The predicament becomes a case study when all the relevant disciplines and concepts are brought to bear on its analysis. In this way, each predicament is examined by candidates from a historical, philosophical, psychological, sociological, and cultural perspective. These examinations are intended to illuminate the uses of the disciplines and to convey to candidates the types of procedures adapted by the profession to the solution of its standard predicaments.

The development of such case studies, however, would require early childhood education to: examine its ideological differences; address questions regarding the diversity of teacher preparation options; develop consensus with respect to which kinds of predicaments characterize the field, and what constitutes standard procedures that all practitioners should be expected to learn and apply; and expand its dependence to disciplines other than child psychology.

## Focusing on Early Childhood Teacher Education

The focus of researchers on teacher effectiveness has distracted attention from what early childhood teacher educators themselves should be expected to know. In discussing the relationship between research and public policy, Phillips (in press) speaks of the creation of a new professional who is knowledgeable in both research and public policy, and brokers the information between these two spheres for scientists and policy makers. This same role function can be applied to teacher educators. Teacher educators may be the "brokers" between relevant theories, and research and practice. They "broker" this information for researchers, practitioners, and students (Goffin, in preparation).

Fein & Schwartz (1982), in arguing a need for a theory of practice in early childhood education, describe the passive role of developmental theory and the activist role of teaching. Shavelson (1988), in presenting his beliefs about the relationship between research and practice, describes the researcher and practitioner as having two different "frames of mind." These frames of mind, which coincide with Fein and Schwartz' (1982) distinction between theory and practice, focus the thinking and activity of researchers and practitioners in different ways. The early childhood teacher educator should bridge these two frames in his or her own thinking and be capable of helping prospective teachers construct their own walkways.

What are the important understandings about child development, early childhood education, *and* teacher education that teacher educators need to know to satisfy the role expectation of "broker"? What aspects of teacher training specific to early childhood education are related to teacher competency? Teacher education is a labor-intensive enterprise; what kinds of organizational backing do teacher educators need to adequately support prospective teachers? These types of questions direct the importance of early childhood content knowledge and pedagogy from the early childhood practitioner to the level of teacher education, and focus the spotlight of teacher effectiveness on teacher educators.

The search for answers will probably need to focus on both teacher education as a teaching enterprise and the early childhood classroom and practitioner. Teacher education seems to require content knowledge, teaching ability, and clinical skills. Acquiring a doctorate or master's degree in early childhood education does not automatically confer these skills.

Furthermore, many departments of early childhood education in colleges and universities consist of only one person. It no longer seems realistic to assume that one person can be proficient not only in early childhood education, child development, and all the subject-matter disciplines, but also in "brokering" this content in both discipline-based courses *and* clinical experiences. After recognizing the intensity and inherent dilemmas of undergraduate teacher education, Katz (1988) questioned whether teacher education could even be implemented at colleges and universities whose mission was expressed primarily through research and publication rather than teaching.

But the gap in knowledge is not only at the level of teacher education. In contrast to the extensive literature on teacher effects in elementary education, very little is known about teacher effects in early childhood education. Furthermore, it is not possible to fully transfer the findings from the available research on teaching because of the distinctive characteristics of early education: the impact of child development on program goals and curriculum planning; the high priority given to social-emotional and intellectual growth over narrowly focused academic learning; the emphasis on child-centered curriculum versus teacher-directed instruction; and greater teacher freedom to determine program content and learning objectives (Goffin, 1989a). Our theories of practice—and teacher education—need to be informed by research on teaching that is specific to early childhood education.

## REFERENCES

Becher, R. M. (1986). Parent involvement: A review of research and principles of successful practice. In L. G. Katz & K. Steiner (Eds.), *Current topics in early childhood education* (Vol. 6, pp. 85–122). Norwood, NJ: Ablex.

Bereiter, C. (1986). Does direct instruction cause delinquency? *Early Childhood Research Quarterly, 1,* 289-92.

Bowman, B. (1989). Self-reflection as an element of professionalism. *Teachers College Record, 90,* 444-51.

Carnegie Forum Task Force on Teaching as a Profession. (1986). *A nation prepared: Teachers for the 21st century.* New York: Carnegie Forum.

Feeney, S., & Kipnis, K. (1989). Code of ethical conduct and statement of commitment: Position statement of the National Association for the Education of Young Children. Washington, DC: National Association for the Education of Young Children.

Fein, G., & Schwartz, P. M. (1982). Developmental theories in early childhood education. In B. Spodek (Ed.), *Handbook of research in early childhood education* (pp. 82–104). New York: Free Press.

Gage, N. L. (Ed.). (1963). *Handbook of research on teaching.* Chicago: Rand McNally.

Gersten, R. (1986). Response to "Consequences of three preschool curriculum models through age 15." *Early Childhood Research Quarterly, 1,* 293-302.

Goffin, S. G. (1989a). Developing a research agenda for early childhood education: What can be learned from the research on teaching? *Early Childhood Research Quarterly, 4,* 187-204.

Goffin, S. G. (1989b). How well do we respect the children in our care? *Childhood Education, 66,* 68-74.

Goffin, S. G. (1990). To be or not to be an early childhood advocate? Is that really the question? *Dimensions, 18*(2), 23-24.

Goffin, S. G. *Program models in early childhood education: An expanded view.* Columbus, OH: Merrill, in preparation.

Goffin, S. G., & Lombardi, J. (1988). *Speaking out: Early childhood advocacy.* Washington, DC: NAEYC.

Gollnick, D. M., & Kunkel, R. C. (1986). The reform of national accreditation. *Phi Delta Kappan, 6,* 310-14.

Hofferth, S. L., & Phillips, D. A. (1987). Child care in the United States, 1970-1995. *Journal of Marriage and the Family, 49,* 559-71.

Holmes Group. (1986). *Tomorrow's teachers: A report of the Holmes Group.* East Lansing, MI: Holmes Group, Inc.

Kagan, S. L. (1988). Current reforms in early education: Are we addressing the issues? *Young Children, 43*(2), 27-32.

Kagan, S. L. (1989). Early care and education: Tackling the tough issues. *Phi Delta Kappan, 70,* 433-39.

Katz, L. G. (1975). Early childhood education and ideological disputes. *Educational Forum, 3,* 267-71.

Katz, L. G. (1980). Mothering and teaching: Some significant distinctions. In L. G. Katz (Ed.), *Current topics in early childhood education* (Vol. 3, pp. 47-65). Norwood, NJ: Ablex.

Katz, L. G. (1984). The professional preschool teacher. In L. G. Katz, *More talks with teachers* (pp. 27-44). Urbana, IL: ERIC Clearinghouse on Elementary and Early Childhood Education.

Katz, L. G. (1985). Teacher education for early childhood education. In M. Dunkin (Ed.), *International encyclopedia of teaching and teacher education* (Vol. 3, pp. 1487-1495). London: Pergamon.

Katz, L. G. (1988). Memo to the Department Chair: Or confessions of a teacher educator. Newsletter of the National Association of Early Childhood Teacher Educators. No. 30, Vol. 93(3) pp. 2-7.

Katz, L. G., & Chard, S. C. (1989). *Engaging children's minds: The project approach.* Norwood, NJ: Ablex.

Katz, L. G., & Raths, J. D. (1985). Dispositions as goals for teacher education. *Teaching and Teacher Education, 1,* 301-07.

McAninch, A. (1989). The case method in teacher education: Analysis, rationale, and proposal. Unpublished doctoral dissertation, University of Illinois, Urbana.

McCarthy, J. (1988). *State certification of early childhood teachers: An analysis of the 50 states and the District of Columbia.* Washington, DC: NAEYC.

Mize, J., & Ladd, G. (1990). Toward the development of successful social skill training for preschool children. In S. R. Asher & J. D. Coie (Eds.), *Peer rejection in childhood* (pp. 338-364). New York: Cambridge University Press.

National Commission on Excellence in Teacher Education. (1985). *A call for change in teacher education*. Washington, DC: American Association of Colleges for Teacher Education.

Phillips, D. A. (in press). Social policy and community psychology. In J. Rappaport & E. Seidman (Eds.), *Handbook of community psychology*. New York: Plenum.

Schweinhart, L. S., Weikart, D. P., & Larner, M. B. (1986a). Consequences of three preschool curriculum models through age 15. *Early Childhood Research Quarterly, 1*, 15–35.

Schweinhart, L. S., Weikart, D. P., & Larner, M. B. (1986b). Child-initiated activities in early childhood programs may help prevent delinquency. *Early Childhood Research Quarterly, 1*, 303–12.

Sears, P. S., & Dowley, E. M. (1963). Research on teaching in the nursery school. In N. L. Gage (Ed.), *Handbook of research on teaching* (pp. 814–64). Chicago: Rand McNally.

Shavelson, R. J. (1988). Contributions of educational research to policy and practice: Constructing, challenging, changing cognition. *Educational Researcher, 17*(7), 4–11, 22.

Shulman, L. S. (1987). Knowledge and teaching: Foundations of the new reform. *Harvard Educational Review, 57*(1), 1–22.

Travers, R. M. W. (Ed.). (1973). *Second handbook of research on teaching*. Chicago: Rand McNally.

White, S. H., & Buka, S. L. (1987). Early education: Programs, traditions, and policies. In E. Z. Rothkopf (Ed.), *Review of research in education* (Vol. 14, pp. 43–91). Washington, DC: American Educational Research Association.

Wittrock, M. C. (Ed.). (1986). *Handbook of research on teaching* (3rd ed.). New York: Macmillan.

Zigler, E. F. (1987). A solution to the nation's child care crisis: The school of the twenty-first century. Unpublished manuscript.

Zimiles, H. (1986). The changing American child: The perspective of educators. In T. M. Tomkinson & H. J. Walberg (Eds.), *Academic work and educational excellence* (pp. 61–84). Berkeley, CA: McCutchan.

CHAPTER 12

# Preparing Early Childhood Teachers for the Twenty-First Century
## A LOOK TO THE FUTURE

Bernard Spodek
Olivia N. Saracho

The material in this volume describes the preparation of early childhood teachers as it has been in the past and as it is in the present. But what of the future? The years ahead will see continued changes in the field of early childhood education, a field that has already experienced rapid changes in the past several years. Some of the future changes will result from the increasing expansion of the field as higher proportions of young children continue to be enrolled in early childhood education programs. In addition, increasingly more diverse populations of children will be included in these programs. Such developments should be reflected in changes in the preparation of early childhood education practitioners.

Evidence of the changes in the field can be seen in the deepening involvement of our nation's public schools in providing early childhood education programs for four- and five-year-olds (Mitchell, Seligman, & Marx, 1989). Child care services, which were once offered by local community agencies and individual entrepreneurs, are now offered by large national corporations. The increasing involvement of women in the work force has been a national phenomenon since World War II. This involvement will increase and become more permanent. The economic situation in the United States has changed to the point where it is virtually impossible for most single wage earner families to support a desirable standard of living. In addition, changing demographics suggest an impending labor shortage, creating a further source of pressure for women, even those who are mothers of very young children, to work. As of this writing, members of Congress are hammering out the final arrangements for a law that will provide federal support for child care services, an indication of the importance of such services to our nation and of the future expansion of the field.

We are also seeing increasing diversity in the children enrolled in early childhood programs. At one time, nursery schools typically enrolled children from middle and upper class backgrounds, while child care centers served children of working class backgrounds. That is no longer the case; middle class families make extensive use of child care centers. A number of special programs have been established to serve a range of children with special needs. Head Start programs, which have been sponsored by the federal government for over 25 years, along with Chapter I prekindergarten programs, serve children of low income families. In addition, a number of states have established prekindergarten programs in their public schools, often serving a population of children who are considered at-risk of later school failure.

More than a decade ago, the federal government, through Public Law 94-142, the Education for All Handicapped Children Act, involved the public schools in the education of handicapped children. That involvement is being extended through Public Law 99-457 to serve handicapped children from their birth.

All of these forces, contributed to the increased need for programs in early childhood education and care and are contributing to the need to prepare increasingly larger numbers of early childhood education practitioners. Other forces are demanding that this preparation be improved and extended.

There have been a variety of responses to the need to increase the number of early childhood practitioners in the field, extend their ability to work in a variety of child population settings, and generally improve their preparation. Not all early childhood practitioners are highly educated, well-prepared professionals. There exists a range of practitioners with different levels of preparation. This was recognized when the National Association for the Education of Young Children (NAEYC), in a position statement, proposed four different levels of professionalism, each with different responsibilities and different amounts and levels of preparation (NAEYC, 1984). These levels include practitioners with a minimum of preparation, practitioners with an associate degree or a Child Development Associate credential, certified teachers with preparation at the bachelors degree level, and highly qualified and experienced practitioners. While this position statement is currently being revised, the new statement will continue to reflect the varied levels of professionalism and professional preparation of early childhood practitioners.

The belief that some early childhood practitioners should be expected to possess the same level of preparation as elementary and secondary school teachers while others should be expected to have lower qualifications is not new. As early as 1929, the field was making distinctions between child care workers and teachers in educational programs (Whipple, 1929). Even within the same program, some individuals (such as teacher aides and teacher assistants, who serve in "auxiliary roles") are generally required to have a different level of preparation based on the responsibility assigned to their role (Spodek, 1972).

Thus, a range of different strategies need to be put into place in relation to the many levels of practice found in the field. Different programs to prepare early childhood personnel need to be implemented, different standards need to be adopted, and different institutions need to be involved in the preparation of personnel at each level. Community colleges, through the establishment of one- and two-year sub-bachelor degree programs, have become and will probably continue to be the main preparers of child care practitioners. More and more, four-year colleges and universities are providing programs to prepare new early childhood teachers who meet state teacher certification requirements and are employed in public school educational programs. These institutions are also providing support for the continued professional development of current teachers, either through in-service work or through graduate level programs. Professional associations continue to wrestle with the issue of what level(s) of professionalism early childhood teachers should manifest. They also continue to refine standards for programs preparing early childhood practitioners.

As we move toward the twenty-first century, there are a number of concerns emerging that will need to be addressed. We will need to prepare teachers for a greater variety of programs that are offered in a variety of settings. Related to these issues is the need to differentiate levels of practice among practitioners in the field.

## TEACHERS FOR A VARIETY OF PROGRAMS

In the United States today there is no single type of program that serves all young children. By contrast, in China the only program differentiation made in early childhood education relates to the ages of the children served: Kindergartens serve children ages 3 through 6, while nurseries serve children below age 3. No differentiation is made there between kindergarten and child care services—all kindergarten programs are extended day programs.

In the United States, however, we have a variety of early childhood programs: kindergarten, child care, nursery school, Head Start, Chapter I, at-risk programs, and so forth. Some of these programs are differentiated by the service they provide—education as opposed to care, for example. Sometimes the programs are also designed specifically for particular child populations; Head Start, Chapter I, and at-risk programs in the public schools tend to be targeted toward children from low income families. Early childhood bilingual programs and programs designed specifically for children of migrant workers, for gifted children, and for handicapped children also exist. All of these programs need to be staffed by teachers and other practitioners.

We must ask whether teachers working in these special programs need to have specific knowledge and competency not expected of teachers in standard early childhood programs. Additionally, we may question whether such special knowledge should be provided as part of the teachers' preservice programs, whether teachers should be provided with preparation beyond that expected of most practitioners, and whether the program sponsors should be responsible for providing whatever additional preparation is needed.

## TEACHERS FOR A VARIETY OF SETTINGS

Teachers of young children must be prepared to work in a variety of settings (for example, public school, private agency, corporate world, home). Though each setting has its own particular requirements of its teaching staffs, programs for early childhood practitioners do not prepare personnel for any particular setting. These programs tend to be generic. With the exception of Montessori programs, early childhood education programs are not designed to prepare a particular type of practitioner. In addition, students enrolled in teacher preparation programs expect these programs to be generally acceptable to a variety of employing agencies. The hope is often expressed that the more broadly prepared such students are, the easier it will be for them to find employment.

The greatest influence on teacher education programs appears to be the teacher certification requirements established by the state department of education (Spodek, Davis, & Saracho, 1983). Since teacher certification is required for employment in public school systems, and since public school systems have the highest salary levels and provide the greatest employment stability, these requirements have tremendous power over teacher preparation institutions, more so actually than do requirements for accreditation by the National Council for Accreditation of Teacher Education (NCATE). Current certification requirements are influencing the preparation of early childhood teachers to serve a wide range of clients. They have led teacher education programs to add courses related to infancy, the handicapped, multiculturalism, and parenting. Also, since early childhood teachers work in child care centers and administer early childhood programs, the competencies needed in these roles also influence the teacher preparation program. Early childhood teachers are also being required to be better educated and better prepared to teach, leading to increases in general education requirements and to innovations in the professional components of such programs (Spodek & Saracho, 1988). Since there is little differentiation in programs that prepare teachers specifically for particular settings, state teacher certification requirements influence the majority of early childhood teacher education programs, whether their graduates expect to seek employment in public school systems or not.

The second major influence on the preparation of early childhood practitioners is professional organizations. Through accreditation agencies like NCATE, standards are established for institutions preparing teachers as well as for programs for specific types of teachers, such as elementary teachers, science teachers, or teachers in any other specializations. Accreditation, however, is a voluntary process. A teacher preparation institution may decide not to seek accreditation and thus not bind itself to any set of accreditation standards.

NAEYC as an organization representing the field of early childhood education has also influenced programs preparing early childhood teachers. In 1982, the association published a set of guidelines for early childhood teacher education programs (NAEYC, 1982). These guidelines influenced teacher education institutions in structuring early childhood teacher education programs along recommended lines. While the association has no power to enforce these guidelines other than the power of persuasion, they have been used by college and university faculty in revising their programs. In addition, portions of these guidelines were adopted by NCATE to be used in accrediting early childhood teacher education programs (Spodek, in press).

These standards for teacher preparatory programs have influenced primarily programs preparing teachers for public schools. They have not influenced either teachers in non-public school education programs or those in child care centers to the same extent, since few of these teachers are graduates of teacher education programs leading to certification. Standards for these teachers are set by state day care licensing agencies and are often minimal.

The programs that do exist to prepare teachers in child care centers are generally non-bachelors degree programs provided by community colleges, vocational training centers, and secondary schools. As Powell and Dunn have noted in Chapter 3, NAEYC has established guidelines for these programs, but there is presently no mechanism for enforcement. NAEYC was also deeply involved in the development of the Child Development Associate credential and is currently sponsoring the agency offering the credential. This credential, originally intended for persons working in Head Start programs, is also being used to credential child care practitioners.

In the United States today, we have two distinct systems for preparing early childhood practitioners: one for teachers in public school programs and another for teachers in child care and non-public school programs. While there is some crossover between the two systems, with some certified teachers employed in child care centers or other non-public school systems, and some graduates of community college programs completing teacher education programs in four-year colleges or universities, they represent two distinct tracks operating in relative isolation from one another. Whether there should be more integration of the two systems, allowing for greater flexibility in employment and employability, is an issue the field still needs to address.

The idea of a career ladder, allowing early childhood teachers to move through stages to higher levels of professionalism, has often been suggested. However, the way in which such integration could be created and the mechanism for such a career ladder have not been established. In addition, whether such a career ladder is feasible has also been questioned (Spodek, in press). Vocationally oriented courses from community colleges may not be transferred to senior college or university programs. Nor are practitioners who enter the field of early childhood education with lower qualifications always willing to continue their formal education. Those practitioners who enter the field with the highest qualifications are more likely to continue their professional education than those who enter with lower qualifications, the opposite of what would be required to establish a career ladder (Spodek & Saracho, 1982).

We must question whether there is a body of knowledge and skills that all early childhood teachers must possess, regardless of the setting in which they practice. We must also question whether there is a common level of competence that early childhood teachers must achieve, regardless of the setting in which they practice. Ott, Zeichner, and Price, in Chapter 7, discuss the notion of a knowledge base for early childhood teachers. Peters and Klinzing, in Chapter 4, suggest a core of child development knowledge, and McCarthy, in Chapter 5, suggests a core of pedagogical knowledge that should be common to all early childhood practitioners. Underlying these discussions is the assumption that everyone prepared to be an early childhood teacher should share some common core of knowledge. It might be suggested that teachers in child care settings need to know different things than teachers in educational settings. This suggestion was made a half-century ago by Beer (1938) and might be worth re-examining today.

The home and school are jointly responsible for the education of young children. Teachers need to know how to nurture the relationship between the home and school. It could also be expected that, as more home-based programs are established for young children and their parents, there will be a greater need for teachers to gain knowledge and competence related to working with parents and to working outside school settings. Teachers need to know about the teaching and learning that occur informally in children's homes; about the processes and conditions within the family that influence children's acquisition of knowledge and skills useful to achievement in school; about the environmental influences on the family's ability to support and enhance learning; about similarities and differences between educational processes in the home and school; and about ways to effect closer liaison between home education and classroom instruction. Teachers need to become sensitive to different family forms, family ecologies, and views of effective family functioning. Knowledge of these influences at the preschool and primary levels, as well as the continuity in the different levels, should be encouraged. Relationships between the social environment of the home and school are considered to interact with the formal educational process, but other settings that function as learning environments (social groups, churches, community recreation groups, and 4-H clubs, for example) merit special consideration as well. Descriptions of learning in out-of-school settings and comparative analyses of learning in multiple environmental settings can increase understanding of the unique characteristics of school instruction and its role in the overall education of young children.

## TEACHERS WITH A VARIETY OF COMPETENCIES

As noted above, we are presently seeing a broader range of children in early childhood classes, and a greater variety of programs are being established to support the education of these diverse children. With the exception of special programs to prepare early childhood teachers of handicapped children, all early childhood teachers are enrolled in the same program. Too often these programs are inflexible, meeting state certification standards, but with little opportunity for elective study.

How best can we prepare teachers for these diverse programs? It may be impossible for preservice teacher education programs to address the needs of teachers of all children in all programs. It may have to become the responsibility of in-service education to serve this need. Such in-service education might be sponsored by school agencies or might be offered by colleges and universities. Either way, these programs must address the specific needs of teachers in these differentiated programs. They should also be articulated with the preservice programs from which the teachers have been graduated.

## A LOOK TO THE FUTURE

Upgrading the level of professionalism among early childhood teachers demands that standards for practitioners be raised. Such a demand has caused the establishment of a credentialing system, a transformation of teacher certification standards, and the preparation of early childhood teachers. Required courses are being added and teaching practice is being changed.

Requiring teachers to have more of what is already required can raise the level of professionalism in the field; however, it may be better to change the nature of early childhood teacher education programs to better reflect what teachers actually do and why they do what they do. Teachers' cognitive processes, the way teachers make decisions, the theories and beliefs upon which their decisions are based, and how teachers function in various settings must be understood. We need to identify a core of practical professional knowledge growing out of early childhood education practice that, when coupled with teachers' technical knowledge of developmental theory and learning theory, can improve and broaden the intellectual base for practice. To help raise the level of professionalism among early childhood practitioners, teacher education programs must integrate these forms of knowledge with the technical knowledge currently offered.

As we look toward the future, we can anticipate that a great deal will change in the area of early childhood teacher education. We can also anticipate that a great deal will remain the same. Based on our best professional judgment, we would predict what follows.

*The field of early childhood education will continue to expand and there will be an increasing need for early childhood practitioners.* The social changes that led to increases in early childhood programs in recent years will remain a part of the American social scene. Young children continue to be born, more often than not into two wage earner families where both parents plan to continue to work, possibly after a relatively short period of parental leave. There will also continue to be large numbers of young children of single parent families and of teenage parents.

*The children enrolled in early childhood programs will continue to be more diverse, making teaching them a more complex task.* Not only will younger and younger children be enrolled in early childhood programs—both home-based and school-based—but the children in these programs will come from more diverse backgrounds and have a wide range of skills and abilities. We will continue to have more children from minority cultural and linguistic groups, both from an increase in the size of our current minority groups and from the continued immigration to America of people from around the world. In addition, there will be continued pressure to educate young children with diverse abilities—from handicapped to gifted—in regular classrooms. As a result, the demands on teachers will increase.

*The role of the early childhood teacher will expand to become increasingly responsible for out-of-class activities.* More home-based programs for younger children will be developed in the near future. There will also be an increase in the range of parent education components in early childhood education programs. Programs will continue to assume increasing responsibility for the health, nutrition, and welfare of the children enrolled. This will require an expansion in the defined role of early childhood teachers, who will need a broader base of knowledge for their practice, not only of education, but of health, nutrition, and social service as well.

*There will continue to be a distinction between the care and the education of young children and between practitioners who provide those services.* There has been a desire in the field of early childhood education to bring the many services to young children together and to wipe out distinctions between care and education. The term *educare* has been used to characterize a combining of the two into a unified service for children. While the idea is a worthy one, pressures abound to keep these programs distinct. Child care programs cost less than education programs. Even when both programs are provided by public schools, it has been noted that the salaries paid to teachers in the child care programs are lower than those paid to teachers in education programs (Mitchell, Seligman, & Marx, 1989). If nothing else, the economics of the situation and the difference in standards for teachers in education programs and child care programs will keep these services and personnel distinct.

*There will continue to be distinct levels of professionalism among early childhood practitioners and varied ways of entering the field.* The field of early childhood education, even when small, was quite diverse, as were its practitioners. Practitioners have always entered the field with differences in levels of preparation. They have also entered with differences in the kinds of preparation they have had. Practitioners have been prepared within the fields of education, child development, child care, psychology, and social work. While programs for the preparation of certified early childhood teachers have had more in common with one another, reflecting similar certification requirements, the continuation of diverse programs for young children within the field, many of which do not require certified teachers, will allow practitioners with a wide range of backgrounds to continue to enter the field.

*We will continue to have practitioners entering the field with a wide range of levels of preparation.* Economic pressures on the field will continue to allow large numbers of practitioners with limited preparation into the field. While many of these practitioners will work under the supervision of professionals, unfortunately many will have primary responsibility for groups of children and a great deal of autonomy in making decisions about children and programs. In addition, an increasing number of professionally prepared early childhood teachers will also be entering the field.

*The move will continue toward better-educated and better-prepared certified teachers of young children, including more programs of teacher preparation that go beyond the four-year degree.* The requirements in general education for teachers have been increasing in many states. Along with this there has been a move to extend teacher education beyond the typical four-year bachelors degree program, in part to accommodate the expansion of general education. Thus five-year teacher education programs and post-bachelor degree programs of early childhood teacher education will become more common. Such programs will give greater emphasis to providing a stronger general education for teachers.

*There will continue to be an expansion of early childhood personnel training programs at the vocational and community college level.* Programs at this level have expanded to meet the need for teachers in child care centers. These programs will continue to expand in keeping with the need for practitioners. Many of these programs will offer preparation for the Child Development Associate credential. Others will respond specifically to requirements of state child care licensing standards.

*There will be an expanded use of electronic media in the preparation of teachers.* While television and computers have had a tremendous impact on our lives in general, they have been underutilized in both preservice and in-service teacher education. This situation should change in the future as television, videocassette recorders, and computers become more common in early childhood classrooms. Examples of good practice, as well as lectures and demonstrations, can be made readily available on videocassettes. This would enable practitioners to participate in teacher preparation programs in their own centers rather than have to travel to teacher education institutions. Computers can be used not only to set up problem-solving situations and simulations, but they can also allow for networking among teachers in children's centers as well as with teacher education institutions, making contact with others in the field — colleagues and experts — more readily available. This could change the way in which knowledge is transmitted within the early childhood field, as it has done in other areas of society.

*While the older ideas of competency-based and field-based teacher education programs will continue to decline, new approaches to field-based programs will be elaborated with the creation of professional development centers.* Years ago there were a proliferation of teacher preparation programs purporting to train teachers in particular competencies required of them as practitioners. As a matter of fact, the original CDA program was based on this approach. There were also numbers of programs that moved teachers-in-training off the university campuses and into schools, reflecting the belief that what could be learned in the field was more useful to teachers in practice than what could be learned in a college or university. Both of these approaches have faded from the scene. The idea of a professional development center, however, a field-based placement, with practitioners who work with children joining university personnel to prepare teachers will expand. The advantages of the professional development center include the fact that novices can develop their practical knowledge in concert with their technical knowledge, providing a sounder base for teaching practice. Such centers also can support the continued professional development of all those involved while supporting preservice teacher training. Thus, they have the potential of raising the standards of knowledge and competency of all those involved in the enterprise of teacher education. How such potential can best be realized needs to be explored further.

*The professional associations will continue to press for higher standards of practice and of entrance to the field of early childhood education.* Organizations such as NAEYC have pressed for higher standards for programs for young children as well as for practitioners who staff these programs. In spite of the efforts made, this standard-setting activity will continue to have limited impact on the field. The voluntary nature of this kind of standard setting allows other pressures and pressure groups to act to keep standards low. The standard setting of professional associations tends to create goals to be achieved by those who are concerned with providing high-quality education to children, rather than to establish floors of practice below which programs would not be allowed to exist.

*The field will continue to expand the knowledge base of early childhood practice.* The efforts, growing out of research about what works in early childhood education, to create an empirical base of knowledge for early childhood teachers will continue. In addition, the theoretical basis for early childhood practice will expand. We will look to other fields beyond child development and individual psychology to help understand what happens to children in schools and families and to develop programs to optimize those experiences. Along with the field of psychology, such fields as sociology and anthropology will provide us with a source of knowledge for classroom practice. In addition, knowledge from fields such as economics and political science will be applied to the role of the early childhood teacher beyond the classroom.

The predictions presented here are statements of possibilities, not inevitabilities. Whether the predictions come true will depend as much on the impact of forces outside the field as on forces within the field. Early childhood educators should realize that they can influence what will happen to the field and not just wait for others to take the initiative and for agencies and institutions beyond their control to create the reality of the future. The technical and practical knowledge of the field of early childhood education should be brought to bear to make that future as bright as possible for the field as well as for the young children who are served by it.

## REFERENCES

Beer, E. S. (1938). *The day nursery*. New York: Dutton.
Child Development Associate National Credentialing Program. (1986). *Preschool caregivers in center-based programs*. Washington, DC: Council for Early Childhood Professional Recognition.
Mitchell, A., Seligman, M., & Marx, F. (1989). *Early childhood programs and the public schools*. Dover, MA: Auburn House.
National Association for the Education of Young Children. (1982). *Early childhood teacher education guidelines for four- and five-year programs*. Washington, DC: NAEYC.
National Association for the Education of Young Children. (1984). NAEYC position statement of nomenclature, salaries, benefits, and the status of the early childhood profession. *Young Children, 40*(1), 52-55.
Spodek, B. (1972). Staff requirements in early childhood education. In I. J. Gordon (Ed.), *Early childhood education, 71st yearbook of the National Society for the Study of Education* (pp. 339-65). Chicago: University of Chicago Press.
Spodek, B. (in press). Linking theory and practice: Partnerships in teacher education. In S. L. Kagan (Ed.), *Early childhood education, 90th yearbook of the National Society for the Study of Education*. Chicago: University of Chicago Press.
Spodek, B., Davis, M. D., & Saracho, O. N. (1983). Early childhood teacher education and certification. *Journal of Teacher Education, 34*(5), 50-52.
Spodek, B., & Saracho, O. N. (1982). The preparation and certification of early childhood personnel. In B. Spodek (Ed.), *Handbook of research in early childhood education* (pp. 399-425). New York: Free Press.
Spodek, B., & Saracho, O. N. (1988). Professionalism in early childhood education. In B. Spodek, O. N. Saracho, & D. L. Peters (Eds.), *Professionalism and the early childhood practitioner* (pp. 59-74). New York: Teachers College Press.
Whipple, G. M. (Ed.). (1929). *Preschool and parental education, 28th yearbook of the National Society for the Study of Education*. Bloomington, IL: Public Schools Publication.

# About the Editors and the Contributors

**Barbara Bowman** is Director of Graduate Studies at Erikson Institute, affiliated with Loyola University of Chicago, where she teaches courses in public policy, administration, and early childhood education. She has also taught in Iran and China. She received her M.A. from the University of Chicago, and a D.H.L. from Bank Street College of Education in 1988. Ms. Bowman is Past President of the National Association for the Education of Young Children (NAEYC), and has served on the boards of the Chicago Institute for Psychoanalysis and the Great Books Foundation. She speaks and writes frequently on issues related to children and families, and currently is directing a project in the Chicago Public Schools to establish developmentally appropriate early childhood units.

**Susan Bredekamp** is Director of Professional Development for NAEYC, responsible for activities relevant to establishing and promoting standards for professional practice, including standards for teacher preparation and accreditation of programs for young children. She has edited NAEYC's *Developmentally Appropriate Practice* position statements. She received her Ph.D. from the University of Maryland and was formerly a teacher and director of programs for young children as well as a college faculty member.

**James M. Cooper** is Commonwealth Professor and Dean of the Curry School of Education at the University of Virginia. He received four degrees from Stanford University, two in history and two in education, including his Ph.D. in 1967. He has written or edited nine books, including *Those Who Can, Teach* and *Kaleidoscope: Readings in Education* (with Kevin Ryan), *Classroom Teaching Skills, 4th ed.*, and *Developing Skills for Supervision*. His books and articles that have appeared in a variety of professional journals address the areas of teacher education, supervision of teachers, microteaching, and teacher education program evaluation. Dr. Cooper was director of one of the U.S. Office of Education Model Elementary Teacher Education Programs at the University of Massachusetts and later was Associate Dean for Graduate Studies in the College of Education at the University of Houston.

**Loraine Dunn** is a David Ross Fellow and Doctoral Candidate specializing in early childhood education, in the Department of Child Development and Family Studies at Purdue University. She holds a master's degree in child development from Iowa State University. She has been a university instructor, head teacher in a laboratory school and Child Development Associate Representative for the Council on Early Childhood Professional Recognition.

**Corinne E. Eisenhart** is a Ph.D. candidate at the University of Virginia in the Department of Curriculum, Instruction and Special Education, specializing in infancy and early childhood development. She is involved in a variety of teaching and research activities. Before pursuing an advanced degree, she taught kindergarten and first grade for 13 years. During that time she was involved in developing a curriculum for young children who were identified as academically "at-risk."

**Stacie G. Goffin** is Assistant Professor of Early Childhood Education at the University of Missouri–Kansas City where she has been teaching since 1983. Dr. Goffin is also a member of the Governing Board of the National Association of Early Childhood Teacher Educators and is co-author (with J. Lombardi) of *Speaking Out: Early Childhood Advocacy*.

**Dorothy W. Hewes** is a professor in the School of Family Studies, San Diego State University. She has a long-term interest in the application of history to current issues affecting management systems and curriculum development in early childhood education. Her doctoral dissertation (The Union Institute Graduate School, 1974) dealt with the introduction of Froebelian concepts into American schools in the late 1800s. She has been a teacher, administrator, and consultant in a variety of early childhood programs during the past 40 years and has written extensively about preschool administration. Dr. Hewes chairs the History and Archives Committee of NAEYC.

**Lilian G. Katz** is Professor of early childhood education at the University of Illinois, where she is also Director of the ERIC Clearinghouse on Elementary and Early Childhood Education. Dr. Katz is editor-in-chief of the *Early Childhood Research Quarterly*, a joint publication of the ERIC Clearinghouse and NAEYC. She has been editor of *Current Topics in Early Childhood Education* and author (with S. Chard) of *Engaging Children's Minds*.

**Dene G. Klinzing** is Associate Professor of child development at the University of Delaware. An experienced kindergarten teacher, she received her Ph.D. in Child Development and Family Relations from the Pennsylvania State University. Her research interests are focused upon communication techniques in pediatric hospital settings. Dr. Klinzing has won numerous awards for her teaching of child development.

**Jan McCarthy** is Professor and Coordinator of early childhood education at Indiana State University. She completed her doctoral studies at Indiana University and has taught nursery school, kindergarten, and primary grades. Her scholarly interests are in teacher education and development of high quality programs for young children. She established the Indiana State University nursery school and child care center, serving infants through five-year-olds; has directed numerous projects for preparing child care and Head Start personnel; and has participated in the preparation of NCATE redesign and preparation of elementary education guidelines. From 1978-80 Dr. McCarthy was president of NAEYC and served on the steering committee for the development of their center accreditation program. She is currently president of the U.S. National Committee of OMEP (World Organization for Early Childhood Education).

**Daniel J. Ott** is a senior lecturer in child and family studies at the University of Wisconsin–Madison, where he supervises student teachers and is also a doctoral candidate specializing in early childhood education, in the Department of Curriculum and Instruction. He has taught early childhood education courses, preschool, and kindergarten, and has served as a cooperating teacher and supervisor of a kindergarten practicum.

**Donald L. Peters** is Professor and Chair of the Department of Individual and Family Studies at the University of Delaware. He received his Ph.D. in Educational Psychology and Child Development from Stanford University. Dr. Peters is the author of numerous articles and several books, including *Early Childhood Education* and *Early Childhood Education: Theory and Practice*. His recent research and writing has focused on early childhood personnel preparation. He is co-editor (with Bernard Spodek and Olivia N. Saracho) of *Professionalism and the Early Childhood Practitioner*.

**Douglas R. Powell** received his Ph.D. from Northwestern University and is Professor in the Department of Child Development and Family Studies at Purdue University. Previously, he was a faculty member at the Merrill-Palmer Institute and at Wayne State University. His research interests include the professional development of early childhood educators' relations between parents and early childhood program personnel, and early childhood intervention. Dr. Powell is the author of numerous scholarly publications, including *Families and Early Childhood Programs*, and serves on the editorial boards of six journals.

**Gary G. Price** is Professor of Early Childhood Education and Graduate Program Chair in the Department of Curriculum and Instruction at the University of Wisconsin–Madison, where he also teaches courses in research and evaluation. He has served as Chair of the Early Education and Child Development Special Interest Group of the American Educational Research Association. Dr. Price received his Ph.D. from Stanford University in 1976, with a specialization in Child Development and Early Education. His research primarily focuses on processes by which experiences in early childhood affect intellectual development.

**Olivia N. Saracho (Editor)** is Professor at the University of Maryland. She received her Ph.D. in early childhood education from the University of Illinois. Prior to that, she taught Head Start, preschool, kindergarten, and elementary classes in Brownsville, Texas and was Director of the Child Development Associate Program at Pan American University. Her current research and writing is in the area of cognitive style, academic learning and teacher education in relation to early childhood education. She is co-author (with Bernard Spodek and Michael D. Davis) of *Foundations of Early Childhood Education* and co-editor (with Bernard Spodek and Donald L. Peters) of *Professionalism and the Early Childhood Practitioner*.

**Bernard Spodek (Editor)** is Professor of Early Childhood Education at the University of Illinois, where he has taught since 1965. He received his doctorate in early childhood education from Teachers College, Columbia University, then joined the faculty of the University of Wisconsin–Milwaukee. He has also taught nursery, kindergarten, and elementary classes. His research and scholarly interests are in the areas of curriculum, teaching, and teacher education in early childhood education.

Dr. Spodek has taught and lectured extensively in the United States, Australia, Canada, China, Israel, Japan, Korea, Mexico and Taiwan. From 1976 to 1978 he was President of NAEYC, and from 1981–1983 he chaired the Early Education and Child Development Special Interest Group of the American Educational Research Association. He is widely published in the field of early childhood education. His most recent books are *Professionalism and the Early Childhood Practitioner* (with Olivia Saracho and Donald L. Peters), *Foundations of Early Childhood Education* (with Olivia N. Saracho and Michael D. Davis), and *Today's Kindergarten: Exploring Its Knowledge Base, Expanding Its Curriculum.*

**Kenneth M. Zeichner** received his Ph.D. from Syracuse University in 1976 and is Professor in the Department of Curriculum and Instruction at the University of Wisconsin–Madison. He serves as senior researcher at the National Center for Research on Teacher Education at Michigan State University. His areas of interest include learning to teach, teacher education, clinical teacher education, and instructional supervision. Among Dr. Zeichner's recent publications are "Preparing Teachers for Democratic Schools" in *Action in Teacher Education*, "Teaching Student Teachers to Reflect" in *Harvard Educational Review*, and "Teacher Socialization" in the *Handbook of Research on Teaching.*

# Index

# Index

Accreditation, 25, 113, 138, 141, 142, 143–45, 188, 193–94, 213. *See also name of specific organization*
Act for Better Child Care, 142
Administration for Children, Youth and Families, 47, 54
Admissions policies, 16, 52–53, 110, 116, 158–61, 163–69, 170–71, 177, 218, 220
Advanced degrees. *See* Graduate programs
Advocacy, 130, 204
Alexander, K., 163
Almy, M., 62, 127–28, 130
American Association of Colleges for Teacher Education [AACTE], 123, 125, 183
American Council on Education, 153, 167
Apprenticeships, 1, 5–7, 12, 96
Assessment/evaluation, 37, 50–51, 93, 162. *See also* Testing
Assistant teachers, 59, 61–62, 107, 112
Associate degree programs, 52, 55–56, 57–58, 111, 138, 140–41, 196, 210
Association for Childhood Education International, 128–29
Association of Teacher Education [ATE], 140, 162
Australia, 111–13, 115–16
Autobiographical inquiry, 86

Baccalaureate programs
 abolition of, 40, 179–82
 admissions policies for, 159
 and certification, 210, 211
 and child development, 70
 and demand/supply of teachers, 156
 and the expansion of early childhood education, 45–46, 196, 210
 in the future, 218–19
 and the NAEYC guidelines, 180–82
 and reform efforts, 179–82, 205–6
 and teacher effectiveness, 45–46
Barnard, Henry, 4, 14

Basic skills, 161
Becker, R. M., 201
Beer, E. S., 215
Beginning Teacher Assistance Program [BTAP], 184–85
Benson, C. E., 15–16
Berger, J., 168
Berk, L. E., 51, 158
Berry, B., 177
Berson, M. P., 51
Blaker, Eliza, 6
Bloom, B., 159–60
Blow, Susan, 9–10, 11–12, 13
Bowman, B., 200
Bradley, Milton, 7
Bredekamp, S., 88, 128
Brokers, 205
Bruner, Jerome, 28
Buka, S. L., 194
Burritt, Ruth, 6

Caldwell, B., 130
California Kindergarten Training School, 9
Career ladders, 59, 61–62, 107, 150, 214
Carl D. Perkins Vocational Education Act, 57
Carlson, D., 160
Carnegie Forum, 39, 116, 142, 153, 176–77, 179–80, 193, 196
Carnegie Foundation for the Advance of Teaching, 155
Case studies, 131–32, 204
CDA [child development associate] credential, 29–30, 46–54, 77, 141, 196, 210, 214, 219
Certification
 alternative, 40, 41, 183–84
 and baccalaureate programs, 115, 210, 211
 and child care, 195, 197
 and competencies, 167

Certification (*continued*)
  and the content of early childhood teacher education, 24–25, 39
  and the crisis in American education, 155, 157
  and the curriculum, 213
  and the definition of early childhood education, 187, 195
  and demand/supply of teachers, 156, 183–84
  and diversity, 188–90, 194–95
  emergency, 140, 183–84
  and enrollment, 188
  and the expansion of early childhood education, 210
  in the future, 216, 218–19
  and kindergartens, 157
  in Korea, 105, 106
  and minorities, 167
  and public schools, 212–13
  purpose of, 190*n*
  and recent interest in early childhood education, 194–95
  and reform efforts, 155, 183–85, 189–90
  and responsibility, 189
  and salaries, 188, 197, 212–13
  and settings, 212–13
  specific/broad forms of, 40, 41, 185–88
  and standards, 139–41, 146–47
  and status, 188
  and tracks in early childhood teacher education, 214
  and unique characteristics of early childhood education, 132
Child care
  and certification/licensing, 24, 45, 140–41, 195, 197, 219
  and corporations, 104, 209
  and demand/supply of teachers, 156
  diversity of, 23–24, 54
  education versus, 23–24, 139, 196–97, 211, 217–18
  enrollment in, 210
  expansion of, 195–97
  in the future, 42, 213, 219
  and in-service programs, 58–60
  in Israel, 115
  reform of, 154
  and salaries, 23, 42, 168, 169, 197, 218
  staff qualifications in, 23–24, 54
  and standards, 24, 139, 156, 211, 213–14, 218
Child development
  and the age range of children, 72–73
  and associate degree programs, 55
  in Australia, 112
  and baccalaureate programs, 70
  and the CDA, 77
  and child care, 59
  conceptual integration of, 74
  and the content of early childhood teacher education, 26, 29–37, 62, 67–81, 86–87, 88
  and curricular vision, 88
  and a developmental perspective, 78
  diversity of content about, 68–72
  and field experiences, 77
  fundamentals of, 73–75
  and graduate programs, 70
  historical perspective of, 69–70, 74
  interdependence of aspects of, 73
  in Korea, 105
  life-span perspective of, 74, 75
  and methods courses, 75
  multidisciplinary origins of the field of, 68–69
  and the NAEYC guidelines, 69
  and observation, 75, 76
  and pedagogy, 83–84, 85
  and practice, 75, 76–78
  quality of research about, 70–71
  and reform efforts, 202, 205
  scientific basis of, 74
  specific content of, 75
  systems perspective of, 74
  teaching, 75–78
  texts about, 68
  and vocational training, 57
Child Development Associate Consortium, 47
Child development associate credential. *See* CDA
Children
  diversity of, 217
  nature of, 196
  views of, 11–12
  vulnerability of, 199–200
China, People's Republic of, 108–11, 115–16, 211–12
Clandinin, J., 130

## INDEX

Clark, C., 85, 160, 162
Clinical experiences, 84, 85, 94, 95–96, 200, 203
Code of ethics, 150, 201
Colonial education, 1–3
Colvin, R., 75
Committee for Economic Development, 153
*The Commonwealth Teacher Training Study* [Charters & Waples], 125–26
Community colleges, 39, 54, 56, 108, 158–59, 211, 214, 219
Community Family Day Care Project [Pacific Oaks College], 60
Community relations, 87–88
Competencies
  and the CDA, 47–48
  and certification, 167
  in the future, 213, 214–16, 219–20
  and minorities, 167
  and reform efforts, 184, 203
  and the retention of student teachers, 162
  and settings, 214–15
  and teachers' roles, 198, 213
  and the unique aspects of early childhood education, 198
Competency-based education, 123, 219–20
Competency tests, 167, 184
Compulsory education, 2, 12
Connecticut College, 169
Content
  ambiguity of, 132
  and associate degree programs, 57
  in Australia, 112, 116
  in China, 109, 116
  and the crisis in American education, 170–71
  in Israel, 114, 116
  in Korea, 105, 116
  overview of early childhood teacher education, 24–39
  and recent interest in early childhood education, 194
  and reform efforts, 179–82, 203
  research about, 119
  of teacher education, 125
  and unique characteristics of early childhood education, 132
  and vocational training, 57
  See also Knowledge base; *name of specific type of content*
Continuing education, 106, 211
Corporations, 104, 209
Cost of education, 162–63, 168
Council for Early Childhood Professional Recognition, 47, 51–52, 71, 141–42
Credentials, 18, 52, 185–88. See also Accreditation; Certification; Licensing
Credit hours, 40, 179–82, 214
Crisis in American education, 153–56, 170–72
Cubberly, Ellwood, 2, 3
Cultural perspectives, 88, 89, 102–3, 115–16, 148, 149, 217. See also Minorities; *name of specific country*
Curriculum, 29–37, 55, 88–90, 178, 198, 202–3, 213. See also Accreditation; Standards

Darling-Hammond, L., 177
Data bases, 61
Demand/supply of teachers, 42, 107–8, 114, 155–56, 163–69, 183–84, 210, 217
Desforges, C., 28
*Developmentally Appropriate Practice in Early Childhood Programs Serving Children From Birth Through Age 8* [NAEYC/Bredekamp], 28, 188
Developmental theory. See Child development
Dewey, John, 14, 28
Doctrinaire approach, 198–99
Douai, Adolph, 14–15
Doyle, W., 119

Early childhood, definition of, 82, 140, 146–47, 153–54, 178, 187
Early childhood education
  defining the issues in, 203–6
  definition of, 104, 114, 193, 195
  ecology of, 71–72
  emergence of term of, 193
  expansion of, 195–97, 209–11, 217
  as a panacea, 189
  purposes/goals of, 195–97, 202
  recent interest in, 193–95
Early childhood specialist, 52–53

Early childhood teacher education
challenges/problems in, 57–58, 61–63, 106–8, 109–10, 113, 115, 157–63
current context of, 193
differences between teacher education [general] and, 171, 192, 195–97, 211, 212
diversity among options in, 23, 82 23, 104–5, 157, 196, 211–12, 218
doctrinaire/eclectic approaches to, 198–99
equivocation about, 83
and experiments with training methods, 62
focusing on, 204–6
in the future, 216–21
and ideology, 198–99
increase in number of programs of, 70–71, 156
influences on, 25, 212–15
and mission, 198–99
predictions about, 216–21
relevancy of, 171
tracks in, 214
unique aspects of, 132, 171, 192, 197–203

*Early Childhood Teacher Education Guidelines for Four- and Five-Year Programs* [NAEYC], 128, 138, 159, 177–78

Early Intervention Program, 91–92
Eclectic approach, 199
Ecology of early childhood education, 71–72
Educare, 217–18
Education
child care versus, 23–24, 139, 196–97, 211, 217–18
crisis in American, 153–56
Education for All Handicapped Children Act [1975], 91–92, 185, 210
Educational Testing Service, 162
Education Commission of the States, 159, 176–77
Effectiveness, 45–46, 119, 127, 205
Eisner, E., 84–86
Elbaz, F., 29
Electronic media, 219
Elkind, D., 127

Enrollments, 155, 156, 172, 188, 210
Entry into the profession. *See* Admissions policies
Entwistle, D., 163
Ethics, 94–95, 107, 128, 150, 201–2
Evaluation. *See* Assessment/evaluation; Testing
Experts, 122, 124–25, 126, 220

Faculty vitae, 148–49
Families. *See* Parents/families
Family day care, 60–61
Federal Preschool Program, 91–92
Fein, G., 205
Feminization of teaching, 3, 5, 8, 9, 16, 169–70
Field experiences
and associate degree programs, 55
in Australia, 112, 116
and child development, 77
in China, 116
and the content of early childhood teacher education, 37–39, 40
in the future, 219–20
in Israel, 114, 116
in Korea, 106, 107, 116
and the NAEYC guidelines, 182–83
negative outcomes of, 77–78
and reform efforts, 178, 182–83
and standards, 147
Fields, C., 166, 167
Financial assistance, 167–68
Five-year programs. *See* Baccalaureate programs
Folio reviews, 143–44, 146–47, 148–51
Foundations of education, 27–29, 86–87, 105, 161–62, 178
Froebelian principles, 1, 5–9, 12, 13–18
Froebel Institute, 11

Gardner, H., 122
General education
and associate degree programs, 55
in Australia, 112
in China, 109, 110
and the content of early childhood teacher education, 25–28, 62
in the future, 218–19
in Korea, 105
and pedagogy, 83–84

INDEX

professional education versus, 157-59
and reform efforts, 178
Gibbs, J., 168
Glaser, R., 126
Graduate programs, 40, 70, 138, 148-49, 211, 218-19
Greeno, J. G., 122, 124

Haberman, M., 41, 62, 161, 167
Hailmann, Eudora & William, 10-12, 16, 17
Harris, William Torrey, 7, 9-10, 11-12
Hatano, G., 122
Head Start, 45, 47, 54, 141, 156, 168, 169, 195, 197, 210, 212, 214
Henderson, J., 86
Herbartian [Johann Frederick] principles, 13-15, 16, 18
Hewes, D., 172
High/Scope curriculum, 28
Hill, J., 91
Hirsch, E. D., Jr., 26
History, 86-87
Holden, C., 166
Holmes Group, 39, 116, 154, 160, 163, 176-77, 179-80, 193, 196
Home-based programs, 215, 217
Home environment. See Parents/families
Honig, A., 88
Howey, K., 131-32
Hughes, James, 13
Hymes, J. L., Jr., 82

Ideology, 123-24, 198-99
Inagaki, K., 122
Individual differences, 30, 88
Individualized education plan [IEP], 92
Infants, 92, 149, 154
Infant schools, 7
In-service programs, 46, 58-61, 196, 211, 216
Institutional atmosphere, 168
Instructional knowledge/theory, 29-37, 178
Interactive skills, 203
Interdisciplinary approach, 220
International Kindergarten Union, 15
International Reading Association, 128-29
Internships, 40, 41, 107
Isaacs, Susan, 28
Israel, 114-16

Jackson, Philip, 160
Jenkins, Anna Louise, 6
Job Training Partnership Act, 54
Jones, E., 171
Journals. See Publications
Junior colleges. See Community colleges

Kagan, S. L., 197
Kamii, C., 126
Katz, Lilian, 94, 127, 129, 132, 171, 205-6
"Kindergarten Crusade," 5-6
Kindergartens
  and apprenticeships, 5-7
  and certification, 157
  in China, 108-10, 211-12
  and diversity in training for, 15-16
  emergence of, 1, 2
  enrollment in, 18, 172
  and the feminization of teaching, 3, 5, 8, 9, 16
  and Froebelian principles, 1, 5-9, 12, 13-18
  and Herbartian principles, 13-15, 16, 18
  and kindergarten training schools, 7-12, 15-16
  in Korea, 103-8
  and the National Education Association, 9, 10, 11
  and normal school preparation, 12-18
  observation, 15
  and Pestalozzian principles, 4-5, 7, 9, 16-17
  as preparation for first grade, 18
  and private education, 9
  and public education, 1, 7, 9, 17-18
  purpose of, 15
  standards for, 7
  and student teaching, 147
  and support organizations, 16-17
  universality of, 195
Kindergarten Task Force, 128-29
Kliebard, H., 120
Knowledge, models of, 124
Knowledge base, 118, 120-31, 178, 194, 200, 214-15, 216, 217, 220. See also name of specific knowledge
Kontos, S., 59-60
Korea, 103-8, 115-16

Krause, John & Maria, 9, 12
Kriege, Alma & Matilda, 10, 12

Lally, J. Ronald, 60
Lanier, J., 77–78
Lazerson, M., 18
Learning, 29–37, 84–86, 88–91, 121, 124
Legal rights of teachers, 94
Liberal arts, 90, 109, 203
Licensing, 24, 45, 139–41, 219. *See also* Accreditation; Certification
Liston, D., 123
Little, J., 77–78
Lombardi, J., 130
Lortie, D., 77

McCarthy, J., 185, 188, 195
McKibben, M. D., 183
Mainstreaming, 91–92
Mangione, Peter, 60
Mann, Horace, 5
Mann, Mary, 7
Martin, A., 130
Marwedel, Emma, 6
Men in early childhood programs, 169–70
Mental representations of students, 122
Methods courses, 28, 29, 55, 75, 105, 110, 147–48, 149, 161–62, 178
Minnesota Early Childhood Teacher Educators, 128–29
Minorities, 62, 159, 163–69, 217
Mission, 198–99
Morals. *See* Ethics/morals

NAEYC [National Association for the Education of Young Children]
and accreditation, 141, 149–51, 168
and associate degree programs, 55–56
and career ladders, 61–62
and the CDA, 47, 52–53, 214
and child care, 59, 214
and the content of early childhood teacher education, 28, 69, 158
and the definition of early childhood, 140, 146–47, 153–54, 187
and ethics, 201
founding of the, 138
goal of the, 138
and graduate degrees, 148–49
influence of the, 213–14
and NCATE, 142–43, 188
and professionalism, 150, 210–11
and reform efforts, 177–88
and standards, 138, 141, 143–51, 187–88, 213–14
and teachers' roles, 127
*See also name of specific publication*
National Academy of Early Childhood Programs, 67
National agencies, 141–42
National Association of Early Childhood Teacher Educators, 148–49
National Association for Nursery Education, 69
National Association of School Boards of Education, 154
National Black Child Development Institute [NBCDI], 128, 130, 153
National Board for Professional Teaching Standards, 142, 155
National Center for Research on Teacher Education, 131–32
National Child Care Staffing Study, 45
National Commission on Excellence in Teacher Education, 193
National Committee on Nursery Schools, 69
National Council for Accreditation of Teacher Education. *See* NCATE
National Day Care Study, 48
*National Directory of Early Childhood Training Programs* [Council for Early Childhood Professional Recognition], 71
National Education Association, 9, 10, 11, 13
National Governors' Association, 176–77
National Kindergarten and Elementary College [Chicago], 16
National Teachers Examination, 162, 179, 184
NCATE [National Council for Accreditation of Teacher Education], 25, 142–45, 148–49, 188, 193–94, 213
Neighborhood Project [Purdue University], 61
Newman, Frank, 177
New York Normal College, 14–15

INDEX

Non-baccalaureate programs, 45–66, 214. *See also* Associate degree programs; Vocational programs
Normal schools, 4, 14–18, 108–9, 110, 115
Nursery schools, 104–9, 192–93, 195, 210, 211–12

Observation, 38, 75, 76, 95, 106, 109, 112, 114
Observation kindergartens, 15
Office of Educational Research and Improvement [U.S. Department of Education], 119
Oppression, 160

Parents/families, 87–88, 92, 106, 115, 147, 154, 196, 201, 215, 217
Peabody, Elizabeth, 7, 10, 11–12
Pedagogy
  in Australia, 112
  and child development, 69–70, 83–84, 85
  in China, 109
  and clinical experience, 84, 85, 95–96
  complementary components of knowledge of, 83–84
  and the content of early childhood teacher education, 82–97
  content of knowledge of, 84–95
  domains of, 84–95
  and general education, 83–84, 157–59
  and materials, 85
  and recent interest in early childhood education, 194
  and research, 84, 118, 119–20
  and student teaching, 84, 95–96
  and subject matter, 83–84, 85
  and teachers' beliefs, 84–86
Perkinson, H. J., 14
Pestalozzian [Johann Heinrich] principles, 4–5, 7, 9, 16–17
Peters, D. L., 53
Peterson, P. L., 85
Phillips, C., 157
Phillips, D. A., 204–5
Philosophy, 86–87
Piaget, Jean, 28, 89–90
Play, 6, 89
Powell, D. R., 60, 214

Practice
  in Australia, 112, 116
  and child development, 75, 76–78
  in China, 109, 116
  and the content of early childhood teacher education, 29, 37–39, 62
  in the future, 220
  in Israel, 114, 116
  in Korea, 105, 106, 107, 116
  and reform efforts, 178, 182–83, 203, 204–6
  and research, 204–6
  and the retention of student teachers, 161–62
  standards for, 138
  and vocational training, 57
  and vulnerability of the child, 200
  *See also* Field experiences; Student teaching
Prior experiences, 121, 122, 131
Private academies/education, 2, 3–4, 9, 14
Professional development, need for a commitment to, 63
Professional development centers, 219–20
Professionalism, 94–95, 108, 126–30, 150, 177, 201–2, 210–11, 216, 218
Professional meetings/workshops, 59, 60, 63
Professional organizations, 28, 42, 59, 69–70, 142–43, 211, 213–14, 220. *See also name of specific organizations*
Project 30, 154
Publications, 58–59, 70, 71
Public education, 1, 7, 9, 17–18, 156, 209–10, 212–13. *See also* State agencies
Public policy, 204–6

Quality, 51–52, 54, 57, 70–71, 116
Quisenberry, N., 172

Racism, 168–69
Ramsey, P. G., 88–89
Recruitment of teachers. *See* Admissions policies
Reform
  and accreditation, 188
  and admission policies, 177
  and baccalaureate programs, 179–82, 205–6

Reform *(continued)*
  and certification, 155, 183–85, 189–90
  and competencies, 184, 203
  and the content of early childhood teacher education, 178, 179–82, 202–3, 205
  contradictory nature of, 178–79
  influence of, 188–90
  and NAEYC, 177–88
  need for, 170–71
  and practice, 178, 182–83, 203, 204–6
  and professionalism, 177
  and responsibility, 189, 190
  and retention of teachers, 177
  and salaries, 177, 189–90
  and standards, 176
  and status, 177, 189–90
  and student teaching, 178, 182
  and teachers' role, 202, 203, 204
  and testing, 184–85
  waves of, 176–77
  *See also* Crisis in American education
Relevancy, 171
Religion, 2, 3, 4
Research
  about child development, 70–71
  domains of, 118
  and early childhood teacher education, 193, 204–6
  and the effectiveness of teacher education, 119
  and expert/novice studies, 124–25, 126
  funding for, 119
  in the future, 220
  and the knowledge base, 118, 120–21, 128, 129, 131
  and learning, 121
  needed, 108, 130–32
  and pedagogy, 84, 118, 119–20
  and practice, 204–6
  and teacher education, 118, 119
Resources, need for more, 109–10
Rest, J., 95
Retention, 161–69, 170, 177
Reynolds, M. C., 123, 125
Rice, Joseph Mayer, 17
Robinson, B., 170
Roles, of teachers, 25, 30–37, 127, 129, 148, 160, 192, 197–98, 202–4, 213, 217

Romberg, T. A., 122
Rousseau, Jean Jacques, 4

•Salaries
  and the CDA, 51
  and certification, 23, 188, 197, 212–13
  and child care, 23, 42, 168, 169, 197, 218
  and costs of education, 162–63, 168
  and the crisis in American education, 172
  and demand/supply of teachers, 155, 156, 169
  and the expansion of early childhood education, 196
  and the feminization of teaching, 170
  in the future, 218
  in Korea, 107–8
  and men in early childhood programs, 170
  and minorities, 168, 169
  and normal school preparation, 15
  and preparation of early childhood teachers, 23
  and reform efforts, 177, 189–90
  and the retention of student teachers, 162–63
  and standards, 139
  and unique characteristics of early childhood education, 132
Saracho, O. N., 30–37, 59, 158, 160
Scholastic Aptitude Test [SAT], 166–67, 179
Schön, D., 86
School environment, 87–88
Schwartz, P. M., 205
Science, 89–90, 109
Seefeldt, C., 127, 129
Selection of teachers. *See* Admissions policies
Selleck, R. J. W., 13
Settings, 113, 114, 119, 132, 193, 195–97, 212–15
Shapiro, M. S., 18
Shavelson, R. J., 205
Sheldon, E. A., 4
Shortage of teachers. *See* Demand/supply of teachers
Shulman, L., 83, 194
Silin, J. G., 70, 120, 129, 130

INDEX

Smith, A. W., 168
Smith, B. O., 84
Smith, Nora, 6, 9
Snyder, H., 165
Social change, 209-10
Socialization, 27, 200-201
Social reconstructionism, 123, 129
Society for Research in Child Development, 69
Southern Association on Children Under Six, 128-29
Southern Regional Education Board, 183
Special education/needs, 71, 148, 185, 195, 210
Spodek, Bernard, 59, 85, 128, 129, 158, 160
Stallings, J., 75
Standardized tests. *See* Testing
Standards
   absence of minimal preparation, 46
   and associate degree programs, 56, 138, 140-41
   in Australia, 113
   and career ladders, 150
   and the CDA, 51, 140-42
   and child care, 24, 139, 156, 211, 213-14, 218
   and the crisis in American education, 157, 170-71
   and cultural diversity, 148, 149
   and diversity in early childhood teacher education, 211
   and the expansion of early childhood education, 196
   and field experiences, 147
   in the future, 211, 213-14, 220
   and graduate programs, 138, 148-49
   in Israel, 114
   for kindergartens, 7
   and the knowledge base, 178
   in Korea, 105-7
   and methods courses, 147-48, 149
   and national agencies, 141-42
   and normal school preparation, 15-16
   for practice, 138
   and professionalism, 150
   and professional organizations, 142-43, 213-14, 220
   and reform efforts, 176
   responsibility for setting, 24
   and salaries, 139
   and state agencies, 139-41
   and status, 139
   variability in, 139-40
   *See also* Accreditation; Admissions policies; Certification; Licensing; *name of specific organization or program*
State agencies, 24, 139-41. *See also* Certification; Licensing
State Recognition System, 144-45
State teacher examinations, 167
Status, 52-53, 54, 139, 155, 156, 172, 177, 188, 189-90, 196
Stipek, D., 75
Stremmel, A. J., 59-60
Student teaching
   in China, 109, 110
   and the content of early childhood teacher education, 37-39, 96
   and kindergartens, 147
   in Korea, 106, 107
   and pedagogy, 84
   and professionalism, 94
   in public school kindergartens, 147
   and reform efforts, 178, 182
   and the retention of student teachers, 161-62
Subject matter, 83-84, 85, 89-90, 157-59, 179-82, 202, 203
Survival skills, 127
Sylva, K., 28

Takanishi, R., 129
Teacher education [general]
   competency-based, 123, 219-20
   and the crisis of American education, 154-55
   differences between early childhood teacher education and, 171, 192, 195-97, 211, 212
   emergence of, 3-5
   in private academies, 2, 3-4, 14
   reform of, 154-55
   research about, 118, 119
Teacher Research Network, 129
Teachers
   beliefs of, 84-86, 162
   characteristics of, 159-60, 200, 202-3
   decision making by, 31, 85

Teachers (*continued*)
    demand/supply of, 42, 107–8, 114, 155–56, 163–69, 183–84, 210, 217
    and a developmental perspective, 78
    effectiveness of, 45–46, 119, 127, 205
    legal rights of, 94
    as models, 31, 37, 160
    and oppression, 160
    roles of, 25, 30–37, 127, 129, 148, 160, 192, 197–98, 202–4, 213, 217
    stages in the development of, 94
    *See also* Assistant teachers
Teaching
    attitudes/beliefs about, 84–86, 155–56
    about child development, 75–78
    complexity of, 217
    *See also* Feminization of teaching
Testing, 93, 161, 162, 165–67, 184–85. *See also* name of specific test
*Theory of Teaching* [Page], 4
Toddlers, 92, 149, 154

Training schools, 7–12, 15–16
Tufte, F. W., 122

Undergraduate degree programs. *See* Baccalaureate programs
U.S. Bureau of Education, 15, 16

VanderVen, K., 53
Vandewalker, Nina, 15, 17
Vocational programs, 39, 56–58, 196, 214, 219
Vulnerability of the child, 199–200

White, S. H., 194
Whole child concept, 4, 197–98, 201
Wiggin, Kate Douglas, 6, 9
Women. *See* Feminization of teaching

Zaffiro, E., 75
Zeichner, K., 123
Zimpher, N., 131–32